*The* **7 Secrets** *of* **Creative Radio Advertising**

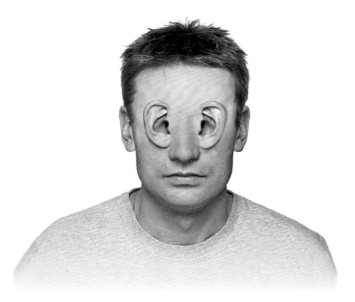

# The
# 7 Secrets *of*
# Creative
# Radio Advertising

## Tony Hertz

# *The* 7 Secrets *of* Creative Radio Advertising

First published in 2013 by
Panoma Press Ltd
48 St Vincent Drive, St Albans, Herts, AL1 5SJ UK
info@panomapress.com
www.panomapress.com

Illustrations by Mela Advincula
Cover design by Michael Inns
Artwork by Karen Gladwell

Printed on acid-free paper from managed forests.
This book is printed on demand to fulfill orders,
so no copies will be remaindered or pulped.

ISBN 978-1-908746-65-8

A CIP catalogue record for this book is available from
the British Library.

This book is available online and in all good bookstores.

# Contents

Introduction   7

A bit about me.   9

The starting point.   15

*Secret #1*   **- Find a Feeling**   33

*Secret #2*   **- Begin with a Picture**   45

*Secret #3*   **- Think About The Person**   79

*Secret #4*   **- One Ad, One message**   95

*Secret #5*   **- Stand in a Different Place**   105

*Secret #6*   **- Characters Not Voices**   117

*Secret #7*   **- Produce with Passion**   125

The Wrap Up.   145

What people have said about Tony's Workshops   149

The Scripts   153

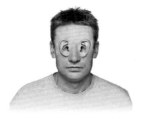

# Introduction

It's taken a long time to get this book out, mostly because I'm a world-class procrastinator. It's been something of an embarrassment to me that at marketing and advertising events and conferences where my presentations and training sessions have been enthusiastically received and I've been hailed as a radio guru, the tables at the back of the room have been piled high with every other speaker's books, except mine. And I'm trying not to think about the number of copies I could have sold over the years.

I must, therefore, give credit to two people for the fact that you're actually holding a book written by me.

The first is Mindy Gibbins-Klein, The Book Midwife. I attended her Thought Leadership Retreat in May 2011 and that, more than anything, gave me the belief that I could do it, the encouragement and the specific tools to help me get started.

The second is Hans De Loos, Marketing Strategy Director of the radio station Q-music in Amsterdam. Hans saw a presentation I did for a European radio association and convinced his management to do a series of seminars for individual Q-music advertisers and their creative and media agencies.

Between November 2010 and June 2012 I conducted my seminar The 7 Secrets of Creative Radio at Q-music 44 times! I know of no other radio station in the world that has made such a significant, long-term commitment to raising the level of commercial creativity – it is a remarkable undertaking. Many, many radio stations talk about the need to do it; Q-music has put their money where their mouth is and I am genuinely proud to be their creative partner.

Somewhere around Seminar Number 38, Hans and Sales Director Rob Beijersbergen announced that they wanted to publish The 7 Secrets as a book for their clients – the sooner the better! It was another kick up the backside so I took some of the material I'd already written for my Mindy book (which I will still do, by the way), began furiously re-writing it in the 7 Secrets format, finishing it the week after my wife and I arrived in the Philippines where we now live.

If you are reading this as a past participant at one of my seminars or workshops, the material that follows will look familiar – it's pretty much what you heard me say at the sessions and I hope it will bring back good memories as well as serving as a reminder. If you're seeing it for the first time, I hope that I've been able to convey on the page something of the enthusiasm that seems to come out whenever I stand up and talk about the advertising medium about which I've been irrationally and unreasonably passionate all my life.

## A bit about me.

I was born in Leeds in Yorkshire long enough ago that radio was simply the only home entertainment: comedy, dramas, the daily serials with their cliffhanger endings, quiz programs, music, King George's Christmas broadcasts. My parents, brother, sister and I would literally gather around the radio at least once every day to listen to our favorite programs. The BBC, literally, brought the world to my ears.

When I was aged 11 my family emigrated to North America – first to Vancouver, Canada and then three years later to Washington D.C. where I spent my adolescence, and radio continued to be a hugely important part of my life. Series like The Lone Ranger, Johnny Dollar, The Green Hornet, soap operas and more quiz programs kept us glued to the radio, but now with an added dimension – commercials – which of course we'd never heard on the BBC. I remember incredibly clearly the first jingle I ever heard – for TIDE detergent. It was not until I was 15 years old that my family owned a television!

Despite the huge exposure to radio and radio advertising, it never occurred to me to consider it as a career. Indeed, I had no idea there was such a business as advertising until the fateful summer of my second year at George Washington University where I was – sort of – preparing to study medicine.

My family was not at all prosperous and I always had to work during the long summer vacations to help pay for university. That year I had a job at a drugstore on Wisconsin Avenue in Washington. It was a typical American drugstore of the period which, in addition to selling all the usual pharmaceutical and health products, had what was called a 'Soda Fountain' which served sandwiches, hamburgers etc. and was a popular place for lunch for the other businesses in the area. One of those businesses was next door, a company named Kal, Ehrlich & Merrick which happened to be Washington D.C.'s largest advertising agency.

I had no idea what an ad agency did, but many of the agency people were regular customers at the drugstore and I quickly registered a few things about them: The girls were very good-looking and bright. The guys wer interesting, laughed a lot (and were also good-looking… and they bought more condoms than other customers!

Think Mad Men! It was that period.

As the summer progressed, they began talking to me and at some point I had to deliver something to the agency and one of the guys I'd been chatting with showed me around. Amazing.

There were people at big drawing boards doing things for work that I did for fun – sketching, coloring, pasting. A man with an airbrush was retouching a photograph of a tire (this was 1960 remember, Photoshop wasn't even a dream yet). And there were people they called 'copywriters' swapping clever lines and stories or fiercely pounding typewriter keyboards; they recognized me and said hello.

And there in a corner was an office piled high with tapes and discs and a guy with a stopwatch reading a commercial out loud. It was a world I'd never dreamed existed and I was absolutely fascinated. And yes, there were those good-looking girls.

The summer progressed and I got in a few more deliveries to the agency. In September, I went back to my studies at GWU but, at the same time, managed to get a part-time job as a messenger/office boy at – you guessed it – Kal, Ehrlich & Merrick!

Many of my deliveries – to radio stations and clients – were for KEM's radio/TV producer, Dave Thomas. He happened to be a big BBC fan and actually knew many of the programs I'd heard as a kid so we became quite close and after a few months I became his assistant.

One evening as I was preparing to leave, Dave came to my desk and said, "I've got a problem, there's a last-minute spot that's needed at a station tomorrow, all the copywriters have gone and I have to leave, can you do it? It's only 10 seconds."

In fact it was just an add-on tag to a recorded commercial but I spent hours crafting it and managed to get it to the station on time. A few days later, driving the company van on a delivery, I heard my 10-second spot on the radio and I felt That is the most exciting thing that's ever happened in my life. And I still do.

So the world lost a probably mediocre doctor and gained a genuine radio freak. I became a part-time copywriter and the following year dropped out of university to do it full time, and even though I made my way up the creative ladder to Executive Creative Director, moved around the world – New York, London, Tokyo, Brussels – and worked on print, poster and lots of television commercials, radio is still the medium closest to my heart and to my creative soul.

## Listen to audio files

Throughout the book I've illustrated The 7 Secrets with examples of radio commercial scripts. When you see the red Play symbol you can listen to the spot either by scanning this QR code, or going to **http://hertzradio.com/qr/**.

And for convenience, the spots are also all together at the back of the book from p155

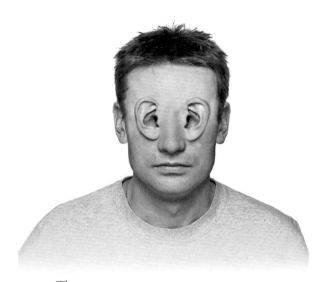

The
# 7 Secrets of Creative
## Radio Advertising

# The starting point.

I have been lucky enough to have been able to talk and teach radio advertising in something like 35 countries over the last 10 years, from Chile to China, Sri Lanka to Slovenia, Ghana to Germany. The one thing common to all these countries –regardless of size, state of development, level of marketing sophistication, language or, indeed, business success of the radio industry – is that **radio advertising is seen to have creative issues or problems.**

Even in countries like South Africa, Australia and the US which have been the major radio award-winning countries, the overall standard of radio creativity is seen to be below that in other media.

Some of these issues are barriers to investment in radio by advertisers:

> If an advertiser maintains, "Our product/brand is so visual, radio can't be effective," that's a creative issue.

> If, for the same reason, an agency doesn't propose radio as part of the media mix (even though it makes media sense) that's a creative issue.

There are advertisers who clearly don't realize that they have creative issues.

If they did, surely they wouldn't be using the commercials they're running.

Finally, and most significantly for purposes of this discussion, it is my personal observation that both agencies and radio are largely unsatisfied with the radio spots they make.

The observation is supported by facts. In 2012 there were 20,337 entries to the Cannes Lions Advertising Festival in above-the-line categories. The chart shows how these entries are broken down by media:

| All Ads | Press | Outdoor | Film | Online | Radio |
|---------|-------|---------|------|--------|-------|
| 20,337 | 29.7% | 23.8% | 25.5% | 12% | 8.7% |

Agency creative directors are the ones responsible for deciding which of their work should be entered for Cannes which is the most prestigious creative competition in the world, and very expensive. Each film (TV or Cinema) entry costs €640; Press, Outdoor and Film Craft €375 and Radio €299. Financial directors scrutinize awards entry budgets heavily and work is not entered frivolously.

So what do the numbers show? That the world's creative directors are between three and four times prouder of their Press and Film than of their Radio.

They're even less proud in the UK. There were about eight times more Film entries than Radio (42.8:5.4%), and in the US the Film to Radio entry ratio was just under 10:1 (50.6

to 5.1%).[1] There are, of course, advertisers who feel that awards are about creative ego, not business, and therefore not worth considering. If you're one of them I refer you to the book The Case for Creativity by James Hurman. In his report on 15 case studies of the link between creativity and business success, he writes:

> *Without exception, those advertisers who have been named Cannes Lions Advertiser of the Year have experienced record share market performance in the year leading up to their awards.*

So to go back to the radio = creative issues/problems premise, the obvious question arises:

Why are radio ads so mediocre or average or less than award-worthy or simply plain bad?

**. . . Well, maybe that's not the right question.**

Why? Because we have to look at radio in the context of all advertising. Is it really that radio is so bad, or is it a case of everything else being pretty amazing.

Spend a few hours in front of your TV or scan through your favorite magazines and what do you see? An incredible variety of amazing images: attractive, sexy people wearing stylish clothes or shaking their hair in slow motion, tantalizing close-ups of delicious food, sleek cars driving through magnificent landscapes or moody cities, special effects that rival those in feature films. You may not like

---

[1] *There were a few countries where Radio fared better. Australia's Radio percentage was 13.6% (Film: 26.5%), Belgian Radio entries were 15.8% of their total and 30% of South African entries were in the Radio category, just about dead level with press. You can see a full list by Googling 'Cannes Lions 2012 entries by country'.*

all the commercials or ads and many of them may not be relevant but they're sure nice to look at.

Here's something I say in every workshop.

You're an agency creative team and you receive a brief to do a TV or cinema commercial for a brand; the details aren't important. My guess is – all things being equal -- that you will not create the same commercial you'd have done last year, or two years ago, certainly not five or 10 years ago.

Why? Because film advertising has evolved, as have consumer tastes and attitudes; technology has improved, styles have changed, you'll have seen and been influenced by what's won at the awards shows. Your job is to produce work that's as contemporary or even ahead of its time as factors will allow. It is what drives the advertising business. And many, if not all, advertisers now appreciate this.

OK, so now you're the same creative team and you're given a radio brief. What will you come up with? Well, I'd bet serious money that you'll write the same radio spot your father would have created 20 years ago if he'd been a copywriter! It might well be a good commercial, well written and produced, but chances are it will be the same ad.

Why? Because radio advertising has **not** evolved, in terms of skills, attitude, approach and desire to be ahead of the curve, so the real question is this:

**Why hasn't Radio kept pace with TV, Print, Outdoor, Digital?**

I believe there are four reasons; three of them are what I would call 'functional':

1. Marketing Communication has become **± 100% visual.**

2. Creatives **are not** taught the skills of radio (nor are CDs, AEs or clients).

3. Lack of **Obsession** and **Passion** for Radio.

Let's examine them one by one.

## 1. Marketing Communication has become ± 100% visual.

Quite simply, this is the reality of our business. Since the launch of the Apple Mac in the mid 1980s, image manipulation has become more and more accessible and sophisticated. This has coincided with the growth in globalization and multinational brands' desire to have their images and campaigns able to cross borders without the barriers that language creates. More and more, advertisers and agencies became reliant on people with visual skills to create easily understandable icons.

Today, the visual is king. Everything is screen-based – YouTube, Facebook, Twitter, LinkedIn, Wikipedia, My Space – and those who have visual talent and skills are in demand at all levels, and have become the world's creative leaders.

And as a result…

**The starting point.**

## 2.   **Creatives are** not taught **the skills of radio.**

There are two realities here. First of all, it's natural that in a visually-oriented industry under pressure – from clients to turn out a high volume of work quickly, and from within to strive for quality work which will keep agencies ahead of the game – the emphasis is on encouraging, mentoring and teaching visual skills.

Add to that the second reality which is that in today's agencies those with the talent and skills to do radio mentoring are in short supply. Who supervises, teaches and mentors young creative teams? Group heads and creative directors (CDs) of course. But today's CDs – say in their 30s or perhaps 40s – are themselves products of the visual age.

When I started in advertising, in Washington, New York and then London, almost without exception agency creative directors were copywriters – intelligent, articulate, usually educated men and women (mostly men I must admit) who could write persuasive headlines and copy and present it passionately and persuasively to clients.

Art directors and visualizers performed an important role but rarely led the creative process.

The opposite is true today and my impression is that creative departments of major agencies are invariably led by CDs who come from the visual side. Many are talented, brilliant thinkers with great strategic insights, the ability to spot ideas that will cut through and to oversee to the tiniest detail of production **in their area of strength,** which is visual. But the sad truth is that they don't know how to get the best radio from their teams because they themselves haven't learned. And the great sadness is that their creative teams rarely hear from them that which they hear as a matter of course when they present visual work:

*"Come on guys, I've seen that idea a thousand times, why not try this direction... or maybe this?"*

And as a result of numbers 1 and 2:

3. **There is a lack of Obsession and Passion for Radio.**

Advertising creatives are by nature obsessive and passionate. We are driven to do the best possible work and will go to incredible lengths to achieve it. The best of us routinely scour the media, the web, the archives and dig deep inside ourselves to find that golden nugget of an idea which will not only do the best job for our clients but will also win us the approbation of our peers in the form of awards and recognition. We can do this because we know we have the skills and expertise to support our passion.

There can be no passion without skill, no obsession without expertise. The lack of radio skills brings with it a corresponding lack of unreasonable desire to explore new ways of doing commercials. It is sad, but true.

**The starting point.**

Those were the three functional reasons why radio hasn't kept pace. There is another, which I would describe as systemic in that it has become almost built into the way radio is bought and sold.

**4.   Advertisers and agencies don't pay enough attention to how listeners consume radio.**

These are the ways most people listen to radio.

*How people* listen:

| | |
|---|---|
| For trusted company | Alone and habitually |

| |
|---|
| While doing something else |

They listen **for trusted company.**

Audience research in many countries shows pretty consistently that while radio audiences of course enjoy the music and features, and appreciate the news bulletins and traffic reports, what they really get from radio is 'company' – the feeling that the DJ is in the room, the car or their office with them.

Let's face it – if all people wanted was music, radio would be dead because there are many better music delivery systems. With Spotify, MSN, Napster, iTunes you can have exactly the songs, in any order, at whatever time and repeated as many times as you want. What listeners really want are the relationships they have with the people who bring them the music, relationships that they trust and feel close to. We live increasingly isolated lives and radio is an easy and effective way of managing solitude. Which brings us to the next point.

They listen **alone and habitually.**

In the introduction I told about my childhood when, as a family, we would sit together to listen to our favorite radio programs. Those days have long gone; families don't even watch television together anymore – all media consumption has become individual – so it almost goes without saying that people listen to the radio by themselves.

Most people have what you might call a portfolio of one or two radio stations that they listen to at pretty much the same time, every day. Forever.

They drive to work between, say, 7:30 and 8:15 five days a week. The radio is already tuned to their habitual station, goes on when the car starts, stays on for the journey and is rarely changed. Maybe on the hour they'll switch stations for five minutes of news, but then they'll switch back. The only reason this pattern would ever change is if the station does something they don't like – such as moving or firing their DJ or changing to another music format. In other words, their radio listening is a habit – a pleasant, comfortable habit.

They listen **while doing something else.**

Radio is often referred to as a 'background' or 'secondary' medium because it's very rare that people listen to it without doing something else at the same time. I agree with radio futurologist James Cridland who prefers to think of it as a 'multitasking medium'. He writes in his blog

http://james.cridland.net/blog/radio-the-secondary-medium/

The starting point.

*'You can't do the gardening while on Facebook. It's hard to read the newspaper while driving. It's difficult to tweet while making love (and you get quite a lot of typing errors). This means that radio is a perfect medium for today's time-poor lifestyle since we can continue to enjoy it even when we're doing something else.'*

In other words, whether they're driving, posting on Facebook, assembling IKEA shelves or making love, people listen to radio. So how do you talk to them? Well here's how a sizeable percentage of advertisers all over the world do it.

How advertisers talk:

| | |
|---|---|
| Talk down to them. | Shout at them, frequently in short bursts! |

Expect them to take in lots of information & detail

Advertisers **talk down to them.**

Thousands and thousands of people are listening to radio stations for company they trust and the reality is that most radio advertising talks to them as though they are not very intelligent. Attendees at my workshops invariably laugh or smile when I say this, but it's kind of embarrassed laughter because many of them know it's true.

Try this test. Take the script of your radio commercial (or any typical spot), stand in front of someone, say 40-50cm apart, and read the words to him or her. How does it feel? How do you think he/she feels hearing it: respected, valued? Do you believe he/she will feel drawn to you? Would you speak to a client or customer that way in person?

**Advertisers shout at them, frequently in short bursts!**

In the average car, the radio speakers, as I described above, are about 40cm from the driver. This is not secret information, so why is it so many radio commercials sound as though they're written to be broadcast from a radio fixed on a pole in the ground in the middle of the town square to a crowd of five thousand people? Imagine someone standing directly in front of you telling you enthusiastically (with energetic music in the background) something like this:

'Hey listen, incredible product or service **Y** is available with **X**% discount, every day this week for a limited time only. For details, call this number and visit this website **zzz**.com/uk/nl/au etc.'

Imagine hearing it two or three times a day for a couple of weeks, along with other commercials with equally incredible offers and discounts, all delivered in the same way and all ending with the same web suffix. How easy would it be to differentiate between them? And more importantly, how much actual connection do these spots make with you?

Frequently in short bursts: The last numbers I saw indicate that the average length of a radio campaign in Europe is 3.2 weeks. What kind of impression do you think that makes on someone who listens every working day all year? Certainly, for actions and promotions with a definite end date, in other words for tactical advertising, this may be appropriate. But it also seems to be the case for brand radio advertising. This is because media agencies worship at the Altar of Frequency. I will talk more about this in succeeding chapters.

Advertisers **expect them to take in lots of information and detail.**

To people who are driving, working, on Facebook, ironing or assembling those IKEA bookshelves while listening to the radio, many advertisers talk as if those listeners are actually waiting for their message, pen in hand, eager to write down model numbers, prices, deals and discounts, telephone numbers and web URLs. Here's some news: they're not.

Yes, radio is a multitasking medium, yes you can interest, remind, amuse, inform and otherwise engage them, but providing detailed information is not the true strength of radio, especially if your information is delivered in the same way, using more or less the same words as everyone else's.

Do you see that there is a **disconnect** between the way people listen and advertisers talk? I call this disconnect **The Gap.**

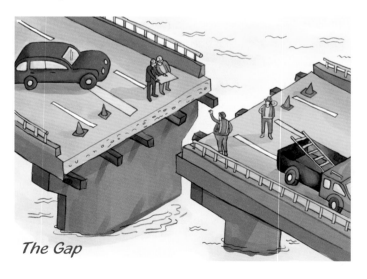

*The Gap*

I am convinced that The Gap is why so many radio briefs everywhere are not actually **Briefs** but rather **Lists,** something like this:

---

**1. What Does the Client Want to Say?**

```
Blah blah OFFERS blah blah FEATURES,
blah blah PRICES blah blah TELEPHONE
NUMBERS, WEBSITE, CALL TO ACTION
```

**2. Needed When?**

```
Don't ask stupid questions
```

**3. Budget?**

```
See previous answer.
```

**4. Tone and Manner**

```
Lively and enthusiastic of course
```

---

As part of my preparation for a workshop or seminar I ask the sponsors to send me examples of radio commercials. As you can imagine, after 36 countries and many sessions (44 in the Netherlands alone in 2011/12), I've heard a lot of radio ads and I must tell you that most of them sound as though they were written to the above brief:

- They are mostly tactical rather than brand ads advertising prices, deals and discounts, and almost always include a web address and or telephone number.

- There is almost always too much content in too few seconds which, of course, means …

- They are delivered in the same Announcer-ish way by – to my anglophone ears – the same four or five voices and sound as though they were done in the same studio at the same time. (When I say this at the seminars in the various countries, there are nods of agreement – yes it's usually the same few people in every market who do most of the Voice-Overs.)

**The starting point.**

27

- There is generally not enough production budget to do it any other way – not that the briefs leave much room for alternative approaches.

But the worst effect of **The Gap** is that it makes it difficult for those who write the commercials to capitalize on radio's two most powerful characteristics:

1. **Radio's power to engage emotions.**

2. **Its unique capacity to evoke personal visual images.**

## EMOTIONS

So much has been written about the emotional power of both radio and sound in general that there is little need to go into it in great detail here, except to remind ourselves that:

Hearing is the first sense that develops in the human fetus, a baby can hear in its mother's womb starting at around 12 weeks! Thus the strong bond between mother and child begins first with sound. Even after birth, the baby hears before it can either see or smell. Radio, done well, can be a continuation of the strongest form of emotional bond.

In his seminal 1964 work Understanding Media: The Extensions of Man, Marshall McLuhan wrote:

*'Radio affects most intimately, person-to-person, offering a world of unspoken communication between writer-speaker and the listener. That is the immediate aspect of radio. A private experience.'*

## IMAGES

Phrases referring to radio as 'The Theatre of the Mind' are as old as the medium itself and tend to be treated – if not dismissed – as clichés. There are so many examples of radio's power to evoke images that, as with emotion, it seems unnecessary to go into huge detail. I offer just two examples – one personal to me, and the other, I guess, to you.

As I wrote earlier, I grew up with radio and as a child my radio heroes existed visually, only in my mind. I had no choice. Stations had no websites, let alone webcams. They did not advertise with photos of their DJs, there were no posters with pictures of my radio heroes: the detectives, criminals, explorers and cowboys who populated the radio serials I listened to faithfully. But I knew exactly how they looked and from time to time when a newspaper or magazine did show a photo, I was invariably disappointed.

Your turn. Be honest now, how many times have you heard someone's voice – man or woman – on the phone, or perhaps behind you in a restaurant, and found yourself attracted enough to want to meet the person? And then been disappointed, because when you saw the person he or she didn't live up to the image you'd created in your mind? That's the visual power of sound and of radio.

So, you're reading The 7 Secrets of Creative Radio, and you've just been presented with items numbered:

1. **Radio's power to engage emotions.**
2. **Its unique capacity to evoke personal visual images.**

Yes, these are the first two of the seven Secrets; here are all of them:

1.  **Find a Feeling**
2.  **Begin with a Picture**
3.  **Think About the Person**
4.  **One Ad, One Message**
5.  **Stand in a Different Place**
6.  **Characters not Voices**
7.  **Produce with Passion**

The first thing to acknowledge, of course, is that they are not secrets. Almost everyone with any advertising training has heard of at least five of my items! There are probably two which are new to you, and if that makes them 'Secrets' so be it. I will devote the rest of this book to explaining all of them.

## *Secret #1*
# Find a Feeling

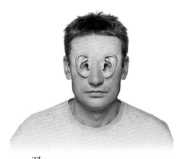

The
# 7 Secrets of
## Creative
### Radio Advertising

## *Secret #1* - **Find a Feeling**

In the last few years an impressive body of evidence has emerged that has convinced most major advertisers that messages with a strong emotional content work better than the traditional fact-filled rational approaches. In my workshops I quote from four well-known ones.

1.  In his authoritative 2008 book The Certainty Principle, Robert Passikoff (the most quoted brand consultant in the US) famously states: **'The decision process in brand adoption, engagement and loyalty is 70% emotional.'**

That's a big claim and a huge percentage, which Passikoff (and his co-author Amy Shea) back up with case histories.

2.  The UK Radio Advertising Bureau (RAB) conducted research in 2010 'Media and the mood of the nation' which they published as 'Radio: The Emotional Multiplier'. It showed very clearly that radio listening lifts people's happiness and energy levels on a day-to-day basis – more, in fact, than the other tested media: TV and Online.

To quote RAB: *'Academic studies have shown that happy and energetic people are more susceptible to advertising messages, which they process with an emotional connection.'*

3. In Germany, Radiozentrale and AS&S did research in 2009: 'Autopilot in den Einkaufskorb' (Shopping Basket on Autopilot), one of the findings of which was: **'Communications that use emotional appeal are more likely to yield strong business results than information- or persuasion-based models.'**

Notice they're not saying emotional appeal yields 'positive impression' or 'good feelings' but rather 'strong business results'!

And finally, a reminder for those advertisers whose spots focus on prices and discounts…

4. Dan Hill, CEO of US research company Sensory Logic and author of Emotionomics states: **'Price-led advertising cuts us off from the wisdom of our emotions and the gut-level instinct we use to evaluate an offer's value.'**

Hill believes, like Passikoff and the others, that our natural tendency is to make purchase decisions emotionally, so at any given time our hearts might tell us to buy Brand A. But if at that moment Brand B is offering a big discount, our heads will tell us to behave rationally and buy the cheaper item.

A win for Brand B, right?

Not necessarily because Sensory Logic's research shows that the inner conflict this switch provokes quite often leads many consumers to make a purchase decision they soon regret, and that's no way to build a business.

He's not saying price shouldn't be a factor but leading with it, without considering the Value Equation (value=price/quality), can be the path to ruin. The full article from which the above paragraphs have been extracted can be found on the Sensory Logic website **www.sensorylogic.com**

So let's look at some examples of radio advertising which make effective use of emotions, spots which 'Find the Feeling'. By the way, it will become clear as we go through the Secrets/spots that there's a lot of overlap; many spots illustrate more than one of – sometimes all – the Secrets.

The first example is a commercial created by Dentsu, Tokyo for the Canon Eos 5 camera and the objective of the ad is to illustrate this camera's very fast start-up time of 0.2 seconds. (In case you're not digitally minded, Start-up Time is how long it takes a camera to reset itself after you've taken a photo so it's ready to take another – important if you're shooting people or things in motion.)

This is a technical point of course; you would expect that there would be some kind of audio/technical treatment to bring this to life, and indeed there is. It's hard to tell it from the script, but when you play the commercial you will hear that every line is spoken in the style of a Formula 1 racing car passing at high speed – exceptionally clever sound design.

But that's not the real reason I think the commercial is wonderful. The copywriter was Wataru Yamamoto and the sound engineer was Hirokazu Suzuki.

▶ PLAY AUDIO  Go to **http://hertzradio.com/qr/** or scan QR Code on **page 12** to listen to this commercial.

**WIFE:** *The baby stood up for the first time.*

**HUSBAND:** *I could see fireworks from my balcony.*

**WIFE:** *The kids were waving at me from the rollercoaster.*

**HUSBAND:** *The groom held his new wife and kissed her.*

**WIFE:** *Our fat cat jumped.*

**HUSBAND:** *Her baby tooth fell out.*

**WIFE:** *My husband did a bungee jump… came back up… and went back down again.*

**HUSBAND:** *My wife finally smiled at me… it's been five years… since she smiled… at me.*

**ANNCR:** *The moments you want captured won't wait for you. Now with a start-up time of just 2/10th of a second – Eos Kiss Digital Camera. Canon Marketing Japan.*

The real brilliance of the Canon commercial is summed up in the Announcer's line 'The moments you want captured won't wait for you'. People who take photos (except for professionals) don't care about Start-up Time, they only care about their lives: their baby standing up for the first time, the husband's bungee jump, the wife's smile. By focusing on the **emotional benefit**, Canon translates the technical feature into a human need! That's what I mean by Find a Feeling.

*The* **7 Secrets** *of* **Creative Radio Advertising**

Here's an example of a commercial that taps into emotions in a different way. It's a spot that my company The Radio Operators did some years ago for a dog food named Go-Dog. On this occasion, I was asked to come up with the idea and script as well as produce the commercial. The brief from the agency was very simple: the commercial had to convey not only that Go-Dog had all the necessary nutrients, in fact more than canned product (Go-Dog was a dry food), but also that dogs really liked it. I had to include their slogan: 'A dog's idea of a complete meal'.

It's well known that the English really love animals (I suspect that they're somewhat fonder of dogs than of children!) and, traditionally, dog food advertising, especially TV ads, featured idealized, country settings with beautiful golden retrievers bounding over hills and leaping fences to return to their loving owners. The agency didn't impose or request a particular style or approach although there was no doubt in my mind that they – and the client – were hoping for a radio version of that kind of spot.

At the time, I had a golden retriever – a sweet handsome dog with a pedigree much nobler than mine (and the best Frisbee catcher ever!), and taking him for walks in London parks was a big part of my life. Watson was an obedient dog; we had trained him well and very rarely had to keep him on a lead – he would come when called.

The same was not true of a lot of dogs I would see on our walks and owners seemed to be in a constant battle to get them to do what they were supposed to. Of course they loved their dogs, and vice versa, but I would observe

*Secret # 1 - Find a Feeling*

37

a great deal of frustration on the part of owners, and it was this emotional relationship that gave me the idea for the Go-Dog commercial.

I decided to create a radio dog-training course and Go-Dog would be the hero. One shake of Go-Dog in its bag (it made quite a satisfying rattle) and even the most disobedient dog would come running.

I presented the script to the agency – I have a vague recollection of doing a lot of panting – and after a few discussions (of course they wanted as much product stuff as possible) it was approved and:

 PLAY AUDIO — Go to **http://hertzradio.com/qr/** or scan QR Code on **page 12** to listen to this commercial.

**TRAINER:** *Today we're going to learn to call a dog using the voice command, come.*

**OWNER:** *Jason, come.*

**TRAINER:** *This command tells your dog to return to the one person it trusts and loves above all others.*

**OWNER:** *Jason, come. Come! Jason come here! Jason, will you come here! Jason! Jason!*

**TRAINER:** *Another method is the new Go-Dog method.* HE SHAKES THE BOX; THE DOG RUNS UP AND BEGINS TO EAT

*Go-Dog is a new kind of dog food – crunchy, meaty-tasting chunks with all the vitamins and minerals dogs need; it has more nourishment than any tinned dog food. New Go-Dog is a dog's idea of a complete dinner. Next time we'll discuss another Go-Dog training situation.*

*The* **7 Secrets** *of* **Creative Radio Advertising**

| OWNER: | *Jason, go away.* |
|---|---|
| ANNCR: | *Special price reductions on Go-Dog beef and liver flavors at most branches of Safeway.* |
| OWNER: | *You're dribbling all over my trousers. Go away!* |

There is a funny story attached to the production of this spot.

The big moment of the commercial, of course, is when the owner shakes the Go-Dog packet and the dog comes running towards him and gobbles the product! I was determined to be as authentic as possible, so on the day of the recording I brought Watson to the studio without having fed him his breakfast so he was really hungry.

We booked quite a large studio, with me at one side holding on to the dog and an assistant on the other side holding a metal bowl containing the Go-Dog. On the signal, I released Watson who ran over, panting, and gobbled the product eagerly. As you can hear in the sound sampler, it was perfect!

Watson then went to sleep under my chair and we got on with recording the actors playing the Trainer, Owner and Announcer, edited and mixed the spot. The agency people were delighted and went off to present it to the client.

The following day, I received an embarrassed call from the producer which is almost a comedy routine in itself:

| HER: | Sorry Tony, we have a bit of a problem. |
|---|---|
| ME: | What kind of problem? |
| HER: | Client doesn't like the eating sequence, says it doesn't sound like a real dog. |
| ME: | That's crazy, of course it's a real dog, you were there! |
| HER: | I know, we've tried to convince him, but he doesn't think it sounds crunchy enough. |
| ME: | !@£$%^&*(!! |

We went back to the studio and re-recorded that segment with the agency producer chewing on crunchy ginger biscuits! Only in advertising! By the way, what you heard in the sound sampler is Watson the Dog – call it the Director's Cut.

It's a cute side-story, but remember the real point of Go-Dog is to illustrate that it's possible to make an emotional connection no matter what the product.

And the next example shows it's possible to Find a Feeling even in the tough, rational, hard-nosed world of tactical retail advertising. It's a commercial by Publicis-Mojo Auckland in New Zealand for Hallensteins, a large retail clothing chain and, in common with almost all advertising in the category, its focus is price.

 PLAY AUDIO    Go to **http://hertzradio.com/qr/** or scan QR Code on **page 12** to listen to this commercial.

### PHONE CALL, FROM THE CALLER'S POV

| MOTHER: | *Hello.* |
|---|---|
| BRIAN: | *Mum, is Dad there?* |
| MOTHER: | *Brian? It's good to hear your voice!* |

| BRIAN: | *Is Dad there?* |
|---|---|
| MOTHER: | *It's been 15 years, I ...!* |
| BRIAN: | *Mum, I really need to tell him something.* |
| MOTHER: | *OK ... It's Brian, he needs to talk to you.* |
| FATHER: | *Brian? Hello?* |
| BRIAN: | *Dad. You can get Lee Rider Jeans at Hallensteins for $49.95.* |
| FATHER: | *Thanks.* |
| BRIAN: | *Oh, Dad ...* |
| FATHER: | *Yeah?* |
| BRIAN: | *Limited time only. I'll see you around.* |
| FATHER: | *Yep.* |

This spot is good on so many levels, and if you go back to the list of Secrets you'll see that it illustrates every one of them, but for the moment let's stick with Find a Feeling.

Canon Eos was a direct emotional approach, linking the product to people's emotional need to record moments in their lives. Go-Dog was less direct about the product but demonstrated the brand's deep understanding of the relationship between owner and dog.

Hallensteins uses emotion in yet another way by touching on a reality that very few retail advertisers ever recognise, which is that, at any given time, not all (in fact relatively few) people listening to a commercial will be in the market for the specific product the spot advertises. Aware that not everyone might need Lee Rider Jeans at $49.95, Hallensteins decides to make the audience like them. In effect, they're saying, 'We're a cool place, we get it, so even if you don't want jeans this week, remember how cool we are when you do need something to wear.'

How do they convey this to an audience of (presumably) young men? Via a little scene, exaggerated of course to be funny but based on truth. A young man calls home, doesn't want an emotional reunion with his mother (whom he hasn't seen for 15 years!) but rather a functional, shorthand conversation with his dad about $49.95 jeans.

Ridiculous? Yes, but through their insight into family dynamics, their understanding that fathers and sons don't have the same conversations as mothers and sons, Hallensteins touches an emotional reality and becomes a cool store.

As I wrote earlier, Hallensteins could illustrate all the Secrets, not least the next one.

## Secret #2
# Begin with a Picture

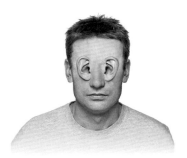

The **7** Secrets *of* Creative Radio Advertising

## *Secret #2 -* **Begin with a Picture**

As I said earlier, my Secrets are mostly common sense rules that could apply to most advertising. Except for this one, which very few people in our business understand.

I'll begin my explanation of it with a simple reality, which is that as an effect of both technology and globalism **Marketing Communication has become ± 100% Visual.**

The Apple Mac came on the scene in the mid-1980s and, creatively, pretty much changed everything. Image manipulation became not only the norm but also accessible to, well, anyone with a Mac. And as major companies and brands expanded into new parts of the world, they developed the need to have brand messages and symbols that were universally understood and did not rely so much on language. Technology made this possible and so today we have an advertising state of affairs which I illustrate in my workshops with this slide:

You may or may not be familiar with Smoke or Flame or Nuke 5 or Motion Control. You may be able to name 10 of the 100 thousand (!) or so typefaces and may well be aware of Photoshop and what it can do, but our Visual Toolbox or Support System is truly awesome.

And it's not just the technology. Along with the software there are designers, illustrators, photographers, editors, film and video directors, lighting cameramen, motion control and VFX (visual effects) specialists, typographers and, of course, creative directors, and this is the slide I use to illustrate the result:

*...see it in your head, do it on the screen!*

There is simply no limit to what can be communicated visually – anything can be superimposed over or turned into anything else. Truly, if you can see it in your head, it can be done on the screen. And you don't need to know how to do it yourself because the Support System includes all the specialists (and more) listed above.

No matter what you want to achieve visually, somewhere in the world you'll find someone who can help you do it.

The security, confidence and feeling of control and power this engenders in creative people is formidable, as is the accompanying need to experiment, to extend creativity, to push the boundaries and stay up with, if not ahead of, the curve. Evidence of this is on every TV and computer screen and in every magazine ad, direct mail leaflet and poster.

And into this inspiring, exciting, creative environment comes a radio brief.

They're the same creative minds, with the same ambition to do good work, to succeed for their clients, to win awards.

But this is radio.

- No pictures
- No clever, easily accessible tools and software and techniques
- No thousands of fonts
- No sound-oriented creative directors or designers

In other words, in sound there is nothing like the combination of technology and people to make up the kind of support system they're used to – or at least, that's what they believe.

All they have is a platitude, a cliché that's existed since the very first radio commercial was aired on WEAF in New York in 1922: **'Radio is Pictures in Sound'.**

It is the copywriter's job, to continue with platitude, to use sound to create images in the listener's mind. And of course, it's the truth.  After all, what is a cliché except the truth told so many times it becomes boring?

So copywriters use sound – words, music, SFX (sound effects) – but the simple truth is that they are limited to the sounds they know or are inspired by.  And while every day they are bombarded with – and thus inspired by – thousands of different sorts of visual images, the range, breadth and depth of audio images they're exposed to is vastly smaller.

So what happens?  They use the sounds they're exposed to.  In effect, those same adventurous, free-thinking, out-of-the-box, push-the-envelope creative teams seek safety in what I call:

## THE AUDIO COMFORT ZONE

The radio *formats*
*and* VOICES *and* SCENES *and* MUSIC *and* SFX
*that* **CREATIVES ALREADY KNOW!**

The Audio Comfort Zone consists of those radio formats and voices and scenes and music and SFX **that they already know!**

You'll see some examples in a minute, but first – courtesy of the aforementioned 'Gap' – let's look at the Client Comfort Zone.

*Client's Comfort Zone*

This is the let's-get-as-much-stuff-into-as-few-seconds-as-possible style of radio advertising which, I'm sorry to say, is all too prevalent. I consider them announcements rather than advertising – tactical, small-space newspaper ads read out loud.

But even without the restrictions and limitations imposed by clients there are various Creative Comfort Zones, and these are pretty much the same all over the world!

# FUNNY OR DRAMATIC CREATIVE SCENE!
## ADVERTISING PART

There's this tried and true format we've all heard a thousand times: a dialogue or scene, amusing or dramatic – husband/wife, salesperson/customer, doctor/patient, friend who needs product/friend who knows about it, mother/child, etc. etc., often illustrating what happens if someone **doesn't** have the advertised product or brand.

## IRONIC MONOLOGUE DONE BY GUY WITH NICE VOICE

Monologues have been big winners in the awards shows for the last few years – Sears Craftsman, Dos Equis, New York Thoroughbred Racing from the US, Virgin Airlines and Mercedes from South Africa, Sky TV from Australia come to mind. Well-written, delivered impeccably – usually ironic or sarcastic. Almost as though the copywriters, who have been taking a back seat to their art director partners for the last few years, have decided to revolt and say, 'Hey look at the power of words!' Sometimes the monologues are accompanied by background scenes or SFX or music.

Here are some of the other Comfort Zone formats widely used all over the world. The Live Phone Call is certainly alive and kicking – advertisers calling unsuspecting customers, or vice versa. Lots of football or other sports commentaries … 'And he scores!! And saves 30% on a brand new XXX!!!'

Well-known songs and voices and, of course, the most widely-used Comfort Zone format – the Voice-Over enthusiastically selling the action or promotion, with music underneath (of course!)

**LIVE PHONE CALLS / SPORTS / GPS / SONGS / FAMOUS VOICES ETC ETC ETC**

The Audio Toolbox may not be anything like as big as its visual equivalent but every copywriter knows that it's possible to sample any sound and then manipulate, repeat, reverse, tune or detune it.  So another category in the Comfort Zone is the Clever-Use-of-Sound-Effects.  Dogs, cats, car-horns played as musical notes.  Words rapidly chopped.  Knives, spoons, doors, bottles played in rhythm etc.  Every year agencies send me two or three scripts of this kind to produce, and I must say they are great fun to work on.

I must make something completely clear: 'Comfort Zone' doesn't mean 'Bad'. The award-winning monologues and dialogues I cited have been immaculately written and produced, as have many of the phone calls, sports commentaries and SFX-based spots. I regularly direct and produce dialogue commercials for agencies and very much enjoy the process; my happiest moments have been spent directing actors in the studio. No, there is nothing wrong with the Comfort Zone in itself; the issue is that it is, well… comfortable. And for both creatives and advertisers, Comfortable is not a great place to be.

For advertisers, Comfortable usually means 'doing what we've always done', and the result is radio commercials for their products and brands which sound like radio commercials for every other product and brand. Commercially, it simply doesn't make sense. Within categories there is already little enough difference between many products and services and I can't comprehend why any advertiser would want to sound like its competitor.

For creative agencies, Comfortable not only runs counter to everything that drives creative people to do better work; it also, frankly, makes even less sense than it does for advertisers.

The reality of our business is that, as a matter of course, creative agencies are driven – even obsessed – by the need to do work that is not only effective for their clients' businesses but also satisfies their passion, their sense of craft and accomplishment and – importantly – gains them recognition from the marketing community. Hence the relationship between creative awards and effectiveness that Furman writes about.

In the visual media they strive to achieve this by being different, by experimentation, by being ahead of the curve and, as you've seen, they have the tools and support system to do it. In radio, they lack the tools and support – or at least feel they do – and thus the Comfort Zone is the manifestation of their inability to summon up the obsession and passion to do something different.

**So what's the answer?**

Believe it or not, the answer is within the same cliché that drives creatives into the Comfort Zone in the first place, i.e. 'Use sound to make pictures'. Except that I turn the cliché on its head.

For many years, in my workshops and seminars I have been using a simple, dramatic example to introduce my cliché-reversing approach to radio. It works because it uses all the elements and features of my workshops: sound, visuals, and interaction between the workshop participants and me. Will it work in book form? Dunno, let's see.

Here's an image. What do you see, or how would you describe it?

I imagine you'll say, 'A man having his back scratched', which, of course, is the obvious – and correct – answer. Certainly it's the first answer spoken in every workshop I've ever done.

What's quite interesting though is that it isn't a precise answer. The back scratching is the story of the picture, i.e. what's happening, but the actual answer to the question 'What do you see?' is 'A hand holding a phone on which there's a picture – a photo – of a man having his back scratched'. I'm quite intrigued by the human tendency to be more taken by the human story than by the factual answer.

Anyway, here we have an image. Now here's a radio commercial:

**PLAY AUDIO**   Go to **http://hertzradio.com/qr/** or scan QR Code on **page12** to listen to this commercial.

WE HEAR A MAN ENJOYING HAVING HIS
BACK SCRATCHED

**ANNCR:**   *Here's something to feel good about, from Blue Band.*

**MAN:**   *Up a bit, bit more... aah great, now in a bit – no that's out! In – to the right.*
*Aaahhh, ooh there, wonderful... oooh.*

**ANNCR:**   *This good feeling is presented by Blue Band Margarine, which is made from only natural ingredients and pure vegetable oils. And that is something else to feel good about.*

It's a very simple spot with a man having his back scratched and directing the scratcher to the exact point that feels best. It was part of a multimedia campaign for Blue Band Margarine in the UK based on 'Good Feelings', i.e. the feeling good about knowing you're serving a natural healthy product. However, the question I now ask is not whether it's a great campaign, I ask, simply:

"Is the Blue Band commercial a picture in sound?" In other words, does it more or less create the picture you see above?

The answer of course is, 'Yes it's a picture in sound', but it is also something else. It is the **sound that the picture makes**, because – here we should insert a big drum roll(!) – The Picture Came Before the Sound!

When I wrote the Blue Band spot I was working in a team with an art director. We had the brief to come up with a continuation of the 'Good Feelings' campaign and, as art directors do, Gwyn scribbled his ideas on a layout pad. One of them was a man with an ecstatic smile on his face as a woman scratches his back.

"What do you think?" he asked.

"I think you've just drawn a radio ad," I replied. I heard the sound that Gwyn's picture was making, wrote it as a script and 'Backscratch' became the commercial you just heard. In other words, The Picture Created The Sound and it is the single most important piece of advice I can offer to anyone writing a radio commercial: **Think first of an image and let the image create the sound!**

It works so well that in every single presentation and seminar and, above all, in my Radio for Art Directors© (Rad4Ad) workshops, I make this promise:

## The RAd4Ad Promise

If you start the radio creative process by thinking in visual terms, I genuinely believe that it will help you in three ways.

1. It will help you Write Radio. Can you see how your creative canvas has just become so much broader? Every one of the visual formats or styles you see in the diagram: Close-Up, a Storyboard, a Cartoon, a Texture and a whole lot more – just about any visual 'ism' you can imagine, including Surrealism – can have an audio equivalent.

   If you are an agency creative, chances are you already work this way. Well don't stop just because it's radio! Draw a storyboard, think of a wide shot, or a zoom or a dissolve or animation. Work as you already may do – as a copywriter/art director team. Visual ideas will lead to more interesting sounds. I promise.

2. It will help you Present. I'll get into this in more detail as we get into the other Secrets, but the simple thought is this: The more advertisers can see in a radio idea, the easier it is for them to buy it, and the overwhelming majority of radio scripts fail to help clients in this regard. At Cannes Lions 2011, I conducted a very well-attended workshop, 100% based on the Radio for Art Directors © Promise. It was entitled 'How to Present Radio so Clients Won't Kill It!'

3. It will help you Produce. I am convinced that if everyone involved with bringing radio spots to life in the studio – writers, producers, engineers, 'voices' – were more aware of the visual intent of the commercials they're working on, there would be many fewer unimaginative, lackluster spots all sounding like each other. Again, I'll go into this in more detail as we go through the Secrets.

The best way to convince you that the promise works is to show you some examples.

The first is a campaign for the Samsung NV10 camera done by Leo Burnett Brussels – three very simple commercials advertising the high definition of the camera's 10 million pixels. The creators were Gregory Ginterdaele and Marie-Laure Cliquennois, production by Sonicville, Brussels.

 **PLAY AUDIO** Go to **http://hertzradio.com/qr/** or scan QR Code on **page 12** to listen to this commercial.

**WOMAN:** *Did you notice?*

*The piece of lettuce… between the teeth… of the guitarist… of the band… on the stage… in the Stade… de France?*

**DIGITAL CAMERA SHUTTER**

**ANNCR:** *Samsung NV Ten. Ten million pixels. For ultra-precise images.*

**SOUND LOGO**

----------------------

**MAN:** *Did you notice?*
*The speck … in the eye … of the priest … on the steps … in front … of the church … on the central square … of the city?*

## DIGITAL CAMERA SHUTTER

**ANNCR:** *Samsung NV Ten. Ten million pixels.*
*For ultra-precise images.*

## SOUND LOGO

----------------------

**MAN:** *Did you notice?*
*The blood vessel... in the eye... of the*
*rabbit... in the mouth... of the snake...*
*on the rock... on the mountain...*
*on the left?*

## DIGITAL CAMERA SHUTTER

**ANNCR:** *Samsung NV Ten. Ten million pixels. For*
*ultra-precise images.*

## SOUND LOGO

----------------------

These commercials are remarkable in that they literally 'Zoom Out' from an extreme close-up – between the teeth – to a wide shot – Stade de France – in one continuous measured movement. Have you ever before heard radio commercials do that?

There's no artifice, no clever tricks, just one person asking you to see what she (or he) sees. And for me, that is precisely the point. The copywriters must have 'seen' the spots first! How could they have written these commercials if not? I don't know whether they drew them or used actual photographs or video, but to me it is simply not possible to describe something you want someone else to see if you can't see it yourself!

There's another great strength to the Samsung spots, and that is their measured pace, and I'll talk more about that in a later chapter.

The next example goes back in time almost 50 years, is one of the great visual radio campaigns of all time and a personal 'Holy Grail'.

The commercial is one of a campaign that the legendary American copywriter Robert C Pritikin created in 1966 for the Fuller Paint Company. There were nine spots, each devoted to a single color, delivered by famous Chicago Announcer Ken Nordine (whose voice Pritikin describes as 'haunting') and each accompanied by orchestrated improvisational jazz – different for each color. They're all wonderful; my favorite is Brown.

 **PLAY AUDIO**  Go to **http://hertzradio.com/qr/** or scan QR Code on **page 12** to listen to this commercial.

ANNCR: *The Fuller Paint Company invites you to stare with your ears… at Brown.*

*Among purists – and you know how many purists there are –  brown was having some difficulty.*

*Some of the purists wanted brown to be more* **(MUSIC)**

*Others wanted brown to be more* **(MUSIC)**

*Still others wanted brown to be…* **(MUSIC)**

WHISPER: *Fuller Paint, Fuller Paint*
*A lesser color might have fallen apart, but*

*The* **7** *Secrets of* **Creative Radio Advertising**

WHISPER: *brown met the problem beautifully by becoming more and more subtle. Brown has become just about as subtle as subtle can get. That's why you hear people saying, "My, what a subtle brown." If that's the kind of brown you want, why want less? Remember to remember the Fuller Paint Company, a century of leadership in the chemistry of color. Visit your Fuller Color Center tomorrow.*

*Or the day after yesterday.*

There's an interesting business side to the Fuller campaign which Pritikin writes about in his book *Christ Was An Ad Man*.

He reports that when the commercials were aired on local stations, around 50% of the time the station Announcer or DJ would rhapsodize about their creativity and unique use of the radio medium etc. These spontaneous ad-lib comments lasted on average 20 seconds which, in effect, gave Fuller Paint a 30% airtime bonus!

I was a young copywriter at the beginning of my career when I first heard the Fuller spots and I was simply blown away – not only by the beauty of the commercials themselves but also by the creative opportunities they revealed. Throughout my 40 years in advertising I have looked for ways to do genuine color radio, and in the late 1980s – 30 years after Fuller Paint – I got my opportunity.

I must be honest and say that I can't actually remember the details of how I came to do a seminar for Unilever in the UK; I believe it was part of an initiative by the commercial radio stations to try to convince the huge multinational (and one of the UK's biggest FMCG companies) to invest in radio. I do remember being questioned closely by their brand people about whether I really believed that products whose benefits were almost completely visual could be advertised successfully on radio. No points for guessing my answer!

Some months later I received a call from the Persil brand team who said they were considering a brand radio campaign in Scotland for their product New System Persil Automatic, and would I be interested in working on it. Are you kidding?

The main claim for the product was that it helped maintain the brightness and intensity of colors. They explained that the normal wear it, wash it, wear it, wash it again routine caused colors to fade – **unless,** of course, you use New System Persil Automatic.

The main advertising for the product so far was an outdoor campaign – bus shelters which illustrated the problem with multiple images of clothing showing the gradual fading. I don't now have a copy of the actual bus shelter poster but the design was something like this:

PERSIL POSTER
-- well, sort of

bright red top
red a bit faded
red more faded
etc

The campaign was aimed at the mothers and wives who did the washing week after week, and the big radio challenge, of course, was to convey the gradual fading which was visualized so graphically – and easily – in the posters.

Each poster – there were three or four executions I believe – focused on one piece of clothing so I decided to do the same thing and do a series of commercials, each of which told the story of a particular garment. I asked the client which clothing items I could feature, and they sent me a list:

> *A woman's blouse/top/shirt*
> *Children's things – like playsuits*
> *Men's sport clothes*
> *Women's exercise wear*
> *A man's business shirt*

The general inspiration, or at least the reference point for my idea, was Peter and the Wolf – Sergei Prokofiev's famous piece in which a narrator tells a story to children in which each character is played by an instrument, or section of the orchestra. So my starting point was a story.

CLAC   CRRRR   WOUZZ

Tell a Story

The main protagonist in this particular tale was a child's playshirt, and I decided it should be pink and would have a pattern of fluffy yellow ducks! And – following Prokofiev's example – this character would be represented by a musical theme.

*The story Hero...*     *...as played by...*

Why pink? Why ducks? It was an arbitrary creative decision arrived at with the help of my musical collaborator for this (and many other) projects, Quito Colayco.  Quito (she's from the Philippines) is a classically trained film composer, used to being asked by directors to illustrate musically a variety of emotions and visual themes.

"Ducks?  Well, Prokofiev used the oboe, that would work!"

So Quito began sketching out pink and duck music and I thought about the big challenge – portraying the playsuit's wear it-wash it-wear it cycle.

What we needed was a shorthand metaphor to express the repeating cycle and I came up with the idea of a little child – I decided to call her Sarah – going out to play in the garden lots of times, and coming back to the house to show her mother what she'd done or found.  And every time she came back in saying, "Look what I found!" you know that whatever she had found or made would have dirt involved.  Something like this:

Look what I found!
Look what I made!
Look what I...!

What on earth?

All good stories need a villain and the bad guy for this one is, of course, the washing machine!  I sampled sounds from three cycles and played them in time with the music.  And, of course, who comes to the rescue but our hero, the product.

CLAC   CRRRR   WOUZZ

The Villain (boo!)        The Other Hero

The nature of the commercial meant that we had to record the elements separately – a kind of Blue Screen radio!

Ten or so classical musicians – mostly from the London Symphony Orchestra woodwind section – played Quito's score, without having a real concept of the commercial other than it had ducks in it,

'In bar 15, could you be a bit more duck-like, and sadder, please,' was Quito's note to the oboe player.

In a separate session, I knelt on the floor as a five-year-old girl obediently ran towards me a few times, saying, "Look what I made, Mummy!"

Nigel Lambert, a talented and very experienced radio actor, read the story in sections, timed precisely to fit with the music.

And my long-time recording collaborator, André Jacquemin (the UK's best sound designer), hit the buttons at precisely the right moment so that the washing machine FX fell in exact time with the music and then we worked together to balance all the elements to make a radio production I'm proud of to this day!

PLAY AUDIO   Go to **http://hertzradio.com/qr/** or scan QR Code on **page 12** to listen to this commercial.

**NIGEL:**   *Sarah is five, and this is her favorite playshirt. It's ♪♫, with fluffy yellow ducks ♪♫.*

**SARAH:**   *It's my favorite!*

**NIGEL:**   *Sarah loves her playshirt, and she wears it to play in the garden.*

**SARAH:**   *Look what I found, Mummy!*

**NIGEL:** *And you wash it, at low temperature (washing machine) and she wears it to play in the garden.*

**SARAH:** *Mummy, look what I made!*

**NIGEL:** *And you wash it (washing machine) and she wears it to play in the ...*

**MOTHER:** *Sarah, what on earth!*

**NIGEL:** *And after a while, the dirt builds up ♪♫. So the pink isn't quite as pink ♪♫. And the yellow ducks aren't as fluffy ♪♫.*

*New System Persil Automatic can help. Its advanced formula can remove ground-in dirt, even at low temperatures. So the pink stays very pink ♪♫. And the fluffy yellow ducks are happy again ♪♫. Wash...*

**SARAH:** *Mummy, look what I made!*

**NIGEL:** *... after wash...*

**SARAH:** *Look what I found, Mummy!*

**NIGEL:** *... after wash.*

**MOTHER:** *Sarah, don't you dare bring that in here!*

**NIGEL:** *New System Persil Automatic. It's all you could want from a powder.*

Here's another one of the spots from the campaign, for a blue rugby shirt. The music idea for this one was simply the word 'blue' sung in close harmony – happy and sad – to a rhythm track.

**PLAY AUDIO**  Go to **http://hertzradio.com/qr/** or scan QR Code on **page 12** to listen to this commercial.

**NIGEL:** *Your husband's joined a rugby club.*
*And he has a brand new rugby shirt.*
*It's deep blue. ♪♫. He puts it on.*

**HUSBAND:** *What do you think?*

**WIFE:** *A winner.*

**NIGEL:** *… and plays in the match on Sunday.*

**WIFE:** *Well?*

**HUSBAND:** *17-6.*

**NIGEL:** *And you wash it at low temperature*
(washing machine) *and he plays in the*
*match on Sunday…*

**WIFE:** *Well?*

**HUSBAND:** *25-0.*

**NIGEL:** *And you wash it* (washing machine) *and*
*he plays in the match on Sunday…*

**HUSBAND:** *Don't ask! Just don't ask.*

**NIGEL:** *And after a few matches, the dirt builds up.*
*And the blues have… a case of*
*the blues ♪♫.♪♫.*

*New system Persil Automatic can help.*
*Its advanced formula can remove*
*ground-in dirt, even at low temperatures.*
*So the shirt stays  bright and the sad blues*
*are happy again ♪♫.♪♫… Wash…*

**HUSBAND:** *12-6.*

*The* **7 Secrets** *of* **Creative Radio Advertising**

| NIGEL: | After wash...♩♫. |
|---|---|
| HUSBAND: | 16-16. |
| NIGEL: | ... after wash ♩♫. |
| WIFE: | You won? You actually won? |
| NIGEL: | New System Persil Automatic. It's all you could want from a powder. |

## The Radio for Art Directors© Game

I realized some years ago that telling the stories and playing examples of visually inspired radio is entertaining, and valuable to an extent, but I also needed to find something that would help workshop and seminar participants begin to engage visually themselves in this exciting form of radio creativity.

The answer was the Rad4AD© Game, which has proven to be an important – and fun – highlight of interactive sessions. If you've attended one of my workshops you'll probably remember how it went. If not – well, playing the game is a lot more engaging than reading a description of it, but I must try to give you an idea of what happens simply because the learning from it is so significant in terms of my visual approach to radio.

Imagine a seminar of say 25 participants; I've played the game with as few as six and as many as 240 but 15 is a reasonable average number. Each participant has a piece of paper with sentences numbered 1, 2 and 3 and there are three different pages distributed so that three people sitting in the same row will have different sentences which are, in fact, descriptions of people, objects, spaces or situations.

## Time to be a Radio Art Director

1. A *Public Space*  Piazza. Museum. Park?  Where?
   A *Relationship* – Personal?  Business?  What do they feel?
   *Something to wear*  Describe it.  Who's wearing it?

2. *Someone at Work* – What is she doing?  What's his name?
   A *Drink* - What kind. how is it served?
   A *Work of Art* - Who is the artist? Describe it

3. *What* do you see?

As you can see, the items for each number differ widely – a drink, a relationship, a view from a window! – and I often adapt the descriptions to the product or brand category of the advertiser whose session it is.

I tell the participants that they are going to hear a piece of music and that, based on what it says on their paper, they should simply write (or draw) **what they see**.  So, for example, if their Number 1 is a drink, they might see a cocktail, glass of wine, café latte, anything.  If it's a relationship, it could be two lovers, two bank robbers, a boss and a subordinate, etc., etc.

"There are no wrong answers!"  I assure them. "No right answers, in fact, just whatever the music makes you see in the category on your page."

I add a further suggestion:

"To give you even more freedom, you are free to change categories, you <u>don't</u> have to follow what's on the page.  If your Number 1 says 'A Relationship' and you see chocolate ice cream, that's perfectly fine!"

They then hear the first piece of music – usually 30-40

seconds – mostly instrumental, selected from my library of around 12 tracks. Often I use sections from film scores but never well-known themes. (Out of the 1,000+ people who've played the game, only one person has ever recognized a piece of music: a Hungarian guy who happened to be a movie music fanatic!)

It's fascinating to watch people writing their 'answers'. Some put down a couple of words, others write lengthy, very detailed descriptions of what they 'see'. Some people begin writing with the first note, others do nothing until the music has finished and then write furiously. Often I observe individuals who up to that moment haven't seemed particularly engaged in the seminar suddenly become deeply involved.

We repeat the process for items 2 and 3. Number 3 is not music but rather a 4-second sound effect – SFX. Then the fun begins; we go round the room asking people what they 'saw' for each piece of music. As they call out their answers, we note them on a big flip chart, and end up with something like this:

As you might expect, the range of answers is remarkable; the same 30 seconds of music evokes a huge variety of quite different images, colors, moods, patterns, drinks, scenes, objects and relationships. And in mixed groups of advertisers, media specialists and agency account and creative people, it's particularly fascinating to me that the most vivid and/or bizarre images rarely come from those participants who are labeled 'creative'!

When we've filled the chart with all the answers, I always ask two important questions:

1. "How many of you took advantage of my offer to change categories and saw something other than what was on your page?"

2. "Keeping an open mind, and remembering that this is just a game, did anyone hear an image from someone else that you honestly felt was just wrong? In other words, that music could not possibly evoke that image."

There are hardly ever any hands raised. In fact, in all the years I've played the game less than one in 50 people has answered yes to either question. Very occasionally there's some discussion around Number 2 but it usually turns out that the person questioning someone else's image actually means to say, 'I personally wouldn't have seen that,' which is not the same as saying, 'It's wrong!'

I believe that the two major lessons we learn from the Radio for Art Directors Game are really important:

First and most obvious is that the same music will evoke a huge variety of different images. Can we therefore simply play a piece of music in our commercial and expect listeners to see what we want them to see? Of course not, but that's where the second lesson comes in.

Given freedom to ignore what's on the page and see whatever they want, 98% of seminar participants follow instructions and **see what they're told to see.** And **they also find what others see believable!** This is really significant. The Radio for Art Directors Game shows us that if we tell people to see a black dress or a mystic valley or strawberry ice cream, and use music to help them, they will see what we want them to see.

Want proof? Go back and listen to the Fuller Paint commercial. Is the music, by itself, really brown? Only brown? Couldn't it be a large dog walking in the street or a glass of red wine? We decided it was brown because Bob Pritikin **told us it was brown and, in the context of the commercial, it made sense!**

In the same way, the Persil was pink with fluffy yellow ducks. Could easily have been something else!

If you tell them in the right way, listeners will see what you suggest they see. Can you see how this widens your choices and gives you so many more creative possibilities?

I'm not saying you have to use music. It can be helpful, but it's not mandatory. What is crucial is that you help your listeners by giving them clues and context – in other words telling them what to see. As do the examples we've already shown and as do just about all the commercials in this book.

## What do we *learn* from this exercise?

You can *create* almost any *image* and
make your audience *see* and *believe* it.
*If* you *help* by providing  *Clues* and *Context.*

---

"In a bit. . .not that's out!"

"700 foot mountain of whipped cream. . . "

"It's pink, with fluffy yellow ducks"

---

Another perfect example is the famous and iconic
'Maraschino Cherry' commercial made in 1957(!) by
American humorist Stan Freburg.

▶ PLAY AUDIO    Go to **http://hertzradio.com/qr/** or scan QR Code on **page 12**
to listen to this commercial.

**CLIENT:**    *Radio?  Why should I advertise on radio?*
*There's nothing to look at, no pictures!*

**FREBURG:**    *Listen, you can do things on radio you*
*couldn't possibly do on TV.*

**CLIENT:**    *That'll be the day.*

**FREBURG:**    *All right, watch this.  OK people!*
*Now, when I give you the cue I want*
*the 700-foot mountain of whipped*
*cream to roll into Lake Michigan,*
*which has been drained and filled with*
*hot chocolate.*

*Then the Royal Canadian Air Force will*
*fly overhead towing a 10-ton maraschino*
*cherry,  which will be dropped into the*
*whipped cream, to the cheering of*
*25,000 extras.*

**FREBURG:** *All right, cue the Mountain!*
(HUGE RUMBLING & GRINDING ENDING WITH A SPLASH)

*Cue the Air Force!*
(FLEET OF WWII VINTAGE AIRPLANES OVERHEAD)

*Cue the Maraschino Cherry!*
(WHISTLING BOMB FALLING, THEN A BIG SPLUDGE)

*OK, 25,000 cheering extras!*
(HUGE CROWD CHEERING)

*Now, you wanna try that on television?*

**CLIENT:** *W-e-e-ll.*

**FREBURG:** *You see radio is a very special medium because it stretches the imagination.*

**CLIENT:** *Doesn't television stretch the imagination?*

**FREBURG:** *Up to 21 inches, yes.*

It's another of my 'Holy Grail' commercials – a tour de force of using sound to create utterly exaggerated – and impossible – images which, at the same time, are also believable because the humor and charm with which the story is told gives us **permission to suspend disbelief** and enter into Stan Freburg's world. At heart, most of us are children and we love being told stories. In the same way, you can give your listeners the same permission and allow them to enter into the world of your brand and product.

I play Maraschino Cherry after the Rad4AD game because game item Number 3 is, in fact, the SFX of the mountain rolling into the whipped cream, edited out of the commercial.

The answers to 'What do you see?' range from 'motorbike crashing into a river', 'huge door of a castle breaking open', 'old house falling down', 'lion roaring before pouncing', 'pirate ship sinking' etc. Nobody, of course, has ever guessed 700-foot mountain of whipped cream! And this is exactly the point. It isn't! It's a collection of carefully edited and mixed sound effects which Stan Freburg tells us is whipped cream. We believe him because he makes us want to. You can do the same.

*Secret #3*

# Think About
# The Person

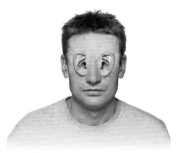

# *Secret #3* - **Think About The Person**

Let's face it, this is not a secret at all, it's kind of obvious! These days, most large agencies and advertisers have an account or strategic planning function – individuals or whole departments who act as the voice of the consumer within the organization and whose main responsibility is to write a creative brief that balances the needs and desires of the target audience with what the advertiser wants to say about the brand or product.

Done well, advertising based on this combination of research and insight will somehow communicate to the target audience that the advertiser understands them.

But listening to most radio commercials, you would get the impression that if such knowledge exists it's been ignored in favor of messages that talk about the product or offer as though the customer's needs – certainly the emotional ones – are an irrelevance.

The objective of Secret #3 is to remember that radio is, above all, personal – a **conversation** between you, the brand and one listener.

I'll illustrate this by asking you to imagine, for a moment, a conversation with someone you've just met, or at least don't know very well. During your encounter, the other person only ever talks about herself.

No matter how interesting or persuasive she is, at some level you may feel a bit ignored and wonder if she actually has any interest in you at all. It's important to remember that you might not be consciously aware of this feeling, but it could well affect your future behavior towards her.

Think about the Person is obviously related to Secret #1 Find a Feeling – you can't really identify an emotional need without thinking about the person whose need it is! So it pretty much goes without saying that all the commercials in this book are very clearly focused on the people they're aimed at.

Here are a couple more examples of campaigns which were created specifically as a result of insight into the thoughts, feelings and behavior of their target audience.

The first is a commercial I wrote when I was Creative Director of McCann-Erickson Central in the UK. It's for Merry Hill, a shopping center in the UK Midlands and it was one of a number of spots we created as part of a Christmas campaign.

The objective was, naturally, to get as many people as possible into the center and therefore, into the stores; the term in the trade is "footfall." Like most malls, Merry Hill believed that the way to accomplish that was to remind potential shoppers of their features and advantages, such as the large number of retailers and restaurants, their late-opening hours – important during the Christmas

Shopping season – and the fact that parking was free – another important consideration (It isn't always in the UK)

It goes without saying that our job is always to help our clients achieve their business objective. But, as creators it's also vital to keep reminding them, and ourselves, of advertising's other, primary, goal, famously expressed by one of the giants of the business.

> *"If your advertising goes unnoticed, everything else is academic"*
>
> WILLIAM BERNBACH

So how did we go about making Merry Hill's Christmas-Shopping message which, let's face it, was pretty much the same as every other mall's – stand out? Luckily, we were dealing with an intelligent and sophisticated Head of Marketing, Julie Haney, who agreed with us that although we were after maximum footfall, the feet in question belonged to human beings, with needs and feelings, likes and dislikes.

I honestly don't remember the actual briefing discussions, but looking through my files I can see we did a TV commercial and 3 radio spots.

And one of the radio ads was specifically targeted at men.

There is apparently tons of very scientific neuro-brain mapping-type research that explains why men dislike Christmas shopping. It's quite possibly to do with our using the right side of the brain much more when we shop than women, who use both sides and get a broader view. Yawn.

The fact remains, most guys just don't like to do it and, reading the brief, I came very quickly to the conclusion that in order to get men to pay attention and take in our wonderful features and information, we'd not only have to get noticed but also – and even more important – show men that Merry Hill actually Gets It. That Merry Hill understands men *don't actually want to go there at Christmas!*

Here is the resulting script:

▶ PLAY AUDIO   Go to **http://hertzradio.com/qr/** or scan QR Code on **page12** to listen to this commercial.

**WOMAN:**   *Right, got something to say to you blokes...about Christmas shopping.*

*Are you fascinated? No! Is your true love expecting a present? Yes! So make it less of a hassle, by shopping late at Merry Hill.*

*It's open weekdays until 10 so you can go after work – I'm sure you can find a creative excuse.*

THE "BLOKE" PHONES HIS GIRLFRIEND

**BLOKE:**   *Hi love it's me. I'm going to be late, something's come up.*

**GIRLFRIEND:**  *Oh, what?*

**BLOKE:**   *A meeting.*   (AWKWARD PAUSE AS HE CONSIDERS TELLING THE TRUTH) *I'm going shopping alright!*

**WOMAN:**   *Call that creative? Anyway, it's less crowded, free parking, places to eat, and there are more than 200 shops.*

*And there are Merry Hill gift vouchers so you don't actually have to go into any of them. And think of the welcome at home!*

GIRLFRIEND: *Get what you wanted darling?*

BLOKE: *None of your business.*

GIRLFRIEND: *Ooh!*

WOMAN: *Late night shopping at Merry Hill.*
*Careful, you might actually enjoy it.*

The commercial started life as a simple monolog. A feisty woman – played to perfection by the hugely talented actress/comedienne Tracy-Ann Obermann – just talking to guys about shopping in a no nonsense humorous manner. (You'll meet Tracy-Ann again later; I had her –or rather the characters she plays – in my head when I was writing)

At a certain point though, I realized there was an opportunity to display a bit more insight into men's shopping attitudes so I wrote in a couple of very short illustrative scenes between the "bloke"- played with delightful grumpiness by Anthony Etherton - and his other half, Amanda Abbington who did wonderful things with 7 words!

The music that sneaks in at the end was composed by Quito Colayco for the TV campaign.

I've chosen as the next example, to illustrate Secret #3, a favorite campaign of mine from the UK for a regional railway company, Chiltern Railways.

As you may know, the UK national rail system was decentralized in the mid-1990s and now consists of a number of individual train operating companies who have the franchises in different areas. Chiltern Railways runs services along the M40 Corridor between London and the Midlands, and this particular campaign is for the route between Haddenham & Thame Parkway near Oxford and London Marylebone station.

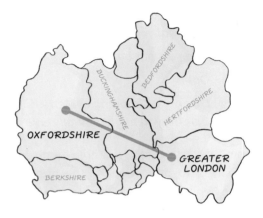

The brief was straightforward: to convince people living close to Haddenham & Thame Parkway station (HDM) that they should take the train to London rather than drive. It's around 67 kilometers from HDM to London Marylebone, pretty much a straight drive down the M40 and with clear roads shouldn't take more than 40 minutes or so. The only problem is that roads are never clear; the M40 into and out of London – certainly around peak periods – is a parking lot!

And it costs a small fortune to park in Central London. In fact there are a bunch of good, rational reasons why it makes more sense to travel in the relative comfort of Chiltern Railways trains.

But reason doesn't always work. HDM is in a wealthy part of the UK and we were talking mostly to intelligent, well-paid executives – mostly men – with work or business in London. Of course they're aware that the train is a more sensible choice than the car, but they drive, in their nice cars, for emotional rather than rational reasons.

So I saw the radio task as not only to communicate the advantages of Chiltern Trains, but also to make drivers feel that their current behavior was, well, not too bright.

The first – and as it turned out, the most crucial – step in the creative process was a meeting with the media agency.

What? Creative and media actually talking to each other – pretty much unheard of these days! Sadly that's true and, in my view, it is one of the major contributors to the overall low standard of radio ads. In this case though, we were lucky. Chiltern's agency was McCann-Erickson, Birmingham and McCann's media arm, Universal Media, happened to be in the same building so at that time meetings between creative and media were actually normal. In this case the meeting proved to be hugely beneficial.

The Chiltern radio campaign would run on two or three local radio stations in the HDM area and UM's Director, Paul Bramwell, suggested that he could place the spots directly before or after the traffic bulletins. In other words, we could tell drivers about the advantages of the train while they were stuck in traffic!

I thought this was a terrific idea and we agreed that I'd work on the scripts while   Paul checked out the time slots and – he said – book the airtime. This was our conversation, as I remember it:

**ME:**   I suppose you'll book 30-second spots
(30 is the UK default length).

**PAUL:**   Probably, unless. . .

**ME:**   Why don't you hang on for a couple of days
until I've written the spots?

**PAUL:**   You're not going to write one of your 60-second
spectaculars are you?

**ME:**   Well I might, but I honestly don't know, just wait
a day or so, the slots aren't going to disappear
are they?

**PAUL:**   Suppose not.

So I went off to write the commercials wondering What can I say to a clever guy who's stuck in traffic that will make him feel just a bit silly?  And how can I say it in a way that he not only won't mind my telling him, but also may even like me?

The answer, and the scripts, actually came quite quickly and after sleeping on them (always a good idea) and polishing them a bit, I called Paul. Again, the conversation is from memory:

**ME:**     I've written the scripts. Are you sitting down?

**PAUL:**   (SIGHS) Go on, tell me. How long do you want?

**ME:**     Ten.

**PAUL:**   Ten seconds? You? You've written 10-second commercials?

**ME:**     Yes, but there's a bunch of them.

Well that made his day. Fact is, 10 seconds was the ideal length because, well, that's all I needed to say in each spot. Chiltern Railways loved the idea and we recorded six spots with a wonderful Yorkshire character actor, Paul Copely. The campaign won regional radio campaign of the year – very unusual for 10-second spots. Here are four of them.

 PLAY AUDIO   Go to **http://hertzradio.com/qr/** or scan QR Code on **page12** to listen to this commercial.

**PC:**   *If you're zooming along the M40, you won't need to know that Chiltern Railways could get you to London in 47 minutes from Haddenham & Thame Parkway.*

*So are you? Zooming, that is?*

----------

**PC:**   *Here's the good news. You could get to London in 47 minutes on Chiltern Railways from Haddenham & Thame Parkway.*

*And the… Well you're probably stuck in the bad news.*

----------

**PC:** *If you were on a Chiltern Railways train to London from Haddenham & Thame Parkway, you'd be looking out of the window, feeling sorry for the people in cars.*

*Unless you were having a nap, of course.*

----------

**PC:** *Chiltern Railways' peak return to London from Haddenham & Thame Parkway is £19.60. So how much do you pay for a day's parking in Central London?*

*That much?*

If we go back to the illustration of How People Listen Xyou'll see that this campaign actually responds to all three points:

**They listen for trusted company.** Our character (Voice-Over if you insist) is a warm, straightforward, humorous guy, talking as though he were in the car with them, which of course he is.

**They listen alone and habitually.** Again, Paul talks to them as individuals and there are enough different commercials that even if they heard the spots a couple of times on each of several days, it's unlikely they'd get bored because although it's the same basic message, it's delivered in different ways.

**They listen while doing something else.** Well, the whole point of the media and creative concept is to talk to drivers while they're actually driving. The spots are, in fact, one half of a conversation with drivers.

The Chiltern spots were 10 seconds long and so far in this book we've looked at commercials of 10, 20, 25, 30, 40, 45 and 60 seconds, so this seems like a good moment to talk about commercial length and answer the question: Is there an ideal length for a radio ad?

*It's not* THAT *hard.*

I don't suppose it will surprise you to learn that over 40 years of writing and producing radio commercials, I've developed a formula for determining spot length. It's simple, it's foolproof and it's in three steps:

**1.** **Write the commercial.** Use the seven Secrets, write, sleep on it, edit, re-write, edit again and get it to where it needs to be.

**2.** **Act it out loud.** Don't count words, just perform what you've written as naturally as you can. If you're not confident or comfortable acting, get someone else to do it.

**3.** **Number of seconds for #2 = Length of commercial.**

In seminar, when I reveal step 3 of the formula there are invariably giggles from various sections of the room. Partly, this is a normal response to being caught out by an unexpected punch line. But there's an element of embarrassment as well because, seeing the formula, most seminar participants realize that radio media planning isn't really planning at all, but a rather mindless habit.

The formula may be simplistic, but it is absolutely not a gimmick or a trick. It is, in fact, simple logic: commercial length should be decided by what needs to be said in the spot – and any media person, client, radio sales exec or creative director who says otherwise is, frankly, talking rubbish! I maintain that the 20- or 30-second length imposed on the vast majority of radio commercials is based on nothing more than a perceived need for a certain number of repetitions, i.e. frequency, without any regard for the message.

Frequency – lots of spots on the Excel sheet – makes media agencies look good, at least superficially:

'See the value we're giving you, look at all the spots you get for your money!'

But frequency is a false god if the radio campaign's content – the images it creates, its emotional relevance and impact, its likeability – aren't also considered.

I am not saying for a moment that creatives should simply be allowed to write long commercials for the sake of 'creativity'. That would be no less irresponsible than allowing media to impose artificially short spots for the sake of frequency. No, what I'm asking, begging, arguing, pleading for is the one simple thing that seems to be so difficult these days: that creative and media people talk to each other!

The 10-second length of the Chiltern Railways commercials was not imposed by a frequency-hungry media planner; it was a creative decision, made in consultation with media. Of course Paul was happy that my creative decision gave him more frequency, but had I told him that I needed 30 or 40 seconds he would have found a way to make it work.

(Incidentally, when I say that spot length depends on the number of seconds to read the script, I mean spot length within the industry disciplines and regulations. In the UK, for example, spots are in 10-second increments, e.g. 10, 30, 30 etc. and a 30-second spot has to be 30 – not 29 or 32 – seconds. I respect and can live with that.)

So the message of this section is a plea to build into the radio process some human communication between media and creative.

The 44 seminars I did for Q-music in Amsterdam reveal a concrete example of frequency-worshipping. Every time I did one, I asked for samples of the current radio commercials for the specific advertiser involved, and I built up quite a collection – around 124 spots last time I counted. The overwhelming majority are 20s but what exacerbates the problem imposed by the short length – and makes most of the spots less than pleasant to listen to – is that in 20 seconds most advertisers are trying to squeeze in 30 seconds of material!

And that leads us to the next Secret.

*Secret #4*

# OneAd,
# One message

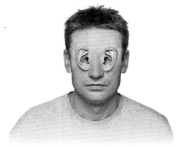

## *Secret #4* – **One Ad, One message**

When you're selling something, it's quite normal to want to say everything you can about your product or service. Surely, the more information prospects are given, the easier it is for them to choose in your favor.

In general terms that makes sense.

But radio is special, and before jamming every product detail into every commercial, let's consider whether it's the best medium for conveying detailed information.

The answer is pretty clear even though we're only halfway through the seven Secrets, and everything we've learned from the first three indicates that radio works best when it's single-minded. Let's remind ourselves:

### *Secret 1:* **Find a Feeling**

Multiple messages, detail and discounts are the antithesis of emotion.

Imagine telling someone how you feel about her and, in the same breath, providing three or four concrete reasons why and suggesting she take advantage of your special love offer this week! Kind of spoils the moment doesn't it? Wouldn't it be more effective simply to tell her you love her in a way that makes her feel good? And then demonstrate with your actions?

The Hallensteins commercial is a perfect example. Certainly, it's a tactical sale ad but by building the story around one item and one relationship it became so much more powerful.

### Secret 2: Begin with a Picture

I hope I've gone some way to convincing you that approaching radio as a visual medium will enlarge your palette of creative possibilities. And if you go back over the examples you'll see that even in the complex ones – Persil for example – there was a single-minded message told in one story about one playsuit.

### Secret 3: Think about the Person

Let's re-look at the way people listen to radio, and remind ourselves that radio is used as Trusted Company.

Doesn't it follow then, that talking to listeners in a way that shows you trust their intelligence reinforces the value of both the medium and your message? To put it another way: if they like you, if they feel you're relevant to their lives, will they not appreciate being considered smart enough to find you?

And for the overwhelming majority, radio is accompaniment to something else they are doing: driving, ironing, working, surfing, reading. The simpler and more single-minded your message, the more likely they are to take it in.

As another example of Secret #4 here's a story of a radio ad that was conceived as a single message and – against all odds – managed to remain single-minded! I'm not a diary-keeper and I'm afraid I don't remember the names of two of the key players in this story, namely the Client and the Account Executive. Sorry guys, if you happen to read this, get in touch!

The client was a car dealer in Bristol, UK – Dovercourt VW (the name has since changed) – and the brief was for a radio campaign to advertise the dealership's move to their brand new showroom on the other side of Bristol. At the time, I was Exec CD of McCann-Erickson Central, based near Birmingham, an agency which had a division specializing in Auto Retail.

In common with the majority of car dealers, Dovercourt saw the move to the new showroom as a big tactical and promotional opportunity, so radio brief was the usual list of 'Opening Day Specials, Deals, Prices, Savings and Discounts'.

But there was also a line in the brief that intrigued me, something like: Be sure to include our Brand Image Slogan, 'The Cream' (cream as in la crème da la crème). I checked their newspaper ads and, sure enough, 'The Cream' was always there, although you couldn't exactly call it Brand Image advertising – it looked something like this (which I've reproduced on the next page from memory):

Nevertheless, I was intrigued by the Cream idea and had the following conversation – again from memory – with the agency account executive:

**ME:** Tell me, will you be doing newspaper ads as well for this move?

**AE:** Oh yes, newspaper, direct mail, inserts, leaflets – everything.

**ME:** That's good, so what I'd like you to do – before we present the radio – is to talk with the client and say that our intention is to use all the visual media to feature the tactical stuff – specials, promotions etc. – but that in the radio we'd like to concentrate on the move to the new showroom, the Brand.

**AE:** That's going to be hard to sell.

**ME:** Well that's why you get the big bucks.

So I did a bit more reasoning and logic, she went off to see the client and I began to pursue my idea which was based on Dovercourt's Cream image.

Suppose – I mused to myself – the Cream moved from one side of Bristol to the other, what would it sound like?

In my head I could hear music, creamy music, and although the production budget was certainly not enough for an original composition, I knew of a specific library music track (production music) which I thought would work. It was in the Carlin Music library and, as it happened, was written by the same composer I'd worked with on Persil and Merry Hill, Quito Colayco. In fact, I'd been present at the recording, which is why it stuck in my mind.

This is probably an appropriate moment to mention that I've been married to Quito Colayco for 27 years. We met in a recording studio in Manila in 1983 and have been collaborating, in more ways than one, ever since!

Anyway, back to the creamy Dovercourt music. In fact, the composition itself had nothing to do with cream, but it sounded creamy to me and, as we learned from the RAD4AD game7, people will see what you want them to see.

I edited the music down to a commercial length and then played it over and over again, writing creamy-type words. What I had in mind was a kind of quartet for voices – two men and two women – a mix of abstract single phrases and short conversations, all about cream and movement.

At a certain point I took what I'd written and a CD of the music to Glyn Evans, a talented Mac designer at the agency, and asked him to create a graphic – a kind of abstract music score – based on the words and music. It wasn't easy to explain; I'd never done anything like it and he certainly hadn't. I remember making waves with my arms, kind of like a conductor, but eventually, after going back and forth a few times, he showed me this and it felt exactly right:

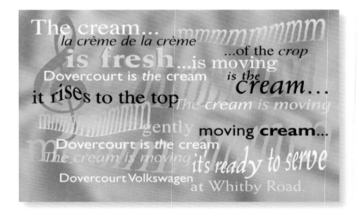

I asked the Account Executive (AE) to make an appointment with the client and a day or so later – with a big color print of the graphic and a couple of CDs of the music – drove with her to Bristol.

It was not the easiest of presentations. To be fair, holding up a big board with words in wavy lines and saying, "This is your radio spot," is considerably more challenging than most clients are used to!

I explained the Moving Cream concept, read the text over the music a few times, told him how interesting and different the spot would be and how it would stand out etc.

He said he liked the music and agreed the whole thing was very tasty. And then said, "And where do we mention the deals and prices?"

I looked at the AE who made one of those 'I told you so!' expressions and I went back to work and did another 20 minutes on Cream and Brand and how newspapers were so much stronger for prices.

In the end I think I just wore him down and finally he told me – and it remains one of the best things a client has ever said! – "Well I still don't really understand this, Tony, but you seem to so I guess you'd better go ahead."

So we did, and this is the final commercial.

 **PLAY AUDIO**   Go to **http://hertzradio.com/qr/** or scan QR Code on **page12** to listen to this commercial.

The Cream - *La crème de la crème* –
*of the crop is moving* moving
*Dovercourt is the cream... is the cream... is the cream...* –
*And the cream is moving*
*Gently moving moving moving moving*
*Softly,*
*Sensuously sliding*
*And slowly slipping*

*Dovercourt   Volkswagen   is the cream*
*Cream rises to the top*
*Fresh, luxurious cream*
*Dovercourt  Volkswagen  is the cream*
*And the cream is moving, Dovercourt Volkswagen is moving*
*I can't wait*
*You don't have to, Dovercourt Volkswagen is now at Whitby Road*

*Come taste the cream*

I'm very proud of this commercial. Proud of it as a concept, as a production and —most of all – proud of the fact that I was able to convince a difficult client to be single-minded in his radio advertising.

And, by the way, the client loved it! He ordered a bunch of CDs, put one in every car in the showroom and told his salespeople to play it to any customer who sat in a car!

And that year Dovercourt Volkswagen won a London International Award.

There are two other significant points to make about the Dovercourt campaign:

The first relates to Secret #2 and the Radio for Art Directors Promise© which is that thinking visually will help you Write and **Present** more effective radio.

The client never saw a script, only the graphic! As a regular script/text, the Dovercourt script not only doesn't look impressive – just a bunch of short phrases – but also would fail to convey the impression of overlapping phrases that I intended.

On the contrary, the graphic helped reinforce the presentation by making it easier for him to 'see' how the commercial would sound.

To my knowledge, there had never before been a car dealer radio commercial like Dovercourt and, as far as I know, not since. It leads us neatly into the next Secret which is a guiding principle to me – not only for radio, but for all advertising.

*Secret #5*

# Stand in a
# Different Place

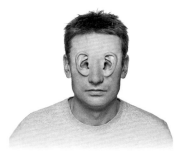

# *Secret #5* - **Stand in a Different Place**

As I discussed at some length in Secret #2, the desire to do work that is new and different is deeply embedded in the psyche of today's creative agencies. And recognition of the direct link between creativity and effectiveness is growing within client organizations too.

The audio Comfort Zone I spoke about in that chapter – the place where the majority of radio resides – is a result of the insecurity of not having the immense support systems that are in place for visual communication. It's why so many agencies and advertisers and radio stations set out to write radio ads that sound like other radio ads.

But Standing in a Different Place isn't just about **sounding** different, not about unusual voices, music or SFX, not about saying the same thing as everyone else in a slightly different way. Secret #5 is about seeing the product or service or user or the relationships involved from a different point of view. It's about focusing on an aspect that, perhaps, hasn't been examined before.

The preceding case, Dovercourt, is an example. This dealer had always used Cream as a slogan but only as a slogan. By making Moving Cream the focal point of the commercial, I was able to create a commercial that not only had a different sound from other car dealer spots but also – and more importantly – put the advertiser in a different, better place than his competition.

I would say that just about all the radio commercials featured in my workshops and in this book are standing in a different place but here are a couple more examples.

I first heard the next commercial when I was on the Cannes Lions Radio Jury in 2005 and have played it in almost every seminar and workshop I've done since then. On the couple of occasions when I haven't, I wish I had.

Unusually for me, I play it without an explanation or description except to say it was written by Martin Mercado of the agency Savaglio\TBWA Argentina for Soleil Factory, a shopping centre in the suburbs of Buenos Aires. Let's do the same here. (Do please listen to the audio while you read the script, it'll make a big difference!)

 **PLAY AUDIO**    Go to **http://hertzradio.com/qr/** or scan QR Code on **page 12** to listen to this commercial.

ANNCR 1:    *We are requesting information to help us find Iginio Gonzalez, Argentinian, 42 years old.*

*He was last seen in the Main Park area, on April 24th of this year.*

*When reported missing, the subject was wearing a beige jacket, an orange polo shirt, blue sweat pants, brown tennis shoes* (HE BEGINS TO LAUGH) *Blue towel socks…* (FINALLY COLLAPSES WITH LAUGHTER) *What a mess…!*

**YOUNG MAN:** *Your old man needs to dress better. Come to Soleil Factory Outlet for Father's Day, and get him the best brands at the prices of the worst brands.*

Soleil Factory is a shopping center and, of course, like all retail stores they live or die on footfall – traffic – numbers of people actually visiting the mall. Most retailers obviously believe that the best way to achieve this is by listing – if not shouting – items, prices, discounts, geographic and web addresses.

It's equally obvious that Soleil Factory has a different approach. Let's examine the commercial, look at some of the differences and how they fit in with the seven Secrets.

First of all, this advertiser has a strong Brand Promise – Best Brands at the prices of the Worst Brands. We've all seen hundreds of Low-Price slogans; this one is particularly strong because it puts it into very human terms. Even more important, Soleil Factory has enough confidence in the promise not to need to give specific price examples. (One Ad, One Message, Think About the Person)

The commercial draws us in by telling a story – a missing person announcement which, historically, is not uncommon in Argentina. We all love stories (Find a Feeling)

It's a wonderfully visual tale too, the really badly dressed man. So badly dressed that the perfectly straight-voiced news Announcer finds himself breaking up with laughter – a wonderful piece of acting. How can we not laugh – or at least smile – as well? (Start with a Picture, Characters not Voices and Produce with Passion)

And then we learn that it's a Father's Day ad, addressed to sons and demonstrating that Soleil Factory knows how most young men feel about the way their dads dress (Think About the Person, again)

But first and foremost, everything about this wonderful commercial stems from the decision to Stand in a Different Place.

The next example is a favorite of mine – not just because it won a bunch of awards, including the D&AD Yellow Pencil, but also because the problems associated with writing it taught me a very valuable lesson.

The campaign is for the Scottish Daily Record, a Glasgow tabloid newspaper and, at the time, the best-selling newspaper in Scotland by far. The Daily Record was a significant television advertiser and the campaign I'm going to describe evolved from a TV commercial.

I no longer have a copy of the TV spot but it's important for the story to show it so I've taken to acting it out in my workshops.

A man in a suit stands against a neutral background reading the Daily Record.

After five seconds or so, an absolutely gorgeous blonde woman in a very skimpy bikini walks slowly and provocatively past him. He doesn't react, just keeps reading.

She walks off. Another few seconds pass and a little terrier dog trots out, sniffs around the man's shoes and then

Creative Radio Advertising_

stands up with his front paws against the man's trouser leg, staring up, panting. The man ignores the dog and just keeps reading.

The dog gives up, gets down and trots off. Another few seconds pass and then BOOM! – all hell breaks loose behind the man. It's a combination of every modern war, uprising or insurgency we've ever seen – missiles, explosions, armored vehicles and men with guns running past! And, of course, our man pays no attention and keeps reading. And over the scene we hear a Voice-Over say: The Daily Record, you can't put it down, read by well-known comedy writer and presenter Dennis Norden.

It was a funny, simple, quite inexpensive commercial and the client loved it – so much, in fact, that they asked their agency, Halls of Edinburgh, to extend the idea into radio. Halls was Scotland's most creative agency at the time and had done quite a bit of good radio, some of it with my production company, The Radio Operators, and Tony Cox, their creative director, had become a good friend.

So Halls set about adapting the Daily Record TV spot to radio. And got stuck.

Let's face it – a man reading in silence, with stuff happening around him, also pretty much in silence (except for a bit of dog panting) until war breaks out at the end, isn't obviously radio material! Try as they might, the copywriters couldn't find a way of translating the story to a sound-only medium.

I learned about their difficulties when Tony Cox called me.

"We could use some help with this and we're running out of time. You're the visual radio guy, would you like to have a go?

I said, "Sure, send me the brief."

They sent me the TV spot which I've just described. I asked if I could have the actual creative brief so I could dig into it a bit more and Tony said:

"We're not looking to reinvent the wheel; all we really want is to adapt the TV spot to radio. You can do anything you want, just make it work on radio. Oh, and you must use the Dennis Norden VO."

I said OK and, full of confidence, got to work. And I also became stuck.

I tried every visual radio technique and trick I could think of to paint a picture of a man doing something in silence, with things happening around him also in silence, and it wasn't working. I became frustrated to the point that all creative people reach at one time or another, saying to myself:

Well, this is it. Today is the day they find out. Today is the day they realize I have no talent, I've been faking it for all these years, it's all over, the world is coming to an end. I'm sure you've been there.

At the time, I had a young assistant, Pam, and after a couple of days of struggling with the Daily Record script, I shared my frustration with her over a lunchtime sandwich.

"… the blonde, the dog, the man keeps reading and the VO says you can't put it down."

Pam chewed on her sandwich and asked:

"Why does he have to put it down?"

"Because that's the strategy! Not being able to put it down is the whole point of the commercial!"

"I still don't see why he has to put it down."

The conversation went round in circles for a few minutes, we finished lunch and I went back to my desk. To continue being stuck.

But what Pam had said was starting to bother me and over the course of the afternoon, in my head, I began to have conversations with myself.

'Tony, would you put it down please.'

'I can't put it down.'

'What do you mean you can't put it down? Just put it down, it's easy.'

'Sorry, I can't put it down.'

'Look, if you don't put it down you're gonna be in big trouble.'

And so on until, in the curious manner of the writer's mind, I found myself in a Western saloon.

You know the scene I'm sure. We're in the saloon and the tall lean Marshall comes in through the swinging doors. He sees the cowboy he's after at the end of the bar and says quietly, menacingly:

"OK Jake, put it down."

And Jake replies, equally menacingly, "Can't put it down, Marshall."

"Am I gonna have to make you put it down, Jake?"

And so on. And then the light switched on. The saloon confrontation was an image I knew – everybody knew – an image with a sound element! And even more important was my realization that I'd been adapting the **execution** instead of the concept! It took a while to sink in, but Pam's innocent question, "Why does he have to put it down?" led to my understanding that 'You Can't Put It Down' was not about someone continuing to read in spite of distractions. It was simply about not being able to put it down and the implication that you ought to be able to do just that.

In other words, I had been standing, stuck, in the same place as the TV, but Pam's question, "Why does he have to put it down?" made me look at the problem from a different place and arrive at a solution.

Here are two of the six 'Can't Put It Down' commercials.

 PLAY AUDIO   Go to **http://hertzradio.com/qr/** or scan QR Code on **page12** to listen to both these spots consecutively.

SCENE: A TYPICAL WESTERN SALOON. MEN DRINKING AND TALKING, PIANO PLAYING. SUDDENLY, EVERYTHING STOPS. THE MARSHALL ENTERS – HE'S LEAN AND TOUGH IN A QUIET SORT OF WAY. HE CALLS OUT TO LUKE, AN ORDINARY COWHAND.

MARSHALL:   *OK Luke, put it down nice and easy.*

LUKE:   *Sorry Marshall, I can't put it down.*

MARSHALL:   *Ain't gonna tell you again Luke,*
*put it down.*

LUKE:   *Sure would like to oblige you Marshall,*
*but I can't put it down.*

*The* **7 Secrets** *of* **Creative Radio Advertising**

MARSHALL: *Boot Hill is full of men who couldn't put it down.*

LUKE: *A man can't put down what a man can't put down.*

MARSHALL: *I guess I'm going to have to make you put it down, now go for your gun.*

LUKE: *How can I go for my gun when I can't put it down?*

MARSHALL: *Put it down first and then go for your gun.*

LUKE: *If I could put it down I wouldn't have to go for my gun!*

MARSHALL: *You've got a point there, Luke.*

LUKE: *See what I mean?*

MARSHALL: *Yes I do.*

D. NORDEN: *The Daily Record, you can't put it down.*

MARSHALL: *We've got to figure this thing out.*

**SCENE: A HOTEL BALCONY REMINISCENT OF NOEL COWARD'S PRIVATE LIVES. A VERY POSH ENGLISH COUPLE – AMANDA AND ELIOT – ARE HAVING ONE OF THOSE VERY VERY BRITTLE NOEL COWARD-LIKE BRITISH CONVERSATIONS.**

AMANDA: *Eliot, have you…*

ELIOT: *Yes Amanda?*

AMANDA: *Have you put it down?*

ELIOT: *You know I can't put it down.*

AMANDA: *You can, you can.*

ELIOT: *My darling, I can't put it down.*

AMANDA: *You must be terribly… strong.*

| | |
|---|---|
| **ELIOT:** | *I've tried frightfully; there isn't a particle of me that doesn't want to put it down.* |
| **AMANDA:** | *Eliot you must. Put it down for our sake.* |
| **ELIOT:** | *I want to quite desperately, but I can't.* |
| **D. NORDEN:** | *The Daily Record, you can't put it down.* |
| **AMANDA:** | *It must be enjoyable.* |
| **ELIOT:** | *Yes.* |

In the 1960s, the American advertising man Jerry della Femina famously said, "Advertising is the most fun you can have with your clothes on." My personal experience of that has always been in the recording studio. There are few things that give me more pleasure than directing talented actors to give great performances of good scripts and the Daily Record sessions will always stand out for me.

And thinking of the process of bringing scripts to life leads us neatly into the final two Secrets.

*Secret #6*

# Characters
# Not Voices

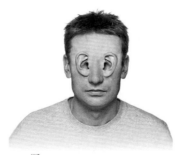

# Secret #6 - **Characters Not Voices**

There's a game that I play when I go somewhere new to do a seminar or workshop. It's part of my preparation, almost a ritual. In the car from the airport, I ask the driver to tune into a local commercial station and, sooner or later, almost inevitably, it happens. I hear the sound I know so well, and exclaim, "That's a radio commercial!"

It's happened in Barcelona and Bucharest, Santiago and Sri Lanka, Moscow and Miami, for products I've never heard of and mostly in languages of which I don't understand a word. It never fails.

How do I know that what I'm hearing is a commercial?

Because in real life **nobody** actually talks like that! No one, anywhere, speaks in that hyper-enthusiastic manner, using those unique sing-song rhythms and modulations **unless they are doing a Voice-Over!** It is a worldwide phenomenon.

So why do VOs sound the way they do?

1. Because they have trained themselves to deliver what they think agencies and clients want to hear.

2. Because agencies and clients have come to believe that kind of a slick, smooth delivery is, somehow, what a radio commercial should sound like (and they actually write scripts to that end).

3. And, saddest of all, because both groups have forgotten the essential truth about radio listening which is that, at their core, radio ads should be like radio itself.

Why do people listen to radio? For trusted company. What is radio's great strength? Its ability to make personal emotional connection with individual people who are listening on their own. Therefore, the brash impersonal tone of the VO who is clearly 'broadcasting' to a large audience is actually a radio contradiction, the antithesis of what radio should be.

In my production workshops – and indeed in my day-to-day production work – I spend a great deal of time showing producers, copywriters and performers how to avoid the 'Voice-Over Trap', and in my book on the craft of radio I cover it in some detail. In this abbreviated version, I will offer two suggestions, which I consider will be the most helpful:

1. First and most important is the script itself.
Write your message the way a real person would talk to someone sitting directly in front of him.
Someone he likes and respects. If you write real, there's a better chance your spot will sound real. If you write in commercial clichés it's difficult to avoid your spot sounding like everyone else's commercial.

2. Secondly – and this is really important – read what you've written out loud, in front of someone.

If you can read it without embarrassment and without making the other person cringe (or boring them), you are probably doing OK.

In this section, I'm not talking about creativity per se – all the different, provocative or amusing ways of telling an audience about your product or service that are illustrated in The 7 Secrets; sometimes we simply need to deliver the message in a straightforward way. The point of this particular Secret is my strongly held belief that the person who delivers your radio message must be exactly that – a Person not a Voice.

Personally, I avoid VOs like the plague; I am simply not interested in how beautiful someone's voice is and how smoothly he/she delivers a message. What I want is, simply, someone who sounds as though he/she is telling the truth. My experience has been that the best way to achieve this is to work with actors in the way they are used to working – that is to be directed.

*Directing actor Tim Bentinck, one of my favorites*

The actor's job is to make the audience believe that the character he/she is playing is real. In other words, being true to that character. I don't want the audience to notice how attractive the voice is, I just want them to believe what the character is saying.

Of course I don't hire performers with unpleasant voices, what would be the point? Most of the actors I work with simply sound, well, 'normal' and some do have attractive voices. But when we are in the studio what I care about is that they sound true to the character I am asking them to play.

If you listen again to the commercials used so far in this book, you will notice the complete absence of standard Voice-Overs. There are, of course, obvious 'characters': the mother and father in Hallensteins, the Marshall and Cowboy and the couple in the Daily Record campaign etc.

But even in those spots which are more like straight messages, the words are also delivered by characters, i.e. real people.

Chiltern Railways is an example: the guy isn't an Announcer – just an ordinary man, someone you might know, asking if you're stuck in traffic. Same for Vicks Vapo-Rub. Even in the Fuller Paint and Soleil Factory commercials, both of which feature men with beautiful, deep, well-modulated voices, the strength of the spots comes from the fact that we believe the stories the characters are telling us.

A commercial which illustrates the point particularly well is the following Australian spot for a health insurance company, HBF, by the agency Meerkats in Perth, written by Kurt Beaudoin and directed by the very talented Ralph VanDijk of Eardrum Australia.

**PLAY AUDIO**   Go to **http://hertzradio.com/qr/** or scan QR Code on **page12** to listen to this commercial.

**MAN:** *It used to be that after a busy day of meetings and phone calls and more meetings, all you wanted to hear when you walked through the front door was… silence.*

*You even talked about it with her, you called it your 'transition time' – a pleasant little break in your day between your work commute and your home life where you could just relax.*

*Not have to hold a conversation.*

*Not have to be a 'good listener'.*

*Just enjoy the sound of… nothing.*

*But then she got sick.*

*And now the thing you hate most when you come home is… hearing the sound of nothing.*

*Your health is all that matters.  HBF.*

This commercial has featured in every workshop I have done for the last three years; I reckon I've heard it more than a hundred times and it affects me emotionally every single time.  It is wonderfully written, going straight to the heart of how so many men – certainly me – feel about their home life with their wives.  And it is delivered, i.e. spoken, in a way that is completely believable.

The guy isn't blessed with a particularly attractive voice, he sounds like a million other ordinary Australian 'blokes'. But when I ask the participants in my workshops the simple question, "Do you believe his wife died?" overwhelmingly the answer is "Yes." And that is precisely the point of this chapter.

For me this is a perfect example of the power of radio advertising: the combination of a beautifully written story, told in a compelling, natural way that draws us in and allows us to suspend disbelief.

And there is another aspect to the HBF commercial worth discussing: the sound design. You may or may not have noticed what was happening in the background as the man told his story. It was something like this:

1. *A CAR PULLS UP*

2. *THE MAN GETS OUT AND SAYS GOODBYE TO SOMEONE*

3. *HE WALKS UP THE PATH TO A DOOR AND UNLOCKS IT*

4. *HE ENTERS AN OBVIOUSLY EMPTY HOUSE, PLACES HIS KEYS ON A TABLE AND SIGHS*

The background scene (Secret #2!) carefully rendered via immaculate Sound Design, not only helps 'illustrate' the story and bring it to life but also – unlike so many radio ads – adds depth, scope and value which enable the commercial to be appreciated through repeated exposure. It is a wonderful example of Passionate Production, the next and last Secret.

## Secret #7
# Produce with
# Passion

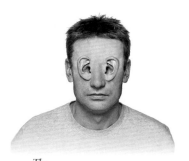

# *Secret #7* - **Produce with Passion**

The first six Secrets are concerned with the radio creative process, the writing. Even Secret 6 – Characters not Voices learning – is about writing because a character is as much about the words he/she speaks as the delivery.

But it all comes to a head with Secret 7. Production is the process of bringing a commercial to life, and if it is not done well – which so often is the case – learning, knowing and even applying the first six Secrets will not improve your radio.

In this section, I will describe, often in some detail, the way I approach radio commercial production.

I should add that half of the commercials featured in this book and in my workshops have been produced by companies other than Hertz:Radio and my former company The Radio Operators, so clearly I'm not alone in approaching radio this way. There are radio specialists in most major markets – I know many of them – and a few dedicated and skilled radio guys within agencies and studios, and we share the same passion.

We also share the experience of being in the minority when it comes to caring about radio.

It won't be surprising to me if you find the production approach I'm about to describe obsessive, perhaps overly passionate – certainly in comparison to the way you may be used to producing radio ads.

My response is simply this: I – and my fellow specialists – produce radio spots in exactly the same way as you or your agency produces your TV commercials and major print ads: with painstaking attention to every step and every detail of the process from preparation to final dispatch.

When it comes to radio, there seem to be two big differences between us and the 'norm' and I apologize for the bluntness of the following statement:

1. My fellow specialists and I really care about doing radio as well as we can; my impression, unfortunately, is that most agencies and clients don't.

2. We know how to do it and we have the experience and the specific skills necessary to achieve the result. Sad to say, in most countries radio production is supervised by agency creatives and producers who simply do not have those skills.

**How I make a radio ad.**

Call me weird, but my idea of heaven – well, work heaven anyway – is recording a radio commercial at Redwood Studios in London with André Jacquemin (with whom I've worked for 40 years!) and as many actors as the script calls for. I find the whole process hugely satisfying and still exciting, even after all these years.

*Listening to a take at Redwood with my longtime recording partner André Jacquemin and Tim B.*

As I write this, it occurs to me that perhaps it's not yet completely clear what my actual role is in the radio production process, so let me explain that now.

I am a radio director and I do for radio commercials what film directors do for TV spots.

The most crucial part of the director's job is to gain a deep understanding of the creative and communication so that he can create a vision – shared with the creative team – of how the film will look and feel. He will then use his skills and experience to achieve it, engaging the appropriate technical people, engaging the right performers, directing them to give great performances and then supervising every step of the editing process to make sure the vision is realised.

Radio directing is no different although, obviously, on a smaller scale. Instead of a crew of 30 or 40 technicians, there's usually one recording engineer – in my case, André. And rather than casting actors for their looks, I look only for their ability to play the character.

And like the film or stage director, the other crucial components of a good radio director's portfolio of skills are understanding of the intent, the vision of the arc of the story, the ability to pull performances from actors and enough technical understanding to know what is and what isn't possible. The following are the steps I go through in the studio, every time:

- Directing the actors so they can use their skills to create characters and get the most from the script. I really love directing, probably because I'm a frustrated actor myself. And actors tell me they like my sessions because, unlike most radio commercial recordings, in mine they have to do actual acting.

- Adjusting the script as we work so that they can act better and make their characters more believable. (I don't remember the last time I left a studio with exactly the same script I went in with!)

- Listening back to the various 'takes' and selecting the best lines – sometimes a single word. We probably do between 10 and 20 takes and André notes my comments on each.

- Assembling the commercials, making timing adjustments, sometimes minute. "André, try adding six frames to that pause," (about 0.25 seconds).

- Watching and listening as André chooses SFX to help make the picture we're trying to achieve. He does movie sound design and has a sound effects library of something like three Terabytes(!) We've worked together so closely for so long we don't need to say very much. I trust him completely and sometimes I go outside to clear my head during this part.

- Placing and assembling the atmospheres and effects and balancing them, making more minute adjustments, sometimes going back to find a sentence fragment we'd previously discarded.

- When we've assembled the commercial, we play it for the agency and client. Sometimes they stay through the whole process; mostly I encourage them to go out for coffee or lunch while we assemble so they can hear the result with fresher ears. As we have begun to do more international work, this process often involves file sharing and Skype conversations.

- We listen to comments, address concerns, sometimes argue for our choices and occasionally yield gracefully!

- Then we mix, that is to say André does his Pro-Tools magic, making even more technical adjustments. He is utterly meticulous and I just let him get on with it until I hear the magic words: "Do you want to listen to this and tell me what you think?"

- I listen – through small domestic speakers, rather than big studio monitors –and might suggest some changes: "That line could be clearer;" "Maybe the door opening should be more to the left." And finally, when we're both satisfied, I send the finished files to the agency or client.

Obviously, commercials vary in complexity; for simple spots the procedure I've just described can take as little as a couple of hours, for more complex productions it can take several days. However, simple or complex, the attention to detail is always there.

As with the other Secrets, the best way to illustrate the production process is with commercials. I've chosen three: a South African spot that I admire a lot plus two of my own. In production terms, they go from simple to complex.

We'll start with a campaign for The Shires, a shopping mall in Leicester in the UK. The commercials were written by a talented copywriter, Nigel Thomas, with whom I've worked a lot. Since writing these at the agency RBH, Nigel has moved on and now has his own agency in the Midlands, The Plain English Agency.

All shopping centres and malls have basically the same message: ' We've got lots of stores and brands and we're open late!' – which is why so many mall commercials sound alike. The brief in this case was to write radio ads promoting the presence of specific fashion brands at the Shires: DKNY, Chanel, Calvin Klein and Boss – usually the recipe for a standard Laundry List commercial.

Thankfully, Nigel doesn't think that way and always looks for an opportunity to say things in a different way. He created characters who happened to have the same names as famous fashion designers and wrote monologues for them based on the confusion that arose around them having famous names, explaining who they were (and who they weren't) and that, like their famous counterparts, they would be at The Shires.

As advertising, the commercials were an opportunity for The Shires to stand out, be warm and human and friendly while conveying their Famous Brand message at the same time.

The producer at Nigel's agency emailed the scripts to me asking for a time-line and, of course, an estimate for the production.

There are always two main questions to be answered at the beginning of every project:

1. Creative: How can I get the best from these scripts so that everyone concerned will be delighted – copywriter, client, myself?

2. Can the scripts be produced profitably, within the agency's budget and to the standard needed within the deadline?

The above items are numbered in my natural thinking order. Realistically though, it's in reverse order; the first thing to sort out is always whether the job is economically viable! As I already mentioned, I'd worked with Nigel and his agency many times before, everyone was pretty familiar with the cost structure, so we could proceed pretty quickly with the production process.

It was obvious that good casting would be the key to making these spots work. In order to identify the best possible actors to play the Coco, Donna and Hugo characters, the first order of business was to have a long conversation with Nigel so I could find out what was in his head.

The great thing about working with Nigel is that while he always writes with clear characters in mind, he's also very open to suggestions and, importantly, happy to go with the flow in a recording session and use impromptu phrases and ad libs. Part of my job as director is to create an atmosphere in which they can happen.

These are the three characters Nigel specified for the commercials:

Coco (Chanel). A young woman, cheerful, ordinary – the opposite of the severe, stylish and very French Coco Chanel. I cast actress Louise Delamere. I hadn't worked with her before but she had done a lot of TV comedy and was strongly recommended by a casting agent I trust.

Donna (Karan). Nigel wanted a slightly older woman, down to earth, self-deprecating, and I immediately thought of the wonderful Tracy-Ann Oberman – a really experienced and delightful comic actress, very experienced in radio drama and with whom I'd already worked many times.

Hugo (Boss). Even though the real Hugo Boss was German, Nigel thought it would be fun to cast him as American and I agreed. We chose Alan Marriott, an actor/stand-up comedian who is Canadian… but close enough, and a very funny guy.

The structure of the 30-second Shires Designer commercials is classic: 24 seconds of comic monologue with a 6-second Announcer payoff at the end, and that was the other 'voice' we needed.

Given my strong aversion to Voice-Overs, I suggested that two of the actors playing characters could be the Announcer in the other commercials (there were actually four spots in the campaign). Nigel agreed readily, the client approved the casting and we spent a fun day in the studio. Here are three of the four spots.

**PLAY AUDIO** Go to **http://hertzradio.com/qr/** or scan QR Code on **page12** to listen to the 3 spots consecutively.

**COCO:** *Hi there, I'm Coco Chanel.*

*People are always asking me if I'm **that** Coco Chanel, and I'm always like, do I look like I've been dead 40 years? I don't think so!*

*And wasn't she French or something? Do I sound French? I'm nothing like Coco!*

*Although, she **is** available at The Shires and I am going there because I need a new outfit for my Christmas party! And parking's free every late night in December.*

**ANNCR:** *Some of the world's biggest fashion brands are available at The Shires. It's in Leicester city centre,*

**COCO:** *And at the shires.co.uk.*

In addition to not much liking VOs I also prefer to avoid the formula in which the comedy is separated from the advertising. In the original scripts, the Announcer's part included the website. I suggested that in order to keep the spots as one unit it would be better –and quite natural – to go back to the character to give the web address. And that's what we did in all the spots.

*Secret #7 - Produce with Passion*

133

**DONNA:** *Hello, hi, I'm Donna Karan. Not* **the** *Donna Karan of course, no. I wish. To be honest, I don't get mistaken for the real Donna Karan that much, even when I do wear her clothes. Maybe because, well, I don't much look like her.*

*But like Donna, I am going to be at The Shires this week because they're open till 8 on Wednesday and I have to go after work to get something nice for my cousin's engagement party next month.*

**ANNCR:** *Some of the world's biggest fashion brands are available at The Shires. It's in Leicester city centre,*

**DONNA:** *And fashion attheshires.co.uk.*

I love the change Tracy-Ann makes in Donna's mood. She starts off feeling sorry for herself and recovers at the thought of going to The Shires. We worked on that. And, although it's not shown in the script, notice when you listen that the character says something like hmm – right after the Announcer's first sentence? It's a trick of mine, again to continue her presence in the spot.

**HUGO:** *Hello, I'm Hugo… Boss. Not the Hugo Boss, sadly he's no longer with us.*

*But I do feel we have this amazing kind of connection, like beyond the grave or something.*

*First of all, we both have the most*

> *impeccable taste. Plus, his clothes are*
> *on sale at The Shires, and I'll be there*
> *this week because their sales are on now,*
> *and they're open New Year's Day between*
> *11 and 5.*

**ANNCR:**  *Some of the world's biggest fashion*
*brands are available at The Shires.*
*In Leicester City Centre*

**HUGO:**  *And at the shires.co.uk.*

Hugo was the surprise of the day. Somewhere in the middle of Take 4 or 5, Alan slid into a gay character – just as a gag. Nigel really liked it and suggested we do the whole commercial in that way. So we did a few gay takes, not believing for one moment the client would ever approve it. But they liked it, and that's the way it went on air!

The next example of passionate production is a South African spot for Handy Andy fume-free oven cleaner, made by Lowe-Bull in Johannesburg. Copywriters were Matthew Brink and Adam Livesey. I first heard it as a Cannes Radio Lions Jury member and I've been using it ever since. It's one of those commercials that could illustrate just about every Secret.

It's not my commercial so I can't really talk with authority about how they actually made it. But everything I hear in the spot makes me believe the director's approach is similar to mine… and I wish like hell I'd done it! We'll analyse it a bit but let's listen first.

*Secret #7 - Produce with Passion*

**PLAY AUDIO**  Go to **http://hertzradio.com/qr/** or scan QR Code on **page 12** to listen to this commercial.

**SCENE: THE KITCHEN OF A SUBURBAN HOUSE OR FLAT. THE HUSBAND COMES IN THROUGH THE FRONT DOOR AND CALLS OUT TO HIS WIFE**

**HUSBAND:** *Hey babe, I'm home.*

**WIFE:** *Sshhhhh.*

**HUSBAND:** *What?*

**WIFE:** *They're listening.*

**HUSBAND:** *Who's listening?*

**WIFE:** *The Green Men.*

**HUSBAND:** *What do you mean the green men?*

**WIFE:** *Over there.*

**HUSBAND:** *Er... baby, that's dishwashing liquid.*

**WIFE:** *That's what they want you to think.*

**ANNCR:** *Rather use an oven cleaner without the fumes?*
*Handy Andy – fume-free oven cleaner.*

First of all, congratulations to Unilever for agreeing to go with this rather edgy approach – a brilliant way of communicating the advantages of their fume-free oven cleaner. This spot is one of a quite extensive campaign.

A man comes home from work; he finds his wife hallucinating about seeing green men, and then an Announcer warns us it's because she used an ordinary oven cleaner with fumes instead of Handy Andy.

Like The Shires and others, it's a classic funny-radio-spot structure, but what makes it exceptional is the execution, in particular the timing of the dialogue between the man and woman is immaculate. Check it out.

*The 7 Secrets of Creative Radio Advertising*

| HUSBAND: | *Hey babe, I'm home.* |
| WIFE: | *Sshhhhh.* |
| HUSBAND: | *What?* |
| WIFE: | (PAUSE 1.8 sec) *They're listening.* |
| HUSBAND: | (BAFFLED PAUSE 1 sec) *Who's listening?* |
| WIFE: | *The Green Men.* |
| HUSBAND: | (BAFFLED PAUSE 1.4 sec) *What do you mean the green men?* |
| WIFE: | (PAUSE .4 sec) *Over there.* |
| HUSBAND: | (ANOTHER PUZZLED PAUSE 2.3 sec) *Baby, that's dishwashing liquid.* |
| WIFE: | (PAUSE 2.3sec) *That's what they want you to think.* |
| ANNCR: | (PAUSE .7 sec) *Rather use an oven cleaner without the fumes? Handy Andy – fume-free oven cleaner.* |

The magic comes from the pauses. For 10 seconds of this 30-second spot we hear nothing but the sound of the room and occasional breathing. We talk about pictures in sound but it is the silences that allow us to see the woman hallucinating! It's the pauses – one almost 2½ seconds long – that let us see the man staring in disbelief at his wife who is high on oven cleaner!

I spend a great deal of time before and during every recording session trying to create breathing space, searching for words to cut so that the characters can speak with the natural pauses and hesitations and thinking time that we use in real life. The Handy Andy commercial is just about the best recent example of this I've come across.

The third and last example of Production Passion is more complex than the first two – more of a radio movie in visual terms. It's for Transport for London, the local government body responsible for most aspects of London's transport system, including advertising road safety campaigns.

TFL's brief to their agency, M&C Saatchi, was to create a radio campaign warning young male drivers, and their parents, about the dangers of speeding. It seems that this category of drivers is responsible for a disproportionate number of speed- (not drink or drug) related accidents simply because their immaturity makes them drive too fast.

During that period I was working very closely with M&C Saatchi's brilliant Creative Director, Graham Fink and he suggested that he and I work together with agency partner and ECD (Executive Creative Director) Simon Dicketts to create the TFL commercial.

They had written the straight Announcer section, which was pretty much proscribed by the client and were looking for a way to dramatize the message. I came up with the idea of a police car stopping a motorist who is driving over the speed limit, and when they ask him to get out of the car, he turns out to be an eight- or nine-year-old child.

We wrote the whole thing out as a script and the two creative directors presented and sold it to the client.

I had a clear idea in my head of how I wanted to produce the spot but it was important to share my vision with everyone involved: agency, client, recording engineer (André of course) and actors. It's my experience and belief that many problems associated with the production of radio ads stem from the fact that, quite often, different parties have different images in their minds. In other words, they are not all making the same commercial!

One way around this is to do what I did in the case of TFL and many other complex productions – use a storyboard. Here's the one I drew. It's a bit crude, I'm not much of an artist but it does help tell the story.

As you can see, we begin inside the police car with the two cops – a man and a woman. Why male and female? The simple answer is, why not? It happens in real life and I thought it would add an interesting color to the spot.

You may notice that the policewoman is driving. Again, a director's decision; we produce in stereo so let's make use of the left and right stereo channels to make a more interesting picture. Also, in terms of the story, I felt it would be better for the following scene for the male cop to confront the driver.

They observe a speeding car, pursue, pull it over to the side of the road and there's a brief conversation about who will get out to talk to the driver (more about this later). The policeman walks from the police car to the speeder. As he approaches, the music from inside the speeder's car gets louder and louder.

He tells the speeder to get out of the car, and it's revealed that the driver is an eight-year-old boy – a metaphor for immaturity. The straight message is delivered by the Announcer, interspersed with protestations from the child. Here's the commercial:

 PLAY AUDIO   Go to **http://hertzradio.com/qr/** or scan QR Code on **page 12** to listen to this commercial.

**SCENE: INTERIOR OF A POLICE CAR, WE HEAR SNATCHES OF RADIO MESSAGES**

COP 1:      *Look at that guy, he must be doing 50.*

COP 2:      *46.*

            *CAR SPEEDS UP, SHORT BURST OF SIREN*

COP 1:      *... Right.*

**POLICEMAN GETS OUT, WALKS TO OTHER CAR. MUSIC FROM INSIDE SPEEDER'S CAR GETS LOUDER AND LOUDER.  HE TAPS ON THE CAR WINDOW WHICH OPENS**

            *Turn the music off please.  And step out of the car please sir.  We clocked you at 46*

CHILD: *miles per hour in a 30 zone. Did you realize you were breaking the speed limit?*

CHILD: *It's not fair! You're always picking on me.*

ANNCR: *Young, immature male drivers are responsible for the largest number of speed-related collisions.*

CHILD: *I didn't do anything!*

ANNCR: *They could lose their license, and along with it their job and social life.*

CHILD: *I'm going to tell my dad!*

ANNCR: *Tough growing up.*

The recording session was complex. Normally I do all the voice recording first and, of course, if it's a dialogue record the participants together. In this case, we had to record the child (whose name I've unfortunately forgotten) in the afternoon after school, so I stood in for him when we recorded the police dialogue with two of my favourite actors, David Charles and Alison Pettitt, and stood in for David when we recorded the kid.

The Announcer was played by Struan Roger, another highly experienced character actor I've worked with for years, with hundreds of TV episodes and films to his name including Four Weddings and a Funeral and Chariots of Fire. The Announcer in this spot is very much a character and I asked Struan for a performance something in between a tough senior policeman and a documentary narrator. I think he did it perfectly.

The storyboard helped André with the sound design as well. We needed different perspectives for the interior of the police car, the exit and, above all, for the policeman's walk from his car to the speeder's car with the music – coming from inside the car – getting louder and louder.

André handled it immaculately as always, but the scene presented us with a problem which meant having to make a significant adjustment to the script.

As written and recorded, there was a brief conversation between the two cops after they'd stopped the speeding car, something like this, lasting 3.5 seconds:

**COP 2:** *I'll get this one shall I?*

**COP 1:** *No, you got the last one, I'll do it. Right...*

It was written to set the scene for the confrontation with the speeder

However, I had always considered that the biggest, i.e. longest, most elaborate scene in the piece, was the walk between the two cars, but as we assembled the commercial we found there just wasn't enough time for it to have real impact.

We could have tightened up pauses here and there and gained an extra second or so but it wouldn't have been enough to make the scene really dramatic, so I took the rather drastic step of eliminating the cops' dialogue scene altogether.

I suppose it was a bit sad that Alison's presence in the commercial was now limited to '46', referring to miles per hour. But it's also kind of cool to have a character say just one word necessary to establish her presence! It's also an

*The* **7 Secrets** *of* **Creative Radio Advertising**

excellent illustration of a key principle of Producing with Passion, which is this:

The creative process should never stop, and I believe that production is as much a part of creativity as the actual writing.

Some clients, indeed some agencies, may find the attention to detail described in this section a little, well, obsessive. After all, 'it's only radio'.

Perhaps it is, but I would remind them that advertising is a business driven by passion. If it weren't for passion and obsessiveness there would be no Cannes Lions, no D&AD, Eurobest, Clio, London International or any other awards programs. I intentionally spent time on the detail of my radio production process specifically to point out that just like great television, print, direct mail, outdoor, online and everything else, great radio needs time, budget, expert attention.

And love.

# The Wrap Up.

So that's it, the 7 Secrets of Creative Radio, six of which, as you've no doubt realised – and which I confessed right at the beginning of the book – aren't secrets at all.

What's important is that if you use them, if they become a habit, a routine part of your approach to radio advertising, they really do work.

1. If you conscientiously set out to **Find a Feeling**, i.e. identify an emotion connected with the purchase or use of your product and show your target audience that you get how they feel, your advertising has a better chance of making a real connection with them.

2. When you visualize your radio and **Begin with a Picture**, not only will you instantly avail yourself of more creative choices, but also you'll be able to develop richer, deeper executions.

3. It seems like stating the obvious, but people are mostly interested in themselves; so clearly, the more you know about your target, the more you **Think About the Person,** the more likely it is that your radio

advertising will connect with them.

4. Single-mindedness is a common feature of all the spots featured in this book, even the complex ones. If you can resist the temptation to say everything in every commercial and stick to **One Ad, One Message**, your radio will improve.

5. One way we can improve your radio is to remind ourselves that we work in a world of parity products and brands. If you **Stand in a Different Place** and make creativity the differentiator, it will lessen the chances that your radio spot will sound like all the others.

6. Picture yourself in your car, the radio less than a meter away. Who would you prefer to persuade you about a service: a normal, sympathetic person you might trust or a hyper, impersonal Voice-Over? If you want to make a human connection, write for believable **Characters not Voices**.

7. And finally, the most emotional, visual, personal, single-minded, differentiated and human script in the world will not make a great radio ad if you don't **Produce with Passion**. This takes skill, experience, time, enough budget and, above all in many cases, a fundamental paradigm shift.

The simple truth is, the Secrets work. But only if you use them and, in most cases, when it comes to radio this will mean a behavioral change because, to quote the old preacher's saying:

If you do what you've always done, you'll get what you've always got!

I'll end this book, as I end most of my workshops, with an ad I wrote in 1976 (believe it or not) for the Scottish Health Council. It was based on a concept by Tony Cox of Halls advertising. It uses all the Secrets – before I thought of them as secrets – and I guess it's my favourite of all the ads I've ever done. And you'll be glad to see it needs no explanation!

I hope you've found this book of some value, that you'll find yourself using the Secrets and making radio ads you're proud of. And if you do, please let me know.

**Tony Hertz**
Silang, Cavite
Philippines

**SCENE: AN ENQUIRY DESK AT A LOCAL GOVERNMENT OFFICE, THE DEPARTMENT OF SUICIDE. A CUSTOMER APPROACHES THE CLERK.**

**CLERK:** *Can I help you?*

**MAN:** *Yes, I'd like to commit suicide please.*

**CLERK:** *I see. Something dramatic?*
*We have an opening*
*on the Forth Road Bridge.*

**MAN:** *Ooh no, I can't stand heights.*

**CLERK:** *Gas oven is still very popular.*

**MAN:** *No, we're all electric.*

**CLERK:** *Pity. How about a nice overdose?*
*That's very quick and neat.*

**MAN:** *I'm not really in that much of a hurry.*

**CLERK:** *Oh why didn't you say so?*
*I've got the very thing. Smoke.*

**MAN:** *You mean cigarettes?*

**CLERK:** *Yes, a natural! It's slow, expensive,*
*unpleasant for those around you.*
*And you can go in so many different ways!*

**MAN:** *Really?*

**CLERK:** *Oh yes – lung cancer, throat cancer,*
*emphysema, heart disease…*

**MAN:** *That's marvelous, thank you very much.*

**CLERK:** *All part of the service. I should warn you,*
*though, that it may take a while, and there*
*is a possibility that you might live.*

**MAN:** *Hmmm. No, I'll chance it. Got a light?*

*The* **7 Secrets** *of* **Creative Radio Advertising**

 **PLAY AUDIO**     Go to **http://hertzradio.com/qr/** or scan QR Code on **page 12**
to listen to this commercial.

# What people have said about Tony's Workshops

*He put a spell on the audience and kept them in the palm of his hands from start to finish. His staggering session took off like a rocket and gave participants a fantastic experience. The vibe in the room was thrilling*

**Christian Kjeldsen**, *Radiodays, Europe, 2010*

*I watched Tony's dynamic Dubai Lynx Seminar. Great content, passionately presented - now I get why his Cannes workshops have always received such high scores and praise from attendees.*

**Philip Thomas**, *CEO, Cannes Lions International Festival*

*Standing ovation for Tony at Radioday 2009; the audience was so fascinated they didn't want him to leave the stage! Thanks Tony for supporting and motivating the radio/advertising industry to make better ads.*

**Lutz Kuckuck**, *CEO, Radiozentrale, Berlin*

*A phenomenal workshop! It was radio plus a lot more, he has a way of getting into creative people's minds, unblocking their dams and unleashing more creativity than they even believe is there.*

**Tony Cullingham**, *West Herts College, Watford*

*7 Secrets*

# The Scripts

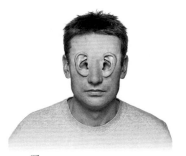

The**7**Secrets*of*
**Creative**
**Radio Advertising**

*Script 1* - **CANNON EOS CAMERA**

**WIFE:** *The baby stood up for the first time.*

**HUSBAND:** *I could see fireworks from my balcony.*

**WIFE:** *The kids were waving at me from the rollercoaster.*

**HUSBAND:** *The groom held his new wife and kissed her.*

**WIFE:** *Our fat cat jumped.*

**HUSBAND:** *Her baby tooth fell out.*

**WIFE:** *My husband did a bungee jump... came back up... and went back down again.*

**HUSBAND:** *My wife finally smiled at me... it's been five years... since she smiled... at me.*

**ANNCR:** *The moments you want captured won't wait for you. Now with a start-up time of just 2/10th of a second – Eos Kiss Digital Camera. Canon Marketing Japan.*

*Secret # 1* - **Find a Feeling**

Script 2 - **GO DOG**

**TRAINER:** *Today we're going to learn to call a dog using the voice command, come.*

**OWNER:** *Jason, come.*

**TRAINER:** *This command tells your dog to return to the one person it trusts and loves above all others.*

**OWNER:** *Jason, come. Come! Jason come here! Jason, will you come here! Jason! Jason!*

**TRAINER:** *Another method is the new Go-Dog method.*

HE SHAKES THE BOX; THE DOG RUNS UP
AND BEGINS TO EAT

*Go-Dog is a new kind of dog food – crunchy, meaty-tasting chunks with all the vitamins and minerals dogs need; it has more nourishment than any tinned dog food. New Go-Dog is a dog's idea of a complete dinner. Next time we'll discuss another Go-Dog training situation.*

**OWNER:** *Jason, go away.*

**ANNCR:** *Special price reductions on Go-Dog beef and liver flavors at most branches of Safeway.*

**OWNER:** *You're dribbling all over my trousers. Go away!*

*Secret # 1 - Find a Feeling*

Listen to the spot either by scanning this QR code on page 12, or going to
**http://hertzradio.com/qr/.**

## PHONE CALL, FROM THE CALLER'S POV

**MOTHER:** *Hello.*

**BRIAN:** *Mum, is Dad there?*

**MOTHER:** *Brian? It's good to hear your voice!*

**BRIAN:** *Is Dad there?*

**MOTHER:** *It's been 15 years, I …!*

**BRIAN:** *Mum, I really need to tell him something.*

**MOTHER:** *OK … It's Brian, he needs to talk to you.*

**FATHER:** *Brian? Hello?*

**BRIAN:** *Dad. You can get Lee Rider Jeans at Hallensteins for $49.95.*

**FATHER:** *Thanks.*

**BRIAN:** *Oh, Dad …*

**FATHER:** *Yeah?*

**BRIAN:** *Limited time only. I'll see you around.*

**FATHER:** *Yep.*

*Secret #1 - **Find a Feeling***

Listen to the spot either by scanning this QR code on page 12, or going to
**http://hertzradio.com/qr/**.

 *Script 4* - **BLUE BAND**

WE HEAR A MAN ENJOYING HAVING HIS
BACK SCRATCHED

**ANNCR:** *Here's something to feel good about,
from Blue Band.*

**MAN:** *Up a bit, bit more… aah great, now in a bit
– no that's out! In – to the right.*

*Aaahhh, ooh there, wonderful… oooh.*

**ANNCR:** *This good feeling is presented by Blue Band
Margarine, which is made from only natural
ingredients and pure vegetable oils. And
that is something else to feel good about.*

**WOMAN:** *Did you notice?*
*The piece of lettuce... between the teeth...*
*of the guitarist... of the band... on the*
*stage... in the Stade... de France?*

## DIGITAL CAMERA SHUTTER

**ANNCR:** *Samsung NV Ten. Ten million pixels. For*
*ultra-precise images.*

## SOUND LOGO

----------------------

**MAN:** *Did you notice?*
*The speck ... in the eye ... of the priest ... on*
*the steps ... in front ... of the church ... on*
*the central square ... of the city?*

## DIGITAL CAMERA SHUTTER

**ANNCR:** *Samsung NV Ten. Ten million pixels.*
*For ultra-precise images.*

## SOUND LOGO

----------------------

**MAN:** *Did you notice?*
*The blood vessel... in the eye... of the*
*rabbit... in the mouth... of the snake...*
*on the rock... on the mountain...*
*on the left?*

## DIGITAL CAMERA SHUTTER

**ANNCR:** *Samsung NV Ten. Ten million pixels. For*
*ultra-precise images.*

## SOUND LOGO

----------------------

*Secret #2 -* **Begin with a Picture**

157

### Script 6 - FULLER PAINT BROWN

**ANNCR:** *The Fuller Paint Company invites you to stare with your ears... at Brown.*

*Among purists – and you know how many purists there are – brown was having some difficulty.*

*Some of the purists wanted brown to be more* **(MUSIC)**

*Others wanted brown to be more* **(MUSIC)**

*Still others wanted brown to be...* **(MUSIC)**

**WHISPER:** *Fuller Paint, Fuller Paint*

*A lesser color might have fallen apart, but*

**WHISPER:** *brown met the problem beautifully by becoming more and more subtle.  Brown has become just about as subtle as subtle can get.  That's why you hear people saying, "My, what a subtle brown." If that's the kind of brown you want, why want less? Remember to remember the Fuller Paint Company, a century of leadership in the chemistry of color. Visit your Fuller Color Center tomorrow.*

*Or the day after yesterday.*

*Script 7* - **PERSIL - PINK**

NIGEL: *Sarah is five, and this is her favorite playshirt. It's ♪♫, with fluffy yellow ducks ♪♫.*

SARAH: *It's my favorite!*

NIGEL: *Sarah loves her playshirt, and she wears it to play in the garden.*

SARAH: *Look what I found, Mummy!*

NIGEL: *And you wash it, at low temperature* (washing machine) *and she wears it to play in the garden.*

SARAH: *Mummy, look what I made!*

NIGEL: *And you wash it* (washing machine) *and she wears it to play in the ...*

MOTHER: *Sarah, what on earth!*

NIGEL: *And after a while, the dirt builds up ♪♫. So the pink isn't quite as pink ♪♫. And the yellow ducks aren't as fluffy ♪♫.*

*New System Persil Automatic can help. Its advanced formula can remove ground-in dirt, even at low temperatures. So the pink stays very pink ♪♫. And the fluffy yellow ducks are happy again ♪♫. Wash...*

SARAH: *Mummy, look what I made!*

NIGEL: *... after wash...*

SARAH: *Look what I found, Mummy!*

NIGEL: *... after wash.*

MOTHER: *Sarah, don't you dare bring that in here!*

NIGEL: *New System Persil Automatic. It's all you could want from a powder.*

Secret # 2 - **Begin with a Picture**

159

**Script 8 - PERSIL - BLUE**

| | |
|---|---|
| **NIGEL:** | Your husband's joined a rugby club. And he has a brand new rugby shirt. It's deep blue. ♪♫. He puts it on. |
| **HUSBAND:** | What do you think? |
| **WIFE:** | A winner. |
| **NIGEL:** | … and plays in the match on Sunday. |
| **WIFE:** | Well? |
| **HUSBAND:** | 17-6. |
| **NIGEL:** | And you wash it at low temperature (washing machine) and he plays in the match on Sunday… |
| **WIFE:** | Well? |
| **HUSBAND:** | 25-0. |
| **NIGEL:** | And you wash it (washing machine) and he plays in the match on Sunday… |
| **HUSBAND:** | Don't ask! Just don't ask. |
| **NIGEL:** | And after a few matches, the dirt builds up. And the blues have… a case of the blues ♪♫.♪♫. |
| | New system Persil Automatic can help. Its advanced formula can remove ground-in dirt, even at low temperatures. So the shirt stays  bright and the sad blues are happy again ♪♫.♪♫… Wash… |
| **HUSBAND:** | 12-6. |
| **NIGEL:** | After wash…♪♫. |
| **HUSBAND:** | 16-16. |
| **NIGEL:** | … after wash ♪♫. |
| **WIFE:** | You won? You actually won? |
| **NIGEL:** | New System Persil Automatic. It's all you could want from a powder. |

*Script 9* - **MAASCHINO CHERRY**

**CLIENT:** *Radio? Why should I advertise on radio? There's nothing to look at, no pictures!*

**FREBURG:** *Listen, you can do things on radio you couldn't possibly do on TV.*

**CLIENT:** *That'll be the day.*

**FREBURG:** *All right, watch this. OK people! Now, when I give you the cue I want the 700-foot mountain of whipped cream to roll into Lake Michigan, which has been drained and filled with hot chocolate.*

*Then the Royal Canadian Air Force will fly overhead towing a 10-ton maraschino cherry, which will be dropped into the whipped cream, to the cheering of 25,000 extras.*

**FREBURG:** *All right, cue the Mountain!*
(HUGE RUMBLING & GRINDING ENDING WITH A SPLASH)

*Cue the Air Force!*
(FLEET OF WWII VINTAGE AIRPLANES OVERHEAD)

*Cue the Maraschino Cherry!*
(WHISTLING BOMB FALLING, THEN A BIG SPLUDGE)

*OK, 25,000 cheering extras!*
(HUGE CROWD CHEERING)

*Now, you wanna try that on television?*

**CLIENT:** *W-e-e-ll.*

**FREBURG:** *You see radio is a very special medium because it stretches the imagination.*

**CLIENT:** *Doesn't television stretch the imagination?*

**FREBURG:** *Up to 21 inches, yes.*

| | |
|---|---|
| **WOMAN:** | *Right, got something to say to you blokes...about Christmas shopping.* |
| | *Are you fascinated? No! Is your true love expecting a present? Yes! So make it less of a hassle, by shopping late at Merry Hill.* |
| | *It's open weekdays until 10 so you can go after work – I'm sure you can find a creative excuse.* |

THE "BLOKE" PHONES HIS GIRLFRIEND

| | |
|---|---|
| **BLOKE:** | *Hi love it's me. I'm going to be late, something's come up.* |
| **GIRLFRIEND:** | *Oh, what?* |
| **BLOKE:** | *A meeting.* (AWKWARD PAUSE AS HE CONSIDERS TELLING THE TRUTH) *I'm going shopping alright!* |
| **WOMAN:** | *Call that creative? Anyway, it's less crowded, free parking, places to eat, and there are more than 200 shops.* |
| | *And there are Merry Hill gift vouchers so you don't actually have to go into any of them. And think of the welcome at home!* |
| **GIRLFRIEND:** | *Get what you wanted darling?* |
| **BLOKE:** | *None of your business.* |
| **GIRLFRIEND:** | *Ooh!* |
| **WOMAN:** | *Late night shopping at Merry Hill. Careful, you might actually enjoy it.* |

Secret # 3 - **Think About The Person**

PC: *If you're zooming along the M40, you won't need to know that Chiltern Railways could get you to London in 47 minutes from Haddenham & Thame Parkway.*

*So are you? Zooming, that is?*

----------

PC: *Here's the good news. You could get to London in 47 minutes on Chiltern Railways from Haddenham & Thame Parkway.*

*And the... Well you're probably stuck in the bad news.*

----------

PC: *If you were on a Chiltern Railways train to London from Haddenham & Thame Parkway, you'd be looking out of the window, feeling sorry for the people in cars.*

*Unless you were having a nap, of course.*

----------

PC: *Chiltern Railways' peak return to London from Haddenham & Thame Parkway is £19.60. So how much do you pay for a day's parking in Central London?*

*That much?*

The Cream - La crème de la crème –
of the crop is moving moving
Dovercourt is the cream... is the cream... is the cream...–
And the cream is moving
Gently moving moving moving moving
Softly,
Sensuously sliding
And slowly slipping

Dovercourt   Volkswagen   is the cream
Cream rises to the top
Fresh, luxurious cream
Dovercourt   Volkswagen   is the cream
And the cream is moving, Dovercourt Volkswagen is moving
I can't wait
You don't have to, Dovercourt Volkswagen is now at Whitby Road

Come taste the cream

**Secret #4 - One Ad, One message**

## Script 13 - **SOLEIL FACTORY**

**ANNCR 1:**    *We are requesting information to help us find Iginio Gonzalez, Argentinian, 42 years old.*

*He was last seen in the Main Park area, on April 24th of this year.*

*When reported missing, the subject was wearing a beige jacket, an orange polo shirt, blue sweat pants, brown tennis shoes* (HE BEGINS TO LAUGH) *Blue towel socks...* (FINALLY COLLAPSES WITH LAUGHTER) *What a mess...!*

**YOUNG MAN:** *Your old man needs to dress better. Come to Soleil Factory Outlet for Father's Day, and get him the best brands at the prices of the worst brands.*

### Script 14 - **DAILY RECORD - SALOON**

**SCENE: A TYPICAL WESTERN SALOON. MEN DRINKING AND TALKING, PIANO PLAYING. SUDDENLY, EVERYTHING STOPS. THE MARSHALL ENTERS – HE'S LEAN AND TOUGH IN A QUIET SORT OF WAY. HE CALLS OUT TO LUKE, AN ORDINARY COWHAND.**

**MARSHALL:** *OK Luke, put it down nice and easy.*

**LUKE:** *Sorry Marshall, I can't put it down.*

**MARSHALL:** *Ain't gonna tell you again Luke, put it down.*

**LUKE:** *Sure would like to oblige you Marshall, but I can't put it down.*

**MARSHALL:** *Boot Hill is full of men who couldn't put it down.*

**LUKE:** *A man can't put down what a man can't put down.*

**MARSHALL:** *I guess I'm going to have to make you put it down, now go for your gun.*

**LUKE:** *How can I go for my gun when I can't put it down?*

**MARSHALL:** *Put it down first and then go for your gun.*

**LUKE:** *If I could put it down I wouldn't have to go for my gun!*

**MARSHALL:** *You've got a point there, Luke.*

**LUKE:** *See what I mean?*

**MARSHALL:** *Yes I do.*

**D. NORDEN:** *The Daily Record, you can't put it down.*

**MARSHALL:** *We've got to figure this thing out.*

## *Script 15* -DAILY RECORD - BALCONY

**SCENE: A HOTEL BALCONY REMINISCENT OF NOEL COWARD'S PRIVATE LIVES. A VERY POSH ENGLISH COUPLE – AMANDA AND ELIOT – ARE HAVING ONE OF THOSE VERY VERY BRITTLE NOEL COWARD-LIKE BRITISH CONVERSATIONS.**

AMANDA: *Eliot, have you…*

ELIOT: *Yes Amanda?*

AMANDA: *Have you put it down?*

ELIOT: *You know I can't put it down.*

AMANDA: *You can, you can.*

ELIOT: *My darling, I can't put it down.*

AMANDA: *You must be terribly… strong.*

ELIOT: *I've tried frightfully; there isn't a particle of me that doesn't want to put it down.*

AMANDA: *Eliot you must. Put it down for our sake.*

ELIOT: *I want to quite desperately, but I can't.*

D. NORDEN: *The Daily Record, you can't put it down.*

AMANDA: *It must be enjoyable.*

ELIOT: *Yes.*

Go to **http://hertzradio.com/qr/** or scan QR Code on **page12** to listen to the 2 Daily Record campaign spots consecutively.

*Secret # 5 - Stand in a Different Place*

**MAN:**  *It used to be that after a busy day of meetings and phone calls and more meetings, all you wanted to hear when you walked through the front door was… silence.*

*You even talked about it with her, you called it your 'transition time' – a pleasant little break in your day between your work commute and your home life where you could just relax.*

*Not have to hold a conversation.*

*Not have to be a 'good listener'.*

*Just enjoy the sound of… nothing.*

*But then she got sick.*

*And now the thing you hate most when you come home is… hearing the sound of nothing.*

*Your health is all that matters.  HBF.*

**Secret #6 - Characters Not Voices**

## Script 17 - SHIRES CAMPAIGN - COCO

**COCO:**   Hi there, I'm Coco Chanel.

People are always asking me if I'm **that** Coco Chanel, and I'm always like, do I look like I've been dead 40 years? I don't think so!

And wasn't she French or something? Do I sound French? I'm nothing like Coco!

Although, she **is** available at The Shires and I am going there because I need a new outfit for my Christmas party!  And parking's free every late night in December.

**ANNCR:** Some of the world's biggest fashion brands are available at The Shires.  It's in Leicester city centre,

**COCO:**   And at the shires.co.uk.

Go to **http://hertzradio.com/qr/** or scan QR Code on **page12** to listen to the 3 Shires campaign spots consecutively.

*Secret #7 -* **Produce with Passion**

**DONNA:** *Hello, hi, I'm Donna Karan. Not **the** Donna Karan of course, no. I wish. To be honest, I don't get mistaken for the real Donna Karan that much, even when I do wear her clothes. Maybe because, well, I don't much look like her.*

*But like Donna, I am going to be at The Shires this week because they're open till 8 on Wednesday and I have to go after work to get something nice for my cousin's engagement party next month.*

**ANNCR:** *Some of the world's biggest fashion brands are available at The Shires. It's in Leicester city centre,*

**DONNA:** *And fashion attheshires.co.uk.*

*Secret # 7 - **Produce with Passion***

Go to **http://hertzradio.com/qr/** or scan QR Code on **page12** to listen to the 3 Shires campaign spots consecutively.

**HUGO:** *Hello, I'm Hugo… Boss.  Not the Hugo Boss, sadly he's no longer with us.*

*But I do feel we have this amazing kind of connection, like beyond the grave or something.*

*First of all, we both have the most impeccable taste.  Plus, his clothes are on sale at The Shires, and I'll be there this week because their sales are on now, and they're open New Year's Day between 11 and 5.*

**ANNCR:** *Some of the world's biggest fashion brands are available at The Shires. In Leicester City Centre*

**HUGO:** *And at the shires.co.uk.*

*Secret # 7 -* **Produce with Passion**

*Script 20* - **HANDY ANDY 1**

**SCENE: THE KITCHEN OF A SUBURBAN HOUSE OR FLAT. THE HUSBAND COMES IN THROUGH THE FRONT DOOR AND CALLS OUT TO HIS WIFE**

HUSBAND: *Hey babe, I'm home.*

WIFE: *Sshhhhh.*

HUSBAND: *What?*

WIFE: *They're listening.*

HUSBAND: *Who's listening?*

WIFE: *The Green Men.*

HUSBAND: *What do you mean the green men?*

WIFE: *Over there.*

HUSBAND: *Er… baby, that's dishwashing liquid.*

WIFE: *That's what they want you to think.*

ANNCR: *Rather use an oven cleaner without the fumes?*
*Handy Andy – fume-free oven cleaner.*

*Script 21-* **HANDY ANDY 2**

| | |
|---|---|
| **HUSBAND:** | *Hey babe, I'm home.* |
| **WIFE:** | *Sshhhhh.* |
| **HUSBAND:** | *What?* |
| **WIFE:** | (PAUSE 1.8 sec) *They're listening.* |
| **HUSBAND:** | (BAFFLED PAUSE 1 sec) *Who's listening?* |
| **WIFE:** | *The Green Men.* |
| **HUSBAND:** | (BAFFLED PAUSE 1.4 sec) *What do you mean the green men?* |
| **WIFE:** | (PAUSE .4 sec) *Over there.* |
| **HUSBAND:** | (ANOTHER PUZZLED PAUSE 2.3 sec) *Baby, that's dishwashing liquid.* |
| **WIFE:** | (PAUSE 2.3sec) *That's what they want you to think.* |
| **ANNCR:** | (PAUSE .7 sec) *Rather use an oven cleaner without the fumes? Handy Andy – fume-free oven cleaner.* |

*Script 22* - **TRANSPORT FOR LONDON**

**SCENE: INTERIOR OF A POLICE CAR, WE HEAR SNATCHES OF RADIO MESSAGES**

**COP 1:**    *Look at that guy, he must be doing 50.*

**COP 2:**    *46.*

*CAR SPEEDS UP, SHORT BURST OF SIREN*

**COP 1:**    *... Right.*

**POLICEMAN GETS OUT, WALKS TO OTHER CAR. MUSIC FROM INSIDE SPEEDER'S CAR GETS LOUDER AND LOUDER. HE TAPS ON THE CAR WINDOW WHICH OPENS**

*Turn the music off please. And step out of the car please sir. We clocked you at 46 miles per hour in a 30 zone. Did you realize you were breaking the speed limit?*

**CHILD:**    *It's not fair! You're always picking on me.*

**ANNCR:**    *Young, immature male drivers are responsible for the largest number of speed-related collisions.*

**CHILD:**    *I didn't do anything!*

**ANNCR:**    *They could lose their license, and along with it their job and social life.*

**CHILD:**    *I'm going to tell my dad!*

**ANNCR:**    *Tough growing up.*

*Script 23*- **SCOTTISH HEALTH**

**CENE: AN ENQUIRY DESK AT A LOCAL GOVERNMENT OFFICE, THE DEPARTMENT OF SUICIDE. A CUSTOMER APPROACHES THE CLERK.**

| | |
|---|---|
| **CLERK:** | *Can I help you?* |
| **MAN:** | *Yes, I'd like to commit suicide please.* |
| **CLERK:** | *I see. Something dramatic?*<br>*We have an opening*<br>*on the Forth Road Bridge.* |
| **MAN:** | *Ooh no, I can't stand heights.* |
| **CLERK:** | *Gas oven is still very popular.* |
| **MAN:** | *No, we're all electric.* |
| **CLERK:** | *Pity. How about a nice overdose?*<br>*That's very quick and neat.* |
| **MAN:** | *I'm not really in that much of a hurry.* |
| **CLERK:** | *Oh why didn't you say so?*<br>*I've got the very thing. Smoke.* |
| **MAN:** | *You mean cigarettes?* |
| **CLERK:** | *Yes, a natural! It's slow, expensive,*<br>*unpleasant for those around you.*<br>*And you can go in so many different ways!* |
| **MAN:** | *Really?* |
| **CLERK:** | *Oh yes – lung cancer, throat cancer,*<br>*emphysema, heart disease...* |
| **MAN:** | *That's marvelous, thank you very much.* |
| **CLERK:** | *All part of the service. I should warn you,*<br>*though, that it may take a while, and there*<br>*is a possibility that you might live.* |
| **MAN:** | *Hmmm. No, I'll chance it. Got a light?* |
| **CLERK:** | *Yes, here* |
| **MAN:** | *Thank you.* (LIGHTS & INHALES)<br>*Ooh, I feel worse already!* |

*Secret # 7 -* **Produce with Passion**

## ABOUT THE COMMERCIALS

This is about credits and permissions.

This book has links to sound files of a total of 25 radio commercials (some of the files are multiple spot campaigns).

Of these, I wrote 14 and directed a further 2. Of the others, eight are commercials, which I came across as a member of an advertising festival jury and have been published on various festival sites. The other two – *Maraschino Cherry* and *Fuller Paint* – were made, I believe, before there was such a thing as advertising awards.

As much as possible I have identified the agencies and individuals responsible and also whenever possible, I have asked for their blessing to use the work in this book.

The tricky part has been "As Much as/whenever Possible."

Some of the ads are for companies, brands and products that no longer exist. And many of the agencies are no longer around and/or the individuals have moved on. In a couple of cases my emails have gone unanswered.

So if you are the advertiser, unnamed creator, director, producer or sound engineer of any of the material, please know this: I have used your spot in my workshops and this book out of admiration and as an example of the best in radio advertising.

If you contact me to correct an omission or error I will do everything I can to make sure it is corrected in the next edition.

# BEST
# BONDAGE EROTICA
# 2011

# BEST
# BONDAGE EROTICA
# 2011

EDITED BY
RACHEL KRAMER BUSSEL

CLEIS
PRESS

Published in the United States by Cleis Press, Inc., 2246 Sixth Street, Berkeley, California 94710.

Printed in the United States.
Cover design: Scott Idleman
Cover photograph: Roman Kasperski
Text design: Frank Wiedemann
Cleis Press logo art: Juana Alicia
First Edition.
10 9 8 7 6 5 4 3 2 1

ISBN: 978-1-57344-426-2

"How the Little Mermaid Got Her Tail Back" by Andrea Dale was originally published in *Fairy Tale Lust*, edited by Kristina Wright (Cleis Press, 2010). "Do You See What I Feel?" by Teresa Noelle Roberts was originally published in *Sweet Love: Erotic Fantasies for Couples*, edited by Violet Blue (Cleis Press, 2010).

# Contents

vii  *Introduction: The Joy of Restraint*

  1  *The Long Way Home* • ELIZABETH COLDWELL
 10  *His Little Apprentice* • JACQUELINE APPLEBEE
 18  *Foreign Exchange* • EVAN MORA
 33  *The Ingénue* • JANINE ASHBLESS
 47  *Reasoning* • TENILLE BROWN
 58  *Subdue* • DUSTY HORN
 68  *Relative Anonymity* • EMERALD
 84  *Closeted* • EMILY BINGHAM
 93  *Vegas Treat* • RACHEL KRAMER BUSSEL
103  *The Cartographer* • ANGELA CAPERTON
116  *The Apiary* • MEGAN BUTCHER
125  *Wired* • LISABET SARAI
141  *How the Little Mermaid Got Her Tail Back* •
     ANDREA DALE
150  *The Lady or the Tiger* • BILL KTE'PI
156  *Sealed for Freshness* • JENNIFER PETERS
164  *Stocks and Bonds* • RITA WINCHESTER
170  *Helen Lay Bound* • SUZANNE V. SLATE
184  *The Rainmaker* • ELIZABETH DANIELS
191  *Do You See What I Feel?* • TERESA NOELLE ROBERTS
203  *Truss Issues* • LUX ZAKARI

213  *About the Authors*
217  *About the Editor*

# INTRODUCTION: THE JOY OF RESTRAINT

Perhaps I shouldn't have been surprised to find, when putting together this anthology, that about 75 percent of the story submissions involved the submissive's, or bottom's, point of view. When it comes to bondage, the feeling of giving in, surrendering, allowing oneself to be placed at someone else's mercy, comes alive on the page, and these authors certainly know how to vividly depict that appeal. Though there are stories here from a top's perspective, told by dominants who delight in the thrill of watching a lover squirm, struggle and submit, most of the stories here go the other way.

Take "The Rainmaker," by Elizabeth Daniels, in which Amy, a bit uncertain, allows herself to overcome her fears and get tied up:

> Darkness and the ropes enfolded Amy like a chrysalis.
> Her mind was clear, finally at peace. After months of
> agonizing over every step of foreplay, after sex that

consisted of checklists and flow charts compiled from hours of research, for once, she did not need to think or plan. Like extradark chocolate, such dependence was not something she would want every day, but for the moment, it was a bite of bitter bliss.

I especially appreciate the stories here that illuminate the leap of faith one needs to make to allow someone else to bind him. In "Truss Issues," Emy repeatedly tells Samir that she's not into bondage, doesn't want to be tied up and yet, somewhere inside, she knows that isn't totally true. "To her surprise, her body didn't sync up to her beliefs. She felt a warm liquid rush flood her cunt... Cursing her body for its betrayal, Emy nestled her teeth in her lower lip and forced her breathing to remain calm, to not come out as a needy whimper." What happens when she surrenders teaches her that she doesn't have to give up all of herself to enjoy the sweet friction and emotional journey that submission to bondage can incur.

In the lesbian scene in Dusty Horn's "Subdue," the narrator finds herself, finds the core of her submission and learns how to be patient.

After what seems like eons without touch, her hot hand on my chin is electrifying. She lifts it up and back, pressing something against my smooth exposed throat. Tugging firmly up on the hair at the nape of my neck, she wraps the rest of the mystery object against the top of my spine where my still body meets my busy mind.

"This is mine," she hums to me as she slides a metal clasp into place. "This is not your collar. It's mine, for you to wear."

> The collar bulges around my neck, a leather halo
> engorged with blood.

Other stories stand out for their unique scenarios. In "The Ingénue," by Janine Ashbless, a young woman finds a bound man outside in the yard, and goes to investigate this curious vision. "How the Little Mermaid Got Her Tail Back," by Andrea Dale, puts a kinky twist on a beloved fairy tale. In "Sealed for Freshness," Mitchell pays for his disobedience with a flogging against his plastic-wrapped skin, while in "Stocks and Bonds," some historical role-play at a Renaissance Festival leaves Kerri begging for mercy.

I was looking for stories that spanned the world of bondage, and boy did I get that! Here, you'll find rope and handcuffs, as you might expect, but you'll also find cling wrap, Ethernet cables, stocks and bonds, silk ties and other implements whose creators probably didn't intend them to be used in kinky play. There's bondage at the office, bondage onstage and under a red turtle-neck sweater dress. There are bondage beginners and seasoned pros, men and women who offer up their wrists, ankles, necks and other body parts to those just itching to play with them.

This is a book for anyone who wants to know what's so arousing about being tied up. Whether you've ever experienced bondage or not, these authors boldly take you along as they negotiate what they are and aren't willing to give up, and illustrate the blissful beauty that can take place, inside and out, when you make the choice to give up some of your freedom and mobility in order to access the world from a new perspective.

If what drew you to this book was the stunningly sexy image on the cover, I can assure you that the stories you'll find inside are just as hot—possibly even hotter. They are about so much more than simply what one looks like while tied up: for instance, what it feels like to wait, longing for release while also hoping the joy of restraint never ends. That push/pull is at the heart of bondage, and that is what you will experience along with the characters, those brave subs, brats, bad girls and naughty boys who offer themselves up so their masters and mistresses—and you, the reader—can savor them, one click of the handcuffs at a time.

Rachel Kramer Bussel
New York City

# THE LONG WAY HOME

Elizabeth Coldwell

W e'll take the long way home tonight," Max says once the waitress has taken our order for coffee. I can't help but smile, knowing exactly what that means.

Bringing me to the White Hart was the clue he might have something planned for us tonight. It's the restaurant where he proposed to me, and the restaurant where so many special evenings have begun in the six years since then. It's been a week now since his design for the town's new community arts center was formally accepted, and I know he's been desperate to celebrate since the moment the contracts were signed. But, as is so often the case for June, it's been far too wet to make driving out into the countryside a pleasure. Only today did the weather break, meaning he was able to book a table for dinner.

We've had a beautiful meal; it doesn't surprise me to learn the chef here was recently awarded his first Michelin star. Max's rib eye steak was rare to the point of bloody—just the way he likes it—and served with a rich red wine and marrow sauce, while my rack of lamb, resting on a bed of creamy champ, was meltingly tender. As for the chocolate fondant pudding and malted milk ice cream that followed, I could happily have licked the plate clean. Max, who is driving, has only had a glass of the excellent Fleurie recommended by the sommelier, leaving me to polish off the rest of the bottle. I never really appreciated wine until I met Max, having neither the palate nor the bank balance for the really good stuff, but he has educated me in so many things.

The waitress returns with our coffees—a double espresso for Max and a latte for me. She catches me applying another coat of blood red lipstick, pouting at my reflection in the mirror of my compact. I catch her eye and she glances quickly away. I know what she's thinking. She's not the first to look at us and make the assumption. Max sits in his shirtsleeves, tie abandoned on the table, looking every inch the serious, hard-working professional he is. Meanwhile, I'm in a PVC top unzipped to show more cleavage than is proper in this environment—I've caught the man at the table in the corner, the one whose wife is clearly boring him, peering over in the hope he will actually catch a glimpse of my nipples—and a short, tight black skirt, and there's half an inch of dark roots showing in my punky peroxide bob. We seem so ill matched, the obvious conclusion to draw is that he's hired me for the evening.

We could dispel the illusion, but it's more fun this way. I wonder what the chap in the corner, or the waitress who thinks she's got me sussed, would say if they knew exactly what we're going to do when Max has paid for our meal and we make our way out to the car.

Max drains his cup, catches the waitress's eye and scribbles in the air in the universally recognized gesture for requesting the bill. She nods, and he gives her one of his trademark tiny winks, guaranteed to send a hot flush of lust rushing through her body.

Oh, but he's handsome, my Max, with his dark bedroom eyes, pepper-and-salt hair and the little dimple that blooms on his right cheek when he smiles, and women never fail to respond to him. He's very good at making them feel as though they are the only person in the room and their every word is of the utmost importance. I often joke that if he wasn't such a talented architect he could have a successful career as a gigolo. Not that I worry he might ever act on his flirtatious impulses. We're too perfectly matched in our desires for him to need to look elsewhere.

Once Max has paid for dinner with his credit card, adding a tip that reflects our satisfaction with the standard of service, he comes round to my side of the table to help me courteously out of my seat. Bending his head close to my ear, he whispers, "Are you ready, my love?"

"Oh, yes," I reply, fighting to keep the excitement out of my voice.

As we walk out of the restaurant, hand in hand, I'm sure my admirer in the corner has his gaze fixed to the cheeks of my arse, outlined almost indecently by my clinging skirt. If only he knew I might be required to remove that skirt before I've even gottten in the car.

In the event, there are too many people sitting at the wooden benches in the beer garden, enjoying the last lingering warmth of the evening, to make such a public display comfortable for me. Max, so attuned to my feelings, merely murmurs, "One day I'll make you do it, Tamsin. I'll let everyone see what you look like in that tiny thong of yours." He knows that's the point where fantasy and reality rub up against each other for me: the thought of being humiliated, of letting others in on our kinky little secrets, never fails to excite me, but I have no wish to actually experience it. Not here, not in front of strangers who would never understand.

The car is parked at the far end of the lot, beneath an over-hanging laburnum tree. I glance back up to the beer garden, but no one is paying us any attention. They may have stared at us as we passed, me in my tarty outfit and my husband in his sober suit, but we were clearly just a one-minute wonder, something to pause and speculate upon before returning to more important matters like getting another round in.

Max opens the passenger door as I stand obediently by the side of the car. He reaches into the glove compartment, roots out the equipment he needs. My pussy lurches, as it always does, watching him play it between his fingers. "Hands out, palms together," he orders, and it begins.

As he wraps the cool, stretchy fabric around my wrists, I remember—as I always do—when I first realized just how much seats belts excited me. My mind flashes back to a journey home, after a day at the coast with my parents. I would have been sixteen, family outings becoming more of a duty than a pleasure, and the day itself is a forgotten blur, mixed up with so many other memories of boring cliff-top walks and huddling behind a windbreak, staring out at the flat gray expanse of the North Sea. But that was the first trip we ever took in my dad's new Nova, fitted out with seat belts back as well as front, as had become required by law a couple of years earlier. Squeezed in the back of the car with my bickering kid brothers, I had found the webbed belt rubbing against my breast, rather than resting comfortably between them as it should. Even beneath layers of clothing, my nipple had sprung to life, responding to the pressure. Combined with the feeling of being restrained in my seat, it had sparked some hidden circuits in my brains—circuits that are still acti-vated every time I click shut my seat belt.

For a long time, it had been my guilty secret. How did you tell a man how you were turned on by something as mundane, as ubiquitous as a seat belt, how you longed to feel it binding your wrists and ankles, and not have him stare at you as though you were mad? Only when I met Max, who understood so perfectly how thrilling it was to have the woman you loved restrained and willingly helpless, was I able to confess.

Now, we have our own little code: the words, the gestures that tell me I'll be ending the evening tied up in the passenger seat. Whatever the company, whatever the circumstances, Max only has to tell me we're taking the long way home to have me squirming in my chair, almost too excited to concentrate on anything around me.

Max helps me climb into the car, something that becomes more difficult than you'd think once your hands are immobilized. When I'm settled in my seat, he takes another length of belt, part of a job lot he bought from a local breaker's yard. He winds this around my ankles, tying my feet together. I can't help but shiver at the caress of the webbing against my bare skin.

Next comes the ball-gag. It's been specially customized by Max, the original leather strap having been replaced with a piece of seat belt, trimmed to the right width. He did a beautiful job, and I couldn't help but admire his ingenuity the day he presented it to me. Not that I enjoy wearing the gag—it's just small enough that my jaw doesn't ache but big enough to leave me drooling slightly—but isn't that the point? It all helps to reinforce that delicious feeling of being utterly at my husband's mercy.

Before he frees the passenger seat belt from its housing and pulls it into place across my chest, he takes hold of the zip on my top and pulls it almost all the way down. If the man who was staring at my chest in the restaurant was here now, he'd finally have the view he was hoping to see: my nipples, strawberry ripe, jutting proudly forward. Max plays with them, tugging and twisting as I moan into my gag. My pussy prickles, just as desperate for Max's touch but knowing that's unlikely to happen for a while yet.

Satisfied I am properly restrained, Max slams shut the passenger door and goes round to his side of the car. Fastening his own seat belt with a nonchalant click that sends another shiver of lust through me, he flicks on the headlights and reverses out into the body of the parking lot. A couple are walking past on the way to their own car. I shut my eyes and pray they won't see me. Unless they're as kinky as Max and me, the sight of a woman being driven away, gagged, restrained and with her bare breasts on display, will have them reaching immediately for their phone to call the police.

"Relax," Max says, aware of my concern, "she's going through her handbag, trying to find her car keys. He's chivvying her to get on with it. They haven't even noticed us."

Relaxing is not an option. Part of me can never quite shake the fear that we'll be caught, either by a curious passerby or a police patrol, lurking in wait for those who still haven't gotten the message about drinking and driving and are willing to take risks on these twisting country roads. Yet it just adds another layer to the thrill.

Max turns on the car radio, turning it from my favorite classic rock station to one playing mellow jazz. The music is strangely soothing, even though I hate jazz. I have no idea how long he'll spend driving around, or whether he will park somewhere before taking me home. There are so many delicious possibilities.

I am continually aware of the insistent chafing of the belt around my ankles and wrists, the subtle pressure between my breasts. From time to time, Max reaches over and tweaks my nipples, keeping them hard and aching. Whenever he pulls his fingers away, I thrust my chest forward, hoping for more, but what happens on this journey is strictly on his terms.

We come to a crossroads I recognize all too well. If Max turns left, home is a little over five minutes away. If he turns right, it takes him out toward an area of Forestry Commission land, deserted at this time of night. He checks the road in both directions, then indicates right. If I could smile around the gag, I would.

Half a mile down the road, Max pulls the car over into a turnout. He turns off the engine but leaves the radio on. The DJ, his voice low and cigarette husky, announces a tune by Herbie Hancock before adding, "And if you're on the roads tonight, be careful out there." Max and I catch each other's eye. The last thing we intend to do is be careful.

He lets himself out of the car and goes to open the hatchback. We've brought my Renault Clio tonight, rather than his considerably more luxurious BMW, because I have the dog guard fitted. Not that we actually have dogs, but the sturdy tubular metal frame, resting flush against the backseat, is the perfect accessory for our in-car games.

I wait patiently till he comes to collect me. He removes the gag first, and my mouth sags open in relief. Then he unties my wrists and ankles, allowing me to rub the life back into them. Finally, he lets me out of the car.

"Skirt off," he orders. I do as he asks, giving him the view he's been wanting to see ever since we finished our meal: my pink lace thong, saturated with my juices and almost disappearing between my fleshy sex lips. He puts his hand between my legs, pushes the fabric even deeper. For the briefest moment, he rubs my clit and sweet pleasure ripples through me, but he quickly decides that's quite enough for the time being.

He urges me into the back of the car. I don't need to be told what position to assume; I simply get on my knees and catch hold of one of the horizontal bars running the length of the dog guard. There are already lengths of seat belt webbing attached to the frame, designed to close with Velcro so I can fasten one in place and Max, reaching over from the backseat, the other.

Once my bonds are secured, Max comes back round behind me and pulls my thong down and off, tossing it onto the floor of the trunk beside me. He pushes my legs widely apart, giving him a wonderful view of my shaven pussy lips and tight anal pucker. "Gorgeous," he murmurs, before planting a soft kiss on each of my bumcheeks.

"Just think what this would be like if we had an audience," he continues, reaching between my legs to stroke my clit as he does. "We could go up to that dogging spot near the golf course, tie you in place and invite anyone who wants to take a turn...."

I can picture the scene in my mind: a queue of anonymous men, condom-clad cocks in their hands, waiting to fuck me. There would be nothing I could do—nothing I would want to do—as they mounted me and plunged into my wetness. Bound as I was, maybe even with the ball-gag in place, I wouldn't be able to direct them, so one might choose to slip into my arse when my cunt became too sloppy and well used for his liking....

It's such an arousing image, yet I know Max would never act on it unless I asked him, and for now his cock is enough. I can hear him undoing his zip, but when he gets into place behind me, he hasn't removed his trousers. It somehow seems even ruder to have him enter me while he's still fully clothed and I'm in nothing but the PVC top from which my breasts spill out, full and perky.

Once Max is lodged nice and deep inside me, he grabs those breasts and kneads them, his mouth nuzzling the nape of my neck as he does. I feel utterly possessed by him, his big body covering my small one, his cock hot and bulky in my cunt. He starts to thrust: fast, powerful strokes that have me almost slamming up against the dog guard with every one. The radio is still playing, the soft, soulful melody of a saxophone solo accompanying our moans and gasps. I close my eyes and give in to the sensations of being so wonderfully fucked.

Max has hold of my hips now, and the manner in which he is speeding up his thrusts lets me know it won't be long before he comes. Despite all the stimulation I've had—both physically from my seat belt bondage and mentally, from the moment Max let me know he would be tying me up tonight—I'm still not close enough to join him. Even though I thrust back hard at his groin, making the most of the heat and friction we're generating, when he calls my name and shoots his seed inside me, I think I'm going to be left high and dry.

Which is when Max springs his final surprise of the evening. He presses something between my legs, and I realize at once it's another piece of seat belt material. Just the feel of that smooth, plasticky webbing rubbing at my sensitized clit is all it takes to make me orgasm as hard as I ever have. "That's it, Tamsin, come for me," Max whispers. When it's over and the colors bursting behind my eyelids have died away to nothing, I'm left hanging in my bonds, weak and sobbing. I'm barely able to shape the words to thank my husband for such an incredible climax.

He unfastens my wrists, holds me close for a moment. We kiss, all our passion and love for each other expressed in that soft meeting of mouths. Then the reality of our surroundings kicks in, and Max hands me my skirt so I can make myself look almost respectable again.

After I've dressed and we've tidied up the trunk, I slip into the passenger seat beside him, Cradled once more in the safe, sensual embrace of my seat belt, I settle back to enjoy the short drive home.

# HIS LITTLE APPRENTICE

## Jacqueline Applebee

I tugged on the belt of my thin dressing gown. The feel of it as it slipped over my skin was like a whispered promise of pleasure. I spent most days covered in grime and dirt, working in derelict buildings. To make up for this, I spent most evenings cosseted by silk. I wound the belt across my wrists. The fabric tightened—the restriction brought my mind into focus. My breathing caught, I sat straighter in my chair. I thought of Sergei—my supervisor, my mentor and my friend. I wished he were the one doing this to me.

Earlier in the day, I had been working hard clearing out a house as part of my painting and decorating apprenticeship. I was learning new messy skills, and I hoped I could start my own business one day. I was the only woman in my group, but Sergei had taken to me almost instantly, showing me the tricks of the trade and protecting me from the other trainees, who seemed to be on a mission to make me feel like shit. It didn't hurt that Sergei was a handsome guy with dark hair and pale blue eyes. He was somewhat older than me. He liked to call me his little apprentice. It wasn't all paternal smiles, though; he would also glance at me sometimes when he thought I wasn't paying attention. I caught plenty of hungry gazes reflected in panes of glass and dusty mirrors.

Sergei and I had both been charged with clearing out a room that had been lived in by an elderly man, before the paint crew came in and worked their magic. When we found an old porno magazine hidden beneath a rug, I didn't know it would ignite something inside me. I'd seen pictures of naked women before, but they had never interested me. Not until that moment.

Sergei laughed, like he always did when he was nervous. "I wonder how old she is now?" He angled the magazine to me. I saw a thin woman on her knees with her arms held out in front of her. Her hands were bound with lengths of rope. From the background clues and the awful beige wallpaper, I guessed the photo had been taken in the seventies. However, what made me swallow hard and then grip the glossy paper in my hands, was the look on the model's face. She was gazing at someone offscreen with a mixture of terror and desire. There was a shadow on the floor, a long thin outline of what I thought to be a man who stood there and watched the whole thing.

Sergei was still talking to me or rather at me. His words were a jumble. I suddenly found it difficult to understand his accent. The only thing that made sense at that moment in time was the hungry anticipation etched on that woman's face. I wanted that. I longed to be exposed, desperate but unable to do anything without the consent of a shadow that loomed above me.

The other trainees called to us as they marched noisily outside, no doubt on their way to the local café for a big greasy lunch. Sergei turned to leave as well, but I reached out, stopped him.

"What do you really think of this?" I couldn't quite meet his eyes.

He shrugged, peered over the top of the paper. "She's not my type."

"But I am, aren't I?" It was probably the most daring thing I'd ever said, but somehow I knew my shyness would not help me in this matter. I was surprised when Sergei blushed.

"Come on, let's get something to eat." He shrugged out of my grip, but he didn't move away. He stared at his feet. Fire started to kindle between my legs. I felt the hairs of my pussy crinkle and smolder. I had the sudden need to rip my clothes off. I launched myself at my friend, kissing him in a flurry.

"What are you doing?" Sergei held me at a distance.

"Please," I whined, pressing forward. Sergei's arms went slack. I felt a surge of relief when he let me come closer. All resistance disappeared as he sprang back into motion and clutched me tight. We pushed at each other's overalls, baring layer after layer of cloth until there was nothing but skin, scalding hot.

"Oh, Carol," he sighed. "Can I touch you?" It was a crazy thing to ask, with me being practically naked; my overalls, jeans and knickers lying in a scrunched heap around my ankles.

"Please." I was on fire. Sergei's cool hands stroked around my breasts, and then he tweaked my nipples. I arched toward him, linking my hands behind my back. "Please, Sergei. Please."

Sergei reached behind me, secured my small hands in just one of his. He cupped my pussy with his free hand. I was shameless. I started thrusting against him like an animal.

Sergei spun me around. "You sure this is okay?"

"Yes!" The room blurred as I was swiftly bent over the back of an abandoned armchair.

I thought he would cool me down, extinguish the fire that raged inside, but when Sergei thrust into me, a new wave of heat descended. He was all friction where I was smooth, dry where I was molten. His hard muscles pulled my arms tighter into a clinch. I could not move, not even a little. Sergei drew my orgasm out of me with brute strength that I could not resist. When he came, he growled in my ear. I imagined he had regressed into a caveman, but that only made me hotter. I made small animal sounds. I became his prey. I let Sergei do whatever he wanted. It was the most blissful thing I had ever known.

I once read that happiness provides in height what it lacks in length. Sergei could barely look at me once we had finished. I pulled up my knickers, shuffled back into the rest of my clothes. I heard the door to the room slam, and I found myself alone. I carefully folded the porno mag, and then I buried it in a deep pocket. Some rational part of me knew that I should have thrown it in the trash, but the greater part of me—the part that had just been shagged over the back of an armchair—wanted more.

I went home later, changed into a silky dressing gown and spent the next few hours looking at bondage sites on the Internet. However, nothing seemed to do it for me in the way that the old magazine had. I held up the picture once more, focused on the shadow on the floor by the model's feet. It could have been another photographer or even someone there to do the makeup. But in my mind, the shadow belonged to a stern man who had commissioned the shoot. He was eager for the photos to be done so he could take his woman home. She would still be bound as he spread her legs wide, unable to escape as he screwed her senseless. But then I thought to myself, *This woman would never want to be free. Who would want to escape such bliss?*

I pictured Sergei pressing me down on a table and then tying me up securely. I would be like Gulliver, restrained so that even the hairs on my head would hold me fast. My pussy clenched at the thought. I just had to convince Sergei that this was a good thing.

The buzzer to my small apartment sounded, shaking me from my fantasy. I opened the door to see Sergei in casual attire.

"I'm a terrible person." He looked up at me, smiled apologetically.

"No, you're not. You're a great guy." I shut the door, ushering him inside. I was so glad he was in my home. My clit began to throb with anticipation. "Can I get you a drink?"

Sergei shook his head. "I'm not staying long. I just wanted to see you, make sure you're okay." He reached out, ruffled my hair in a paternal way. My heart fluttered. Sergei was not my father. I knew deep down that he didn't see me as his little girl, either.

"About what we did…" I started, but I didn't get a chance to finish.

"What we did cannot happen again." His voice was hard.

"But I liked it. You liked it. It was the best sex I've ever had."

"You're young. You'll meet somebody one day who's decent." Sergei wrung his hands together as he spoke.

I made a face. "What if I don't want decent? What if I want to be tied up?"

Sergei put his hands in his pockets. "You don't want that."

"I do. I really do." I knelt at his feet. Sergei's hand went instinctively to my short hair. He petted me as if I were a child. But I was not a child. I'm a grown woman. I knew what I wanted, and what's more, I had some idea of how I could get it. I reached up, stroked my hands over the rough fabric of Sergei's jeans. My fingers traced the outline of his cock, small but getting bigger with every moment. "Please, Sergei," I whispered. I undid the buckle of his belt, and then pulled it out in a whoosh. "I really want this." I felt his cock twitch against my face. I had my answer.

I mouthed his erection through the barrier of denim, but as he started to thrust against me, I held up his belt. "Restrain me."

I felt Sergei freeze for a moment, but after a few rapid heartbeats, he began to move. I stood and looked into his eyes, the pupils that had dilated wide and deep. I held out my hands, offered myself up to him like a sacrifice. Sergei quickly bound my hands together with his belt. My knees wobbled. I had to sit down or I would collapse, but Sergei had other plans. He pulled me by my wrists until we were against the wall where my jacket hung. Sergei yanked it off, and then placed my bound hands over the now empty coat hook. He stepped away, and for a moment I thought that he would make his escape, but then he brought his hand down on my backside. I yelped and turned to see him rub his hands together. He slapped me again, this time harder. Sergei was a strong man. His hands were calloused through hard labor. I felt every mark and line as he continued to beat me. My legs widened. I desperately needed them to be restrained, too.

"You still want this?" Sergei's voice sounded tight.

"Yes. Yes, I need this."

"You want me to use you like a cheap slut?" He slapped my arse as he spoke, punctuating the words.

"Yes."

"Ask nicely."

"Please, Sergei. I'm yours. Do it, please, do it."

The next thing I felt was hot breath against my shoulder. Sergei bit into my flesh, and then he pushed his cock against me, running it over my backside. It felt like an eternity before he finally shoved inside me. We both groaned as he angled himself to thrust deeper. A trickle of sweat rolled over my nose, down to my lips.

"Slut."

"Yes." I could barely get the word out.

"Mine."

"Always." I meant it.

I started to come. A quake centered on my clit and then radiated out until my whole body shook. The fire that raged inside made a final roar of heat, and then it was silenced. I felt Sergei come seconds later. The echoes of his cries traveled back and forth across my skin.

Sergei took me off the coat hook after a while. I sagged against him as he led me to the sofa.

"We can't do this again." He sounded broken. It hurt when I realized that I was the one who had fractured him. He swept my dressing gown to the side, ran a hand gently over the skin of my arse. "You're red. You must feel so sore right now."

"I feel incredible," I countered.

"My little apprentice," he said softly, running a finger over my nose.

I jerked away from him. "I'm not little. Trust me, Sergei."

Sergei turned away. "It's just a phase. A phase you'll get over."

"Just a phase?" I was suddenly angry. "Was it a phase when you made me beg?"

Sergei stood up. "I knew this would happen." He roughly untied my hands. I felt bereft now that I was free. "Look after yourself, Carol."

I couldn't believe this turnabout. "Why are you doing this?" I asked as Sergei stood at the door.

"Because I care about you. I don't want to hurt you."

I stumbled over to him, inched myself between his body and the door. "Then don't hurt me." I cupped his face, stood on tiptoes and then kissed him. "Make me happy." I put every ounce of my desire into the words. He just had to believe me.

Sergei held me tight. "Carol." I could barely hear his voice, but I could feel his smile against my cheek. "Making you happy is all I've ever wanted." He squeezed me even tighter. I felt the smolder begin once more. I must have moaned a little because Sergei started laughing. "You really are a slut, aren't you?" He increased his hold on me, restrained me with bonds of living flesh. Strong arms and legs held me still while he ravaged me once more. I knew I would never be truly free again. And that suited me just fine.

# FOREIGN EXCHANGE

### Evan Mora

Things are different in New York than they are at home; everything seems edgier and more aggressive. It's not like Toronto's that far away, but it's more than geography that separates us. We've come from the land of "please" and "thank you," the place where people apologize first and ask questions later. New York seems less forgiving somehow, more arrogant, more self-assured.

The city itself makes me tingle just a little. It exudes the kind of cool confidence that makes the submissive in me want to prostrate myself at her feet, to lie naked before her and tell her to do with me what she will. Graham feels her, too, though differently than me. I see her creeping into his eyes and under his skin. We grow hungrier, he and I, the longer we're here, and we're here for a very long while.

Graham has taken a position at a teaching hospital in Brooklyn, an exchange organized by the hospital where he works in Toronto. We're two months into a twelve-month stint, both

settled and unsettled. Our apartment on Garfield Place is well
situated, a two-bedroom on the fourth floor of a brownstone
only a few blocks' walk from the hospital and close to everything we might need. Closer still are the neighbors who fuel our
imaginations, who are everything in their bold American ways
that we are not.

"You must be the new tenants—welcome!" A woman in a
tight black sheath offers with a blood red smile, extending a
gloved hand to Graham and me in turn.

Her beauty is captivating and her smile is genuine, but
the man she has leashed and collared behind her makes our
answering smiles falter and our reciprocating greetings trail off.
She continues to speak, asking where we're from and how we
like the apartment, as though there's nothing unusual going on,
as though this is a commonplace occurrence.

"Say 'hello,' Jay," commands the woman, Giselle.

"Hello," he says.

Nothing more.

"Did you like that?" Graham growls, his hand on my throat,
fucking me in our apartment soon after. He's as hard and aggressive as I am open and receptive, painting a crude picture with his
whispered words, a picture of Giselle and this man.

In the aftermath, we are quiet. There is newness in this space:
a prickle on my skin; a flicker in the periphery of my vision.
We are sadist and masochist, Graham and I, but we are not,
have never been, dominant and submissive. Ours is a communion in the giving and receiving of pain, but it has never been an
exchange of power. Not really.

Graham gives everything of himself: everything, to everyone.
He is as selfless a man as I have ever encountered. That inflicting
pain satisfies a need in him is secondary to the fact that I need to
*feel* pain. I need to feel it, and so he gives it to me. But if I didn't,

he would swallow his own need without a word.

Paradoxically, therein lies our impasse. I need more than pain. I need to submit. I need the exchange of power, and although Graham would give me anything, he cannot give me his selfishness.

In my fantasies, I am used. I service. In my fantasies, Graham calls me a dirty whore and fucks my ass for his own pleasure. It is an ecstasy better than any orgasm I can imagine. But in reality, telling me to get up and get him a coffee makes Graham uncomfortable.

And yet…with his hand wrapped around my throat and his cock stabbing my cunt, I felt for a moment that I *was* being used, that he was lost in his vision of Giselle and her boy, and that I was no more than his vessel.

We encounter our neighbors again a few nights later, walking along Sixth Avenue. Though not bound by leash and collar this time, Jay maintains a perfect stride slightly behind and to Giselle's right, as though invisibly tethered to her. Giselle invites us over for tea, which seems at odds with our admittedly speculative image of her, and being both curiously fascinated and politely Canadian, we accept, despite feeling somewhat awkward.

The layout of their apartment is a mirror image of ours: a small foyer, master bedroom and bathroom to the right, and to the left, a second bath and bedroom, then a narrow corridor leading to a central kitchen, opening finally into a large living space. We pass by the second bedroom, with door wide open, en route to the living room and gape like motorists at a traffic accident at what is quite obviously a fully equipped dungeon. Though we do not stop our forward progression, in those brief seconds I register a wide assortment of floggers, paddles and canes all neatly displayed along the wall, as well as a padded leather spanking bench and some strategically placed hooks.

Our hostess throws a deceptively casual glance over her shoulder, but her knowing eyes and small feline smile suggest that nothing she does is accidental, and that our interest has been accurately gauged. I feel the heat of a blush rise quickly in my cheeks and lower my gaze, but not before Giselle raises her eyebrow ever so slightly, as though to say, *And now I know to whom each role falls....*

As we pass the kitchen, Jay leaves our procession; presumably it falls to him to make the tea. The rest of us continue on to the living room, which is modern and minimalist and tastefully furnished. Giselle sits at one end of a black leather sofa, and Graham and I move to fill the matching chairs opposite her.

"Sarah," Giselle's voice stops me before I can be seated, and she pats the cushion next to her in invitation, "won't you sit next to me? You don't mind do you, Graham? It just feels so formal with the two of you over there; I prefer a cozier atmosphere...." Her voice trails off in a manner I can only deem suggestive and I look to Graham hesitantly for direction, though he only shrugs slightly and gestures toward the sofa. Giselle seems oblivious to any discomfort her words may have caused and pats my thigh approvingly when I take the seat next to her.

"Lovely," she murmurs, shifting seamlessly into conversation with Graham about his work at the hospital, which leaves me with little to do other than to sit quietly beside her and listen. Giselle is animated in her conversation, laughing easily and punctuating Graham's replies to her questions with clever witticisms, and each time she does so, her hand finds my thigh again. I don't know if she means to make me feel included in their conversation with this brief contact, or whether it deliberately serves another purpose, but deliberate or not, I find myself increasingly aware of her touch, which both confuses and excites me.

Jay returns, and the diversion of tea gives me an opportunity to seek out Graham's gaze. Has he noticed Giselle touching me? Has he marked my response? Am I reading too much into this? So many thoughts swirl in my mind and I try to convey them all to Graham without speaking, but if I have been successful, he gives no sign.

"Mmm! Sarah," Giselle calls my attention back to her, "try one of Jay's cookies—he's an excellent baker." Instead of offering me a cookie, though, she breaks a small piece from the one she has bitten and holds it out to me expectantly. It is a curiously intimate gesture and without thought I lean forward and take it gently from her fingers with my mouth, as I am clearly intended to do.

"Such a pretty mouth..." Giselle says. "I'd love to see it put to good use." Her words send a thrill through me, and heat floods my cheeks and clit in equal measure. It's the way she says it: that perfect tone that implies my permission is not being sought and that compels my immediate compliance. I want to sink to my knees and press my lips to the leather of her fine, high-heeled boots.

Giselle's eyes swing from my mouth to Graham, pinning him with an unblinking stare. The silence in the room is absolute. Graham's composure is rattled, and that it is apparent angers and humiliates him. This isn't what he—or I—expected, though if pressed, I'm not certain either of us could properly say what we *had* expected.

"Oh, come now," Giselle voice is steel wrapped in a seductive purr, "we both know this is where it ends, I've only skipped the courtship. You strike me as a man who appreciates directness. Am I wrong?"

Graham scrubs his hand across his face and through his hair, telltale signs of his agitation, and shifts uncomfortably in his seat, exhaling loudly and staring fixedly out the window. Seconds pass by in the pregnant silence as Graham collects himself before he replies.

"Look—I appreciate your directness," he says, his voice tight with anger, "but your presumptions are too great. We're complete strangers. You know nothing about our lives or our desires...." Giselle arches one graceful brow and a flush steals into Graham's cheeks, but he doggedly continues, "and to invite us here under the pretext of a friendly cup of tea only to then ambush us with lewd propositions is bad form and, well, it's downright...rude," he concludes somewhat weakly. But having made his point and set up his exit, Graham rises to his feet and holds out his hand to me.

"Come on, Sarah, we're leaving," he says. On the other side of the apartment threshold, Graham pauses.

"Thank you for the tea," he says properly.

"Oh, you're most welcome." Giselle smiles, making no secret of her amusement. "And should you ever change your mind... you know where to find me." She winks at Graham and closes the door.

Things are different after that. On the outside, our lives are the same as they were before. Graham works at the hospital five, sometimes six days a week. We avail ourselves of the many fine restaurants Park Slope has to offer, often with one or another of Graham's colleagues; on the weekends we enjoy leisurely brunches and walks through Prospect Park. But there is something growing beneath the surface, something dark and heavy that is living and breathing alongside and between the two of us.

When we play, there is a new edge in Graham's voice, a different set to his jaw. Where before he gave me pleasure by giving me pain, now it's more complex, more about control. He binds me now, too. He never used to; he's never needed to. My wrists, my ankles; with either or both he binds me to the bed, to the curtain rod, to the chair he bends me over. He binds me, and then he beats me, and when he's finished beating me, he fucks me.

"You're mine," he says when he tightens the knots, and his possession ties me to him in ways that rope could not. He lights into my flesh like a cruel inquisitor, and the harder he is, the softer I become, the more I melt into his hands, lift up for his blows. And only when my flesh is on fire, when my ass and my thighs and my breasts are red and striped from his ministrations, only then does he lay down the implements of my punishment and cover my body with his.

He fucks me like he can't fuck me hard enough, deep enough, like he's trying to get *inside* me, to brand me, to fill me up with his come. Sometimes he is relentless in demanding my orgasms, making me come more than I think I can, as though only when I'm spent and trembling and weary beyond belief is he satisfied. But other times, it's different.

"Get on your knees," Graham says, and I sink to the floor in front of him, raising tear-streaked cheeks in silent offering. He grabs my hair and pulls my mouth to his cock, pushing between my lips, watching as they stretch apart to accommodate him.

"Such a pretty mouth…" he whispers, his eyes fixed on the wide-stretched bow as his cock rocks back and forth, disappearing and reappearing wet with my saliva. I wonder what he thinks of when he fucks me like this; when his body shudders and hot jets of semen fill my throat; when his eyes finally close. I wonder if he knows how this has to end?

It's one of these other times when it finally happens. Graham is still in the aftermath of his orgasm, his hand still clenched in my hair. He withdraws from my mouth, studying my swollen lips intently, grasping my face in his hand and squeezing almost as though he's not aware of what he's doing. Then, abruptly, he lets go. I look up at him, at the myriad emotions that I see passing across his face—pleasure, anger, sadness, uncertainty, jealousy—and I think that maybe he is lost, that maybe this will be our undoing.

I'm rocked out of my thoughts when Graham's open palm connects with my cheek. Tiny starbursts flash behind my eyes, and my head snaps to the side and I gasp, throwing out my hands to brace myself when I would otherwise fall. He's never slapped me before.

"Whore." Another slap. My cunt clenches wildly. I've asked him to slap me in the past, but he's always refused, always said it was too degrading.

"Slut." Another.

"More!" I gasp.

"No."

He walks away, and I am left alone, heart racing and cheeks burning, with no idea what to do next. But Graham is not gone long, and he returns before I've moved from the floor. He's dressed now, and he deposits a couple of items onto the sofa before coming to stand in front of me again.

"It excited you, didn't it? When she said what she did?"

"Yes." I won't lie to Graham, but I feel ashamed of my answer.

"I saw it. You would have done whatever she told you to do. You would have been *happy* to do it." The last bit comes out a jumbled mix of pain and anger and incredulity.

I nod silently, swallowing around the lump in my throat and blinking back the tears that threaten. I hate myself for wanting these things and for not being able to deny his accusation. I hate that we have come to this crossroads, to this place he doesn't want to be.

"I can't stop thinking about it. I keep imagining this woman—this stranger—using you like some...some kind of prostitute—" He breaks off, pacing restlessly.

"And do you want to know the craziest part?" It's torturing him, I know. I've known it for some time. "It *excites* me. How sick is that? The thought of giving you to her—to them—of them using you while I watch *turns me on*."

"I know." I whisper the words quietly into the silence that follows his admission, accepting him, accepting what he's not sure he himself can accept.

Graham turns away from me, moving to the window and staring out into the night sky. He takes a deep breath and exhales slowly, the way he does just before he heads into the OR to perform a difficult procedure. It's transformative; the tension leaves his shoulders and the emotional turmoil he's been broadcasting disappears. When he turns to face me, he is calm, collected and in complete control. I feel a little flutter in my stomach.

"She was right, you know," he says, advancing toward me slowly. "It's inevitable. If it wasn't then, it certainly is now."

The flutter becomes a knot of anxiety and excitement. Does he mean what I think he means? And surely he doesn't mean *right now?* Graham picks up one of the items he'd placed on the sofa, a slim leather collar with a drop ring on the front, and kneels in front of me.

"Hold your hair up," he says, and I automatically comply. I search his face, but his features, usually so open, are unreadable, remote. He fastens the snaps.

"Okay?" he asks.

It is snug, but not overly tight. I swallow compulsively three or four times, feel the accelerated beat of my heart in my chest, the dampness of my palms. It's one thing to fantasize, but to actually have that fantasy realized? What if it all goes horribly wrong? What if Graham can't handle it? What if I change my mind? What if—

"Sarah," Graham's voice calls me back. "Does it feel okay?"

I nod, not trusting myself to speak.

"Look," Graham's hand is gentle on my cheek, making me meet his eyes. "I love you more than anything in this world. You belong to me, and I won't let anything jeopardize that. This...this *thing*...is eating us both from the inside out, and the only way we're going to exorcise it is to let it play out in its entirety. But if you don't want to do it—if you honestly don't want this—you need to tell me now."

I'm nervous and scared and oh, god, excited. Oh, yes, definitely excited. My lust returns full force, and I know that Graham sees it shining in my eyes.

"Good," he says, planting a kiss on me that is devastating in its thoroughness, and that leaves no doubt, really none whatsoever, about whom I belong to.

And so we find ourselves again at the threshold of Giselle's apartment, though this time, I'm wearing only a collar and trench coat.

"Graham," Giselle greets him like an old friend, kissing him on both cheeks and stepping back to usher us in. "I'm so glad you could make it." She's wearing a stunning black leather corset and matching bikini panties, overlaid with garter belt, stockings and black stilettos. Opera-length gloves complete the ensemble, and with her perfect red lips and a sinister-looking flogger dangling from her fingertips, she is Bettie Page incarnate, and I feel myself bending toward her, yielding to her, though she does little more than glance in my direction.

When the door closes and pleasantries conclude, my coat is

removed and I am directed, on hands and knees, to precede my two masters into the dungeon, encouraged by the steady fall of Giselle's flogger on my already heated backside.

"Lovely color," Giselle comments.

"Thank you," Graham replies.

Jay is naked in the center of the room, his wrists encased in heavy leather restraints bound together and pulled taut above his head, so that only the tips of his toes touch the floor. His chest is heaving and a sheen of perspiration coats his trembling body, which is painted like a sunset in varying shades of purple and red and pink. His head hangs down and does not rise when we enter, not even when Giselle informs him that she's brought him a present, by which, I presume, she means me.

I am brought to kneel at Jay's feet, close enough to smell the musk of his sweat and arousal and to see the drop of moisture that glistens on the head of his painfully engorged cock. Giselle kisses Jay, and his cock twitches with excitement. My cunt twitches, too, watching her tease her tongue up his jaw, hearing her whisper that he's been a good boy. Graham seats himself in a chair by the wall. He is, I understand, only an observer, a voyeur on this journey we are taking.

Giselle grasps Jay's cock near the base and strokes his shaft, eliciting a groan from him and forcing another drop of precome to well up. Then, quickly, I forget everything, all the anxiety, all the fear and lean in toward him, lapping his head, dipping my tongue into his slit to taste his semen, letting Giselle guide his cock into my willing and waiting mouth, which still carries Graham's taste. I hold on to Jay's thighs, but Graham protests.

"No," he says. "No hands. Just her mouth. Only her mouth."

"As you wish...." Giselle ties my hands behind my back, and each time the soft rope circles, each time it draws tighter, I feel more and more free. I move my mouth lovingly over Jay's cock, kissing and tonguing it, learning its shape and texture, so similar and yet different from Graham's cock, finally taking him deep in my mouth, into my throat, nuzzling my nose into the soft mat of his pubic hair and eliciting another tortured groan from his throat.

Giselle moves to stand behind Jay, and a moment later I register the crack of leather biting skin at the same time that Jay's body jerks forward, nearly sending me over backward. I struggle to keep my balance and to keep Jay's cock in my mouth, a task made difficult by my bound hands.

"Now, Jay," Giselle says, tsking, "you nearly knocked the poor girl over. You're going to have to stay still for this to work."

"I'm sorry, Madam." Jay's apology is delivered in a choked whisper, and the next time Giselle's flogger makes contact, his body tenses and shudders but does not move. Giselle settles into an easy, seductive rhythm that I fall into with hedonistic abandon, my mouth rising and falling on Jay's cock in time with her strokes. I am liquid with need, drowning with want and yet conscious—ever conscious—of wanting to please her, this imposing mistress, my master's proxy.

Jay's breathing is erratic, punctuated by moans and grunts, the dual sensations of my mouth and Giselle's flogger swelling his cock to painful fullness. It won't be long, I sense, and redouble my efforts, sucking his cock lustily, taking him deep in my throat. A harsh cry tears from Jay as his orgasm overtakes him, filling my mouth, spilling from my lips.

"Such a good boy…" Giselle croons in his ear, kissing his neck and patting his backside approvingly. His cock begins to soften, and I stroke my tongue along his length, cleaning him, then kissing each of his thighs in thanks. Giselle lowers the rope that has held his cuffed hands aloft, helping him gently to the sofa tucked against the wall.

When she returns to me, she cups my chin, raising my head so she can look at me, or rather, my mouth. She runs a gloved fingertip over my swollen lips, first one and then the other, collecting the remnants of Jay's semen, then inserting her finger into my mouth, which I gratefully suck clean.

"Mmmm…" she murmurs, "I was right about that mouth of yours…so pretty."

She withdraws her finger, leaning down, ever so slowly, so that her mouth is a mere breath away from mine. Her tongue retraces the path of her fingers, tasting first one and then the other before slipping in between, exploring my mouth with a slow deliberation that nearly makes me come. I whimper just a little and she raises her head with a chuckle.

"Oh, don't worry," she says, smiling wickedly, "I'm not finished with you yet. Come."

She turns away and walks back to the couch where Jay is recovering, and I follow awkwardly on my knees, my hands still bound behind my back. Giselle removes her panties and positions herself on the edge of the sofa, reclining into Jay's waiting arms like a queen, spreading her thighs so that all of her treasures are revealed. Her glossy black pubic hair is closely trimmed, her lips glistening with moisture. I am humbled by her beauty, grateful for the chance to worship her, anxious only that I won't please her. It's been so long since I've touched another woman, college explorations that predate my relationship with Graham.

Giselle and Jay share a kiss, and I look to Graham for guidance. His face is a tight mask of pleasure, his pants open, his hand slowly stroking his cock.

"Go ahead," he says, his voice rough with arousal, "kiss her."

So I do. I close the distance between us until I am kneeling between her thighs, her perfume intoxicating, so different from that of a man. I place reverent kisses on the inside of each thigh, nuzzling my face into her folds, spreading her lips with my tongue. Giselle sighs into Jay's mouth, and his hands are on her breasts, cupping their weight, teasing her nipples into tight peaks.

I delve deeper, pressing my tongue into her heat, wishing I could penetrate her more fully, satisfying myself instead by tracing the line of her cleft to her most sensitive part, circling her clit, teasing it with the tip of my tongue before returning to dip into her heat once more. I lose myself in the taste of her; in the softness of her skin; in the breathy sounds of pleasure she makes. I return to her clit, so beautifully hard, focusing my attentions there, drawing her into my mouth, scraping her gently with my teeth before settling into a steady rhythm with my tongue. Giselle moans her approval, her hips writhing restlessly beneath me, her thighs trembling and then halting abruptly as she cries out, arching off the sofa and into my mouth, filling me with joy as release floods through her. Graham's moan follows on the heels of Giselle's, and I sink back onto my heels, nearly weeping with gratitude that he has found pleasure in this, too.

The room is quiet, save for the sounds of our breathing, and in this moment of solitude, all of my body's aches slowly make their presence known. I am sore, wonderfully sore, and my jaw aches from tending to the needs of so many. My clit is an unrelenting ache between my thighs, and yet I am filled with a bliss more profound than I can express.

Someone gives me some water—it's Graham—and then he guides me to my feet, gently removing my bonds and helping me into my coat. Farewells are exchanged, though I am only distantly aware of them, and then we are in our own apartment once more, and Graham is in the shower with me, bathing my wounds, washing me clean. He towels me dry and helps me to bed, and as I lie there, looking up at him, a dreadful rush of anxiety returns. Does he feel ashamed of me, that I so obviously enjoyed being used by these people, servicing them like some kind of wanton slut?

A whisper of a smile pulls at one corner of Graham's mouth, and he eases his body down next to mine, pulling me into the warmth of his embrace.

"You did well," he whispers into my hair. He takes my face in his hands, kissing my eyelids, my cheeks, my forehead, my mouth, each time whispering that he loves me, that I belong to him, that nothing in the world will ever change that. And now, I know, nothing ever will.

# THE INGÉNUE

Janine Ashbless

Through the window of the music room on the upper floor of the villa, Zephine could see the man crucified in the rose garden below. She felt her heart thump against her breastbone as she realized what she was looking at. Her fingers fell from the pianoforte keyboard.

"*Cui-cui*," sang the sparrows in the cherry tree, into the silence.

He was quite still, his arms spread as if embracing the world, his head tilted back and to the side. He seemed to be naked. Zephine pushed back her stool and stood, feeling light-headed. The scales she'd been practicing still sounded in her head, like the echo of hurrying footfalls. She wondered if she should follow the descending notes down the stairs and out into the garden; they must have escaped that way.

Had the man out there heard her play? Should she find her aunt and ask her what was happening? She'd been told to stay out of the way because every servant in the villa was busy preparing for the party and the house was in chaos; that was the only reason she'd come up to the music room of her own volition. She didn't know if going out into the garden would count as getting underfoot, though she knew there was a long table being laid with fine white linen on the terrace and that the gardeners had been hammering the iron spikes of great flambeaux all around the grounds. Zephine rather feared annoying her aunt, to whom she owed so much.

She went down anyway, past the maids polishing the crystals on the chandeliers and the housekeeper directing the arrangement of hothouse flowers in the hall and the footmen carrying furniture from room to room. She slipped out through the veranda doors and down through the *parterre* to the rose garden beyond. From ground level, it seemed a far more private space, and it took her a moment to spot the man through the bushes.

The scent of the roses lay heavy on the still afternoon air. Her little boots clicked on the brick paving. She did not quite have the courage to approach him directly but stopped and stared through a tangle of green leaves and white blossoms.

No, he was not entirely naked; there was a gray silk scarf knotted loosely about his hips and the dangling ends veiled his private parts. That was a relief; more so, that he was not in fact nailed to the wooden cross that had been planted in the rose bed: his arms and ankles were secured to the beams with crimson rope, much like the ones that held back the velvet drapes in the drawing room. But it certainly looked cruel, with his arms out at full stretch and his shoulders pulled back. To Zephine, it was eerily reminiscent of the carved crucifixes she was used to seeing in church, even down to the slight angle of his hips in their makeshift loincloth and the ragged dark hair framing a drawn and unshaven face. He was a Christ formed in flesh and bone—if Christ had had Slavonic cheekbones and a broken nose and hair sprinkled with gray.

He was, she guessed, one of those foreign poets her aunt cultivated at her salons—or perhaps an anarchist, although his beard wasn't really long enough for that. He certainly looked lean enough to be an artist of some description, with none of the mutton-fed plumpness of the monied classes. His muscles stood out like the charcoal lines of an anatomical study and under his rib cage, his stomach was stretched flat and taut. Zephine pursed her mouth, deeply uncomfortable. Her aunt did so encourage those frightening, half-civilized men, and the more they railed against bourgeois hypocrisy and sneered at the moral bankruptcy of the ruling classes—as they helped themselves to her wine and her canapés—the more she seemed amused by them. Of course, Zephine was rarely allowed to stay and listen at the salons, despite being no longer a child. In deference to the way her late mother had brought her up, her aunt took care not to expose the young woman to the offensive language or shocking opinions of such a radical circle.

"Good day, *monsieur*," she started to say, but the words died in her throat. She clenched her hands in helpless embarrassment. It seemed crazy to address a near-naked prisoner in such feebly polite terms, but she had no idea what else to say. She didn't even know if he was conscious.

Cautiously she began to circle the man, always keeping a rosebush between herself and him. What on earth could he be doing here? Was this part of some artistic endeavor, some *tableau vivant* being prepared for the party? She knew her aunt's pastimes were unconventional and that her reputation raised eyebrows. But really, this was in terribly bad taste. The man was all but exposed: she could see his whole torso and his bare thighs and the contoured cheeks of his buttocks. His skin was rather pale—they were all pasty, those artists; they spent too much time lurking in dark cafés, drinking disgusting herbal liqueurs that did them no good at all—and his body hair very dark in contrast. There was a line of it up his belly, all the way from the silk loin-cloth to the fan of hair that nested his nipples. Zephine was a little startled to see that those nipples—dark, unlike her own pale buds—were standing proud. She hadn't thought that men's would do that in the same way that hers did, reacting to a cool breeze or a stray thought. Right now, under the silk and cotton layers of her dress and her corsetry and her undergarments, her nipples were tingling almost painfully, as if in sympathy with his.

She licked her dry lips.

"You can come closer, if you like," he said, opening his eyes and turning his head to fix upon her; it made her jump as if guilty, though what she should be guilty of was something she couldn't have expressed. His eyes were gray, not dark: as pale as the plumage of her aunt's parrot, the one that lived in a gilt cage in the conservatory and quoted Rousseau. She found the bird quite frightening, with its wicked beak and its inscrutable stare, and her reaction to this man was not dissimilar.

"Why are you tied up?" Zephine asked. It was not a polite question at all, but she was flustered and nervous. She even retreated a couple of steps.

He smiled a crooked, most un-Christlike smile, but didn't answer. Those pale eyes had that intensity she associated with poets and lunatic radicals.

"Does it hurt?"

He looked from one forearm to the other, opening and clenching his hands experimentally. "It's not comfortable."

Concern jumped within her. "I'll untie you," she said, starting forward, but he stopped her with a frown.

"I wouldn't do that if I were you. Madame de Villiers would be very angry."

Zephine swallowed. She knew her aunt possessed a cold but formidable temper at times. And she had no wish to upset the woman who had provided her with a home, and who had been so good to her. "She's my aunt."

"Then you know why I'm tied up."

Zephine shook her head. "I don't… I'm not allowed…"

"I am part of the entertainment for the party tonight."

Her imagination simply could not encompass what that might entail—except that she suspected blasphemy. She bit her lip.

"What's your name, *chérie*?"

"Zephine."

"Well, you don't need to hide, Zephine."

She shifted her feet but did not step away from the shelter of the rosebush. "What's yours?"

"Piotr."

She'd been right about him being foreign, then—and his French was accented, though only a little. An educated man, from his speech. It didn't make her feel less jumpy. "Saint Peter was crucified upside down," she pointed out.

"Ah…you're convent-educated, are you, Zephine?" For some reason, that seemed to amuse him.

She nodded.

"Come closer," he repeated, lowering his voice. "Let me see my inquisitor."

She shuffled forward from cover, reluctantly. His dark half-smile was discomforting. Everything about him made her feel wrong within herself, as if her skin no longer fit.

"That's better." He did not bother to hide his scrutiny of her, from the pale blue hair ribbon to the matching toes of her satin boots—and all the territory in between. Judging her, no doubt, she thought. Such a well-dressed young lady as she was must rouse the particular derision of a political radical. She found herself annoyed at the thought; annoyed that he should be finding her so amusing. Everyone always looked down upon her—the orphaned niece. The naive girl, the pretty, inconsequential young woman. But he had no right, she thought, not tied up as he was, so pathetically helpless, so undignified in his *déshabillé*. What had he to feel superior about, with his bare feet planted in the rose bed among crumbs of horse manure?

She drew up her chin and met his gaze.

"You're pretty," he observed. "Small, yet you look strong. Your lovers must be fighting one another for your favor."

Blood flared in her cheeks but she set her jaw. "What are you suggesting, *monsieur*? I have no suitors yet; I have been most gently raised."

"You must be cruel to them, Zephine."

"What?" she said, forgetting her manners in her surprise.

"Cruel. So that they will love you. Spurn them; mock them; hurt them. They will worship you."

"That's a terrible thing to say!"

"It is human nature." The man—Piotr—drew his upper lip through his teeth. "We love those that beat and break us. Men love the lamia, women love the brute. When you fall in love, little Zephine, it will be with a man who ignores you most of the time, whose eyes turn constantly to other women, and who, when he makes carnal use of you, will do so roughly and with savage appetite, not sparing your tender body as he takes animal possession of it."

His crude words sent a wave of heat through her skin. "You're quite wrong. I am determined that I will marry a kindly man."

"I don't doubt it. Yet afterward you will fall in love with one who will take your tranquil heart and cast it in the flames of Hell. As I said, it is human nature."

"We yearn to be unhappy, you think?" she scoffed.

"If you like. Rather, we yearn to be mastered."

Her voice was a little unsteady now. "That's a strange thing for an anarchist to say, isn't it? I thought your kind claimed that we all strive to be free?"

"Am I an anarchist, then?"

"Are you not? You've just damned all of civilization."

A slight lowering of his eyelids admitted she had a point. "I am a man," he answered, "who recognizes the dark beast within himself. And lest it make me the lickspittle slave of a society whose rotten soul I see only too clearly...I let the beast feed here."

"Here?"

"In this garden. At the pleasure of Madame de Villiers."

Zephine could not answer. She stood with her lower lip thrust out, glaring.

"Come closer," he said for the third time, his voice dropping again, soft and dark as soot. "Touch me."

"Why?"

"Because you want to."

The anger twisted in her entrails once more. "You presume a great deal."

"Have you ever touched a man's bare flesh before?" There was a gleam in his eye. "I thought not. So naturally you wish to know what it is like."

She wanted to slap him for his rudeness.

"After all," he added, jerking his wrists to demonstrate his constraint, "it's not as if I can hurt you."

She would have liked to laugh at him, but her face was all hot and stiff. She wanted to prick the bladder of his arrogance and, as she turned away, see him slump, crestfallen, but his eyes wouldn't let her. His eyes held hers. They saw past her pride and her agitation to the animal curiosity that had drawn her down from her high window into the garden.

Something about that truth in his eyes drew her.

Clenching her jaw, she stepped forward. If his arms had been free she would now be within their compass. She couldn't help checking with little flickering glances that the crimson crisscrosses of his bonds were real, that his forearms really were secured to the timbers. The ropes were not tight, she thought—they didn't really bite into his flesh the way she'd thought they would—but they seemed to be snug. She lifted a hand and touched him on the lower ribs, and Piotr took a deep breath so that she felt his chest expand. His skin was surprisingly warm; she thought the music practice must have cooled her fingers. Warm and smooth, like satin, and ridged with bone like the corset she wore beneath her dress.

"You smell so sweet," he whispered. "Fresh as spring."

She thought to herself that she could not return the compliment. The scent that reached her own nose—bare skin and a little sweat—was not at all unpleasant, but it was an aroma that seemed to demand attention: savory-sweet and yeasty like a hot oven full of new-baked bread. Her throat worked at the thought. Was she hungry? Everything was confused: sensation and conscience and understanding all mixed up and nothing clear any more, least of all how she came to be standing here face-to-face with a crucified anarchist, touching him. She felt as light-headed as she had looking out of that music room window, and she knew if she lifted her hand away from his skin it would be trembling.

"Not that scary," she said under her breath. From his exposed armpits jutted tufts of dark thistledown hair. They looked utterly incongruous against those ridges of muscle; in fact they looked so soft that she felt an urge to stroke them. Instead, she shifted her touch to his stomach, to the vertical stripe of hair that divided his torso like a road across an alien landscape. Her fingertips rode its length, exploring the texture of the short hairs. Piotr made a noise in his throat, and she saw his chin dimple as he bit the inside of his lip. Something made her look down, and her jaw dropped: "Oh!"

Below where her fingertips lingered, something had changed. When she'd approached the bound man, the silk scarf that preserved his modesty had hung flat, or nearly so. Now it leaned out from his body, draping the thing that swelled beneath— something that moved. Zephine's lips shaped a circle of shock. She froze as the blood rushed up into her cheeks and started pounding in her eardrums. Suddenly her clothes felt too tight and too hot.

"Oh, look what you've done to me, Zephine." His voice was soft, thick…heavy. Loaded with the knowledge of that forbidden tree in Eden.

"Me?"

He smiled. "Take a look."

It would be easy to uncover him. The moving aside of a flap of silk, that was all. "I…I mustn't."

"Don't you want to know what a man bears between his legs, little Zephine?"

"I know." As his voice grew deeper, hers was becoming higher and more wispy. "I mean…I've seen the statues in the Louvre, of course." The statues of the Roman gods and heroes, so incongruously nonchalant in their exposure. And she'd sat gossiping with other girls at school and listened to the stories, the rumors as wild and unbelievable as any classical myth. Of course she knew. But Piotr's smile became more mocking.

"Oh? The Louvre? I think you're in for a shock, Zephine."

"Why?"

"Take a look." When she did not obey, he added, "Are you

afraid? How can you be afraid of me, Zephine?"

How could she be? Her pride prickled. He was bound, spread-eagled—helpless. He could not be more vulnerable, nor less of a threat to her. Why, then, was she feeling like this?

Clumsily, she pulled aside the flaps of silk. They clung to him a little, as if his skin was damp, and she felt against her hand the impatient nudge of what lay beneath. Then the cloth was gone, and she could see.

He was nothing like a statue from the Louvre. He was flushed dark, hairy—and erect. His phallus stood out at an impossible angle, grown to what seemed like a monstrous size. It looked like a weapon.

"Now touch it." There was no mistaking the authority in his voice. And Zephine had run dry of protest or questions—of any words at all. She looked once into his eyes and then obeyed, running her fingers down its shaft. It kicked against her as if in irritation and she jumped.

"Take it in your hand. How does it feel?"

Her fingers barely circled its girth. "Hot," she whispered. "Hard." There was a peculiar satisfaction to its bulk and strength, too, though she couldn't put that into words.

"Do you like it?" His voice was a murmur now. "It likes you, Zephine—very much."

She didn't know if she liked it. She just knew that this made her feel as if nothing else in her life had ever mattered, in comparison. "My aunt will be so angry," she said, with wonder. To her surprise, a surge ran through the flesh in her grasp and it grew even harder.

"Yes." His eyes were darker now, the pupils dilated. "She will beat me."

Zephine's own eyes, which had been strangely heavy, shot open. "Surely not!"

"She will. With a riding crop, or a garden cane, or a leather strap."

"She can't do that to you!" Doubt crept in, then. "Can she?"

"She's done it before, Zephine. She left me covered in broken welts, all across my chest and my thighs and my *derrière*."

"What for?" In her shock, Zephine could not help thinking of the flagellation of Christ. In the church at her school, the Stations of the Cross were depicted with wax models of startling realism. One in particular—the whipped and bloody body of Christ, kneeling in his agony—always drew her, horrified and fascinated and full of pity. She feared it, but she'd spent hours gazing at it. She wondered if Piotr would resemble that, if he were to be horse-whipped.

"For her pleasure."

She swallowed. "I will let you go." Yet her hand did not desert its post gripping his thick meat. He shook his head, just a twitch.

"I don't want you to, Zephine."

"But it will hurt!"

"Very much so."

"Aren't you frightened?"

"I'm sick with fear." His lip crooked in a thin smile. "You're my only comfort, *ma chérie*. Move your hand, Zephine; move it up and down my cock."

"I...I don't think I should."

"But you must. And if you do, I will tell you what else happens at these parties your aunt throws."

Zephine bit her lip, but her resistance was only momentary. She wanted to know; indeed she felt she had to, now. Her hand began to slide up his shaft, stroking the hot flesh.

"Good girl. A little firmer. Oh...yes, that's right." He cleared

his throat and blinked, his eyes starting to lose focus. "Tonight...
Oh, there'll be so many people here tonight, Zephine, after you
are tucked safe in your virgin bed. People from the highest and
most respectable echelons of society and from the lowest, though
the poor must be very beautiful to be invited inside these walls—
or prodigiously talented. In the twilight, the torches will be lit,
musicians will play, and all the food and drink you might ever
want will be laid out upon the tables. Our salvers will be the
bare bodies of young women and men, their nipples garnished
with cream and gold leaf, their open thighs displaying the most
delectable of banquets. A bath will be filled with champagne,
and in it will lie a young beauty, offering her cup for anyone to
drink from. From under the trees, in the dark, will come soft
cries of pleasure and sharper gasps of pain.

"But do not worry, Zephine: on a night such as this, the pain
is only part of the pleasure. The world is turned upside down
in this place, and the ancient ironclad laws of civilization are
dissolved. Men are used as women; women rule as men. The
rich bow before the poor, and the great beg indulgences of the
lowly. Tonight, were you to mingle with the guests, you might
see a bishop on his hands and knees, a bridle about his head
and a bit in his mouth, being ridden by a fair whore clad only in
spurs, while another jade plunges a huge horse-tail plug between
his willing cheeks. You might see a general of the army spread-
eagled upon the lawn, and a queue of matrons taking it in turn
to straddle him and lift their skirts so that they might relieve
themselves upon his face. You might, if you were inclined, seek
me out here among the roses."

Beneath her hot, tightly corseted dress, Zephine was melting,
her body dissolving into trembling boneless weakness, her long
drawers clinging to her moist skin and growing sodden with the
flow of her sex. She felt almost as if she would faint, and it was

all she could do to cling to the great solid stake in her hand. "And what ...what will they be doing to you?" she asked.

"They will do anything they like to me; I'm bound tight and cannot defend myself. Oh, I will thrash and strain against my bonds and cry out in protest, but they will laugh at my rage and mock my entreaties. Some of them will be cruel and hurt me: they'll strike me and tie weights about my ball-pouch and abuse my manhood. They'll slap my face and bite my nipples and stroke my crotch with stinging nettles until my cock and stones burn. Others...others will be kindly, and that is worse: they will caress me until my balls are bursting, but deny me satisfaction until I am screaming with lust. I will not be able to turn anyone away: man or woman, young or old: anyone may make easy with me. As for Madame de Villiers... Oh, she likes best to administer a good hard whipping. She likes to hear me plead for mercy."

His hips were juddering now and his cock like iron. Zephine could only imagine what it would take to humble this man and his proud member. Part of her was horrified at the thought and another part avid.

"Eventually she will tire of seeing me on the cross, and she will give the signal for my deposition. But that won't mean I am free. My hands will be tied to the ring at the base there, so that I am kneeling. My legs will be bound apart to an ox-yoke. You would be able to see my most private parts exposed, Zephine, if you were there."

The narrative hung. She was expected to respond. "How terrible for you," she whispered.

"It is unbearable. That is the point when Madame de Villiers will give permission to any man whom she favors, that he might take carnal pleasure of me. Thus my humiliation will be complete, and everyone will witness it as I am used and sodomized. Oh, good god, Zephine—use your nails—dig your nails into me—please—now!"

She hardly knew what he meant, but she sank the nails of both hands into the base of his cock and raked it from root to crown. Confusion lent her spite and she was not gentle—Piotr gave a great gasp; there was a sudden warm, wet gush in her hands, and she looked down and saw white gouts of semen spurting from his member onto her dress. Zephine shrieked and tried to stop the flow, but the jets only pulsed out between her wild fingers and turned her grip into a slithering caress. Even as he gave himself up to his crisis and heaved up against his bonds, muscles straining and body taut—even as he called blasphemously upon God—his teeth were bared in joy.

Zephine slapped him across the face.

Then she ran. She ran out of the rose garden and across the lawn and through the gate into the vegetable patch beyond. She didn't stop until she reached the gardeners' shed with its iron pump outside. Shame and guilt and a dark and triumphant glee boiled between her legs. She ached to the core with a hot need. Heaving up on the handle, she raised enough water to wash her hands, but the spurting gush of the water itself made her tremble.

There were loops of pearly spunk splashed across the blue silk bodice of her dress. She scrubbed at them with wet fingers, but she could not erase the stain.

# REASONING

Tenille Brown

The simplest way Carlotta could explain it was that she was tired, plain and simple. She was tired of hearing about it, tired of arguing about it and tired of tiptoeing around it when she knew it was on his mind.

And Carlotta was sick to death of avoiding it, avoiding it to the extreme that not only were she and Ray no longer sleeping in or sitting on the damned thing, they weren't fucking there either.

But they *were* fucking, which was a plus, and boy, were they fucking. Unfortunately, the mega–fuck fest had to take place on the couch, the kitchen table or the floor, the carpet burning her elbows, knees and forearms when she rode him or when he fucked her from behind. Of course, it all became mundane, so they tried it on the chair—well, Carlotta couldn't really complain about the chair. She rather liked straddling him on the chair, but that wasn't the point.

The point was, Ray was trying to fuck her to death. She

pondered the idea as she stepped out of the bathtub and gently patted her middle dry, making sure not to rub because she was still sore from this morning's ravishing. Not that she was complaining about the ravishing itself, just the meaning behind it—the principle, so to speak.

It might be different had he just come back home or if he had missed her while he was gone. No, that wasn't it. It was that he had heard about that one night she gave in and fucked long-legged, buck-toothed Bennie Marshall, that one night when Carlotta had simply grown tired of waiting on Ray to come back.

*That* was what Ray was trying to fuck out of her: the feeling, the reflection, even though, truth be told, Bennie Marshall wasn't even that good a lay. His reputation was actually a little exaggerated. His cock wasn't nearly as large as rumor led people to believe, and once their clothes were off, Bennie needed some coaxing to really get things going, and once things *did* get going, it was over and done with just like that, which was *why* there had been just that one time and one time only.

But, Carlotta thought, as she finished drying and slipped into her T-shirt and shorts, Ray didn't have to know all that. *He* was the one who up and left last year and spent three months who knew where, doing who knew what to who knew *who*. Hell, let him use his goddamn imagination as to what really went on with Bennie.

But Carlotta supposed Ray *had* been using his imagination. *Had* been painting the sordid pictures in his mind when he couldn't get a straight answer out of her, which was how he came to the solution.

*His* solution.

It didn't matter how Carlotta felt about it. Matter of fact, Ray never asked how she felt at all.

He just up and made the statement one night while they were lying there watching the news. "We gotta get a new bed."

Carlotta was as cool as could be when she asked, "New bed? Why, Ray, your back bothering you? We could always flip the mattress."

Ray grunted. "My back feels fine."

Carlotta propped herself up on her elbows. "Then, why?"

Which was when Ray began to rattle off his prepared speech: "This was our bed, Lottie, ours together, and now it's ruined, tainted with the memories of you and, and, that other guy."

So, as Ray had given his reasons, Carlotta gave hers:

"First of all, we can't afford a new mattress, let alone a new bed. And this bed, it's practically an antique now. And like you said, we bought it together, so I'm a little sentimental about it, too. It's a good bed, with high, heavy posts, and they just don't make them like this anymore."

It was as if she hadn't said a word.

Ray said, "We could sell it, get good money for it and buy a new one."

"One of those trendy, cheap-looking sleigh things they're selling now will last five years before we have to replace it with some other cheap, trendy thing."

Ray exhaled. "Just see if you can get off work early tomorrow."

It was mind-boggling to Carlotta that she had to go through such hell to make up for such a bad lay. Maybe if the sex had been worth it, the torture that came behind it would have at least been bearable, but she never even thought about Bennie, avoided him in grocery stores, pretended not to see that buck-toothed grin when she ran inside the gas station to hand the cashier her thirty-five bucks.

And Carlotta might have entertained the thought had Ray

posed it as a suggestion or asked in any kind of way what she thought, but, no, it was a demand, and Carlotta didn't take too kindly to demands these days.

So, Carlotta had said, "No," just like that, and it really hadn't felt bad at all. It had felt damned good, in fact.

Foolishly, Carlotta thought Ray would just get used to the idea, but he kept steady at it, eventually moving out of the bed altogether and Carlotta, like a fool, followed him. And sleeping on the floor or on the springy pullout couch was no more comfortable now than it was then.

Carlotta became a whole other kind of pissed off as she thought about it now, puttering around the kitchen, stirring up some breakfast before Ray woke up out of his sex sleep. She shook her head. He slept so comfortably there on the bedroom floor—too comfortably.

He was back to being the same old Ray Porter, king of all, the boss of everything. But there were a few things Mr. Porter didn't know. Carlotta had discovered a little something called liberation while he was gone.

She didn't come running when he called anymore. She didn't cook three times a day; hell, some days she didn't even turn the stove on. She let him iron his own clothes for work, and she simply stepped over the ones he discarded at the end of the day. She had grown comfortable that way and just a little cocky. In fact, she was kind of bitter that he had come back and interrupted it all.

Of course, Carlotta had let him come back. Because no matter how hard an exterior she had developed over the months, somewhere tucked deep inside, she still had a soft spot for Ray.

She was damning that soft spot right now, of course, wishing she had held fast to that independent fire that had ignited a few weeks after Ray had stormed out.

Ray wasn't one to listen to reason. His head was hard as a brick. But she would find a way to reason with him; yes, she would.

He wanted to golf this morning. Get in a few rounds before the heat got too bad, but Carlotta, she had other plans.

She tiptoed into the bedroom, stepping across a sleeping Ray. She walked barefoot across the soft carpet and opened her closet. She stepped way into the back. In a dusty old chest was their equipment, the things they referred to when they were feeling especially frisky. Neither was feeling all that frisky lately, though.

It didn't matter today, though, because Carlotta wasn't shooting for frisky, and she wasn't shooting for kinky.

Carlotta removed and fingered the leather cuffs; the silver chain links that connected them still held their sparkly newness even though they were his favorite out of the whole pile. And she liked the way they felt on her wrists, whether they bound her to a door frame (if he chose to keep her arms above her head; they made her tits perkier, he said) or to a chair or to the bed. Oh, she liked it indeed, but today, this morning, Ray would be giving them a go, whether he enjoyed it or not.

Not that it mattered. Enjoying it wasn't the point. Being still so she could say her piece, however, was. And location, location was key. It had to be the bed. No matter how boring or how trite. He would get there and he would stay there. She would use the whip if she had to, if he struggled or tried to make problems for her, and the clamps, too. She would use the clamps in places he wouldn't like, wouldn't like at all.

She gathered everything she'd need as he lay sleeping, and it was the one time she could recall being thankful for his dead slumber, for his unbelievably loud snoring. He didn't even know she was in the house, let alone standing over him.

Carlotta awakened him. "Get up." She pushed her bare foot into his side. "I need you to do something for me."

Ray rubbed his eyes. "What?"

Carlotta jerked her head toward the bed. "Just come here."

Ray sighed, moving with the enthusiasm of a drunken snail. He stopped just near the side of the bed. He shrugged. "What?'

Carlotta pointed to the ceiling, at something invisible to all, but enough to get Ray to lift his chin, place his hands on his hips and just for a second, lower his guard.

It turned out a second was all Carlotta needed.

She pushed him hard enough to send him face-first into the mattress so that his feet flew outward and upward.

He lifted his head. "What the hell?'

But by the time Ray began to struggle to his feet, Carlotta was on him, bringing him over to his side and rolling him completely onto his back. The struggle ended with Ray length-wise in the bed and Carlotta on top of him, one knee on either side of his waist, holding him still with her powerful thighs.

She grabbed one of his thick wrists while he was still trying to catch his breath. Lucky for Carlotta, Ray was out of shape.

Carlotta talked as she worked, strapping each wrist and each ankle to the bedposts.

"Yes, Ray, this is the very bed I fucked Bennie in. So what? You weren't here and from what you said when you left here, you didn't plan on coming back! What was I supposed to do? Go chaste? *Die*?"

"We can buy another bed!" Ray shouted as he fought to lift his head.

Carlotta went ahead and added the mask for good measure. Besides, it would help him relax, and it actually got Carlotta a little tickled. She didn't let him see her laughing, though. He'd be pissed for sure, then.

Carlotta gripped Ray's chin in her hand and held his face still. "And then what? It would just be a new bed. Different mattress. You can't erase him out of me. He was still in this room. Maybe we should tear this room off the house and build a new one. Now that I think about it, he walked to the kitchen for a glass of water afterward. Better get rid of that room, too. Oh, and we watched television in the den first. Better get a new one of those, and a living room suite and a new tub and toilet... You see, Ray, the whole thing is stupid!"

Carlotta took a minute to breathe and as she did, she looked again at her beloved bed. Damn she loved that bed, and ugly assed Bennie Marshall would *not* be the reason she had to replace it.

"You say the bed is tainted, Ray, but what about you? According to the grapevine, you sampled more than your share while you were a free man, so what good are you to me? Should I just go and get rid of you?"

Carlotta stopped there because she knew that Ray knew that she damn well could, if she wanted. The way he exhaled and twisted his lips confirmed it.

So she left him alone there in the bed to ponder the thought, and returned to making breakfast.

As Carlotta suspected, Ray began to struggle shortly after she left the room. The rattling of the chains was a little nerve-wracking at first, like death slowly coming to get her. She was standing over the skillet flipping a pancake, because, when all was said and done, Ray did have an appetite like a savage. Then came the subtle rubbing of rubber against wood. The straps were thin, but they were strong; Carlotta knew that from experience.

Carlotta finished breakfast and made sure that Ray ate,

feeding him small spoonfuls through the small mouth hole of the mask. He kept his lips pressed tight at first, but Carlotta assured him that he should eat; after all, they were going to have a good, thorough talk, and she tended to be long winded.

And so, Carlotta talked.

And Ray, he rolled his eyes and pursed his lips.

Carlotta talked some more.

Ray interrupted.

Then, most unexpectedly, there in the middle of the godforsaken bed, Ray's cock rose to attention.

Carlotta tilted her head, unnerved. Ray was hard, harder than Carlotta had seen him in months.

He was hard lying on the bed. He was hard *despite* the bed. Before, it was an unattainable feat.

Carlotta was left with a decision. What on earth to do with the cock that rose and waved slowly from side to side as if in surrender? What on *earth* to do?

To *take care of it* would have been too easy, predictable even, and this whole charade would have been a moot point.

Or would it?

When she thought about it, long and hard, really, Carlotta had won.

Carlotta climbed in and lay upside down next to Ray, who was too mad to speak. Her feet were near his head, her head next to his calves.

She crossed her arms over her chest. "You mad about the straps, Ray?" she asked. "Or the bed? Or the straps?" She raised her head. "Or the *motherfucking bed*?"

Ray grunted.

But Carlotta continued. "You know you've disproved your own theory, right? Mad or not, you're turned on. I could fuck you silly right now...if I wanted."

Ray pulled pointlessly against the restraints.

And Carlotta lay there next to him, feeling as restrained as he was. She did want him—needed him was probably more accurate—but she needed more to be heard, to put an end to this madness.

Carlotta twitched and squirmed. She was becoming wet, soaking through her panties, soaking clear through to her spandex shorts. She wanted Ray to touch her, but she also wanted him *not* to. She wanted to torture him the way he had tortured her.

Carlotta went over it all in her mind, but it was hard to concentrate when Ray was displaying that tree of a cock. It was hard to remain focused and firm when all she wanted to do was strip off her clothes and mount him.

And suddenly, Carlotta's steady concentration was broken as she felt wetness on her toes.

She maneuvered to see that Ray had turned his head, had begun to slowly lick at her bare feet.

Carlotta was wetter still.

"Stop, Ray," she said softly, and she was certain she *did* say it, but Ray kept right on, ran that long pink tongue up and down the bottom of her feet, between each toe, sucking on them at random.

Carlotta squirmed. It would have been simple enough to snatch her foot back, to get up and leave the room completely, but she was paralyzed there in that place.

He was trying to get her to lose her bearings was all, wanted to twist the situation in his favor, but it wouldn't be that easy.

Things were going her way this time.

Hesitantly, Carlotta pulled her foot away.

But so unsettled and so turned on was she that she began using her fingers. She pulled her shorts and her panties aside and quickly, intently began to finger herself.

She heard Ray groan, watched the veins in his hard cock grow deep and blue.

Carlotta clasped her knees together, clamped her pussy tight against her own fingers, but still she found no release.

She finally crawled up near Ray, crouched over his head and lowered herself onto his open mouth.

"Yes, Ray, you can kiss, but you won't touch."

Ray seemed satisfied with that. He clamped his lips tight over her wet pussy and seemed to be pulling out of her what she had desperately been trying to hold back.

The reasons, the reasons, the reasons...

"Fuck you, Ray," she said, "I don't know why I ever let your simple ass come back here." Carlotta said it through short gasps.

But Ray kept right on. And as he licked, as he sucked, as he gently nibbled and gnawed, one by one the reasons came rushing back to Carlotta.

Ray *was* one hell of a fuck and a pretty good guy once you got to know him and never had been scared of work and...

Carlotta loved him...just a little.

The admission brought on a gush of an orgasm. She came in his mouth. The thrusting of his hips into the air sent his cock waving frantically and after a few minutes, he came too, shooting hot seed up and out.

After a few minutes for them both to catch their breath, the straps were loosened, the mask removed. Carlotta stood next to the bed and held her tools out in front of her.

"Back in the closet, then?" She raised one eyebrow.

Ray gathered his bearings and lifted himself into a sitting position, slowly, carefully. He shrugged his shoulders. "Would make more sense to me for them to be under the bed. You know, for when we need 'em. We could just reach under...easy access that way."

Carlotta nodded, swore to herself that she wouldn't smile, not even a little, and pushed the things under the bed with her foot.

# SUBDUE

## Dusty Horn

Daddy tells me to close my eyes.

Goddamnit, I hate this.

"I know you hate this," she grins, rich even alto, calm dom intuition.

That grin is the last thing I see as I brattily narrow, then lower my lids.

"Good girl. Now. Down."

I do as I'm told. I may be a sass-back, but I ain't dumb. Kneeling in the corner with my feet cradling my ass, I wait hungrily for morsels of orders.

A moment ago, I was rushing up the stairs to our apartment, a million miles a minute. I was everywhere at once, or at least I tried; every point on every line in every direction. Tearing off my clothes; ready for action, for attention, for satisfaction; rushing to offer myself. No need for seduction! No time for mystery! I am ready to glut myself on everything I can get my hands on and allow myself to be used by everything that can get its hands on me.

Ordered to be still, I am antsy, lunging at every excuse to refuse this command, to bolt.

After all, nothing is technically tethering me here.

Daddy is taking her damn time. When is she going to touch me? When do I get what I want? I cycle through worship, resentment, anticipation, lust, indignation, adoration, defiance, devotion.

It is very difficult for me to sit still, especially when I am horny. Why sit still when there is so much to do? My pussy starts to weep in longing and my ass itches to be grabbed, spanked. My nipples swell and ache as my chest rises and falls.

Fortunately the body, with its sensory experience fixed firmly in the present, is relatively tamable. If I move, I will be punished. If I want attention, I must obey. It's impressive what pain and discipline will do to train the physical.

The mind, with all its hidden powers and emotions, contemplating the past and anticipating the future, is more challenging to subdue.

The longer she takes to act, the more my mind rebels against my Daddy. Who does she think she is, making me *wait*? What kind of sick sadistic pleasure does she get out of making me squirm? It's not *fair*. I don't have to do this. I hate this! She can't make me! Why am I allowing this? What else could I be doing? Whose idea was this? When am I gonna get what I want? What *do* I want?

My mind is a hurricane of spinning plates, my irons in the fires, my thumbs in all the pies. I am flapping tongues. I am an ever-generating list.

I am tireless, but this is ridiculous.

Still no action from Daddy. No pain, no pleasure, no attention, no delicious words. No recourse but to accept my fate and practice patience. My willfulness begins to falter, and I have no option but to surrender.

My closed eyes cross and slowly my busy mind begins to settle itself.

Sensitivity shuffles into the following priority: hear, feel, smell, taste. Each of these senses grabs greedily at information. Weight and movement come into clearer view. The ambient sound of the afternoon outdoors going about its business rotates out of my periphery and into sharp focus. The shifting of matter imperiously displaces space. Air pours back into the vacuum, endlessly chasing the ghost of mass.

As if following a cue in the movement behind my eyelids, Daddy chooses this moment to take hold of my head.

After what seems like eons without touch, her hot hand on my chin is electrifying. She lifts it up and back, pressing something against my smooth exposed throat. Tugging firmly up on the hair at the nape of my neck, she wraps the rest of the mystery object against the top of my spine where my still body meets my busy mind.

"This is mine," she hums to me as she slides a metal clasp into place. "This is not your collar. It's mine, for you to wear."

The collar bulges around my neck, a leather halo engorged with blood.

Daddy moves back and away from me, and there is no movement or noise. She is gazing at me, watching me, knowing that I am unmoving because she told me not to move.

"This is so I can chew and bite on your neck as much as I want without killing you."

She knows and I know that I am free. Nothing is tethering me except my will to be tethered, my need to ask and allow someone else to call the shots. My collar says this is what I want.

*I want you.*

Around my ankles and wrists, my Daddy attaches leather cuffs.

I don't always know how to be good. I don't even know if I always want to be good. I want to do the right thing, but I don't always know what that is. When I am collared to my Daddy I am given instruction, orders. I am being told what to do. All I have to do is obey and I am being good. I get the affirmation and praise I crave: simple call and response.

I am bound to her because I am free. Neither of us would have it any other way.

As loud and sharp as she was just silent and obtuse, Daddy barks what I have been craving: an order to follow.

"Stand up!"

Frantically, I try to spring into action but my legs are stiff from kneeling.

Daddy is amused. "Try again. You're not going to get there any faster if you rush."

I take a deep breath and then I take my time, even trying to be slinky, sexy.

I am aware of my Daddy's arms engulfing me, her lips taking mine in.

"Open your eyes."

I find myself staring into her deep, natural, gorgeous androgyny.

"Time to get ready, little girl. We have guests coming over."

Daddy goes first. She lifts her hands over her head and waits. Her pursed lips of expectation are the adrenaline of an athlete at the starting line and the excruciation of a patient awaiting the necessary pain of a bone being reset. Her shoulders are broad and built, square and set like a comic book hero.

I place an Ace bandage on her spine, the meridian between her shoulder blades. Tenderly, I uncoil the cloth under armpits and across ribs. Lighter even than the "flesh"-colored binding, her soft pink tits are a delicious contrast to her pronounced upper body strength. I am sad to see them go, but Daddy wants her sensitivity tucked away.

I dance around her, careful to be precise, to keep the bandage taut as I flatten her femininity away. Like a kingly Scarlett O'Hara, she wants it tighter, tighter! I always loosen it as I climb up her chest, sneakily preserving the openness of her lungs and heart.

"All done, Daddy."

She pulls a black, ribbed tank top over her head and buttons up a similarly black dress shirt. Her cotton tighty-whities hug her hips as she pulls dress pants over them.

I am staring in the mirror at my collar. It looks so small and thin compared to the way it felt when she initially wrapped it around my neck.

Coming up behind me, she wraps more black leather around my body in the form of a waist cincher. The corset encases my core, compresses me, squeezes me like a tourniquet. Unencumbered by a bra or panties, my flesh bursts out from either end like cookie dough from a tube. I slip into gold closed-toe six-inch stilettos, but otherwise I am naked and available.

Daddy kisses my forehead and encircles me yet again, this time wrapping an opaque black nylon stocking around my eyes.

In our apartment, a sling harness hangs as sensibly as any piece of furniture might in yours. A web of black leather and silver buckles on a wooden frame, it is arranged so that the occupant's hole is level with the average standing person's crotch.

It is this position, the position of the hole, that I am instructed to assume.

I am made bereft of my sight again, more forcefully this time, but I can guide myself, blinded as I am. I know this choreography like the back of her hand.

When it's just me and Daddy, I can be trusted to control myself, to be controlled. I can keep my eyes shut and stay still. These physical tools—the stockings around my eyes; the leather around my wrists, ankles and neck; the sling—are reserved for nights of overstimulation, when I surrender my body and lose my mind to arousal and power and fantasy, dictated by her, welcomed by me.

I sit my ass on the edge of the harness gingerly, testing my weight. As many hours as I have lain here, there is still, from time to time, that initial moment of disbelief in its capacity to support me. Why else should we hesitate before jumping into water when we know full well that the surface is only an illusory boundary between our world and cool quiet submersion?

I take a deep breath and leap.

When I lean back, I am cradled in the air as if in a hammock between two trees. I squirm about, settling in.

Her voice growls, "Spread your legs."

Like a ballerina, I point my toes and spread them as far apart as they will go. As soon as I open myself in this way, I shift my senses outward again and discover we are not alone. Bodies have begun to shuffle unobtrusively into the room. Some of them approach me with their warmth while others hold back. It is impossible to tell how many enter from their breath and steps alone, but there is no doubt in my mind that their numbers are steadily increasing.

My defensive instincts being heightened, I can tell they are hungry.

Their presence is confirmed when I feel more than two hands attaching my cuffed ankles with carabiner clips.

I am officially not going anywhere.

"Open your arms."

I realize I have been gripping my fist with my other hand, elbows and shoulders in, as if it is a cold day and I can retreat inside myself for warmth. Tentatively, I uncoil and open my chest.

Yes, there are many hands on me now. Those that don't attach my wrist to the chains holding me up begin to caress, pinch, slap and grab at my available flesh.

I know it is Daddy pulling on the collar loop at my throat, know that it's her hand that grabs my ass.

"This is mine. I do what I want with it."

"Yes!"

A hard slap to my pussy. "This is mine, too."

Again, I moan an affirmation.

Her voice in my ear drips with primal aggression and human restraint. She is holding herself back.

"I am giving you to all my friends. You are going to make me proud. You are going to take it from all of them, in all of your holes. You are on display, available to the party. You have no choice. You are everybody else's good time. I am just going to watch. You are going to entertain me. The moment you think you can't take any more is the moment when I am going to have you. By then, you will just be a thing that belongs to me."

As she purrs at me, the groping alien hands ease toward my spread-open cunt and asshole and get to work.

"Good. Now. You listen to me. Don't you dare fucking come."

I gulp. A challenge.

"No, Ma'am."

My own voice sounds dreamy and distant.

"I want to be the only one you come for."

I sigh like a deflating balloon, and my ego drops out of my stomach, through the floor.

I surrender.

"Yes, Ma'am."

How many eyes are on me?

I completely lose track of how long I am fucked. It is impossible to tell how many people are involved. Warm, malleable dicks fill condoms with jizz, their balls slapping against my ass. Stiff silicone strap-ons drill away at me. My ass expands over the widest girth of teardrop-shaped plugs and retracts, swallowing them. Freezing steel dildos are inserted and pressed up like levers against my G-spot. I fight them all, squeezing my tight pussy to push them out. But they persist, and their numbers grow even as I conquer them one by one. They warm me, tenderize me.

Every so often, Daddy slips into the realm of my senses and whispers in my ear, "That's a good girl. You're Daddy's little slut, aren't you?"

The black leather fixes my body in a single point in space and time, and reminds my mind that it is located at a single point in a multidirectional web of control and power.

After hours of tireless attempts to use me up, the cacophony of attention dwindles. There is less and less presence in our apartment until the final touch is removed from me, slowly fading out and away. I have thought countless times that I could not take any more inside of me, only to be subjected to twice as much. Yet I am not broken. I am just being pulverized for the one I want.

I feel each restraint being uncuffed, and the cold air on my exposed wrists and ankles. As she releases my physical attachments, my senses expand outward again and I realize that the chatter of the party is dying and movement receding.

There is no sound or movement in the room, but I know she's standing there, taking in the tableau. I am so divorced from sight by now that I can't even conceive of how I look to her.

My Daddy stalks over to me and brushes my skin with hers with excruciating patience. I know that she is naked now, her chest released, because I feel her tits against my belly. She is a rock climber, reaching out and grabbing at my flesh, pulling herself up. I am being sucked into her through her nose as she inhales me.

I feel her cock against my cunt as she rips the blindfold off. I am pierced by her eyes and pinned by her cock. I reach out to grab her, to wrap my freed self around her, to feel her heat against mine.

"No! Lie back. Haven't you learned anything?"

Whimpering, I relax again.

"You listen to me." She is grinding now ever so slightly, sending the countermovement of the sling out and back onto her, like Newton's cradle.

"You don't move. You don't fight back. I want you. You are just a hole to me. You take it."

I swallow the entire room into my lungs and, like a good girl, do as I'm told.

I thought I knew what it was like to be fucked before I met my Daddy. Uh-uh. No one has ever really gotten inside until the first time she pounced on me. I've resisted everything that has ever attempted to penetrate me. I guess I just don't want to go down without a fight. Most have given up as soon as they met resistance, content to bunt away, relaxing on my front porch. My Daddy marched right up to my door and barged inside, straight to the inner sanctum of my body, where I had always been curled up, asleep.

Impaled, I am an object. She trains me to let go of a body that binds me to everything worldly, pries me open like a book, guides me to do what I already know how to do, which is let go.

I am floating in water so intensely hot that the only way to stand it is to float perfectly still. I am melting.

Daddy fucks me and I moan and wail and come and squirt and gush and forget I know how to close my legs, my arms.

I forget I am not attached, and I remember that I am free.

# RELATIVE ANONYMITY

### Emerald

She and David had married young. They'd known each other all their lives—their parents had been good friends since high school—and at the time, it seemed the thing to do. And they were in love. So at the tender age of twenty, they were married in the town's small Baptist church surrounded by the people they'd known all their lives.

They lived happily enough for seven years on their own farm two miles from her parents, three miles from his. It was beautiful and charming and calm, the routine of the farm as steady and predictable as the rise and set of the sun that marked their workdays.

Carly wasn't sure when she started to realize it, and she wasn't sure when David did, either. But she remembered the day the two of them stood in the kitchen, when their gazes had locked and they knew: They loved each other—but not as husband and wife. The same connection that had been between them as long as they could remember, that had allowed them to know each other more intimately than anyone else, allowed them to see with undeniable clarity what they both knew the moment their eyes met that day. Tears had fallen from both as they'd moved into a silent embrace.

The divorce was as quiet and intimate as their tiny country wedding had been. David had chosen to stay on the farm in their rural Nebraska town and live in their house. Carly wasn't sure how she knew leaving was the right thing for her to do, but she did. Nebraska held everything in life she loved, yet she felt there was nothing left there for her.

When David had called her three weeks before and said there was something he wanted to talk to her about, she had invited him to go ahead. He said he wanted to tell her in person—that it wasn't urgent, but he was wondering when she next planned to visit.

Carly had guessed David was seeing someone, that it was getting serious and that he wanted them to meet. She'd smiled softly as a pang of nostalgia pulled her heart. She could understand his desire, and since she hadn't been back since Christmas and had always enjoyed the early-summer atmosphere of her rural hometown, she'd checked her schedule and booked a flight.

The farm looked precisely as she remembered. She had seen David in the three years since the divorce, but always gathered at his or her parents' house or somewhere as part of a get-together. This was the first time she had returned to the home they had shared.

The screen door squeaked open, and David stood framed. He smiled and waved, and Carly slammed the car door and waved back as she headed up the driveway to the yard.

She met his gaze. He looked great, though there was

something different in his eyes. They looked darker, deeper, less like the carefree blue gaze she had always known; something solemn lay behind them now.

Settled with iced tea at the kitchen table, Carly leaned back and rested her feet on the rung of the chair beside her. There was no indication of anyone else around, and she wondered if her suspicion had been erroneous.

"I'm moving away," David said.

Carly looked at him in surprise. "Away from here?"

He nodded. He appeared calm, fairly unmoved by the idea, which surprised her. But as she looked at him, she understood suddenly that he was feeling the exact way she had when she had left three years before.

"Well, wow. I had no idea. No one said anything to me about it, amazingly enough. When?"

"They don't know." David looked at her. Peace, she noticed with a start: that was the new depth in his eyes. Carly felt surprise because she had never thought of David not at peace, but the impression, though understated, was precise.

"They don't know you're leaving?" Carly guessed he was referring to their respective families and other acquaintances in this small town—which was virtually everyone.

David shook his head. "I'll be asking Dan to take over the farm, which I'm pretty sure he'll be fine with."

Carly nodded. She wanted to ask how his brother was doing but sensed David had more to say.

David tipped back his glass and stretched his long, jeans-clad legs out in front of him. There was silence for several minutes as his gaze rested on his cowboy boots.

"I need to ask you to keep this in confidence, Carly. And I really mean that," he said, turning his head to meet her gaze.

A bit taken aback, she said, "Sure."

"I trust you, that's why it feels okay to me to tell you this, but I'm serious."

Carly stared at him. She had no qualms about keeping a secret, and she understood how much of a challenge that was in a small town. His trust in her was not misplaced, but she couldn't fathom what he had to say to her.

He stood and motioned for her to follow.

David led her down to the basement, where their old farming tools, extra and reject horse equipment and other farm paraphernalia were stored. The basement was mostly unfinished, but its existence was what had been important to them—tornadoes were not taken lightly in this part of the country.

Carly walked behind him down the steep staircase in the dark, glancing ahead to the shadows on the concrete floor. She narrowed her eyes at a large shape she didn't recognize as they reached the bottom.

David turned on the light. Carly blinked.

The basement no longer held farm equipment; at least, not in sight.

She looked around, keeping her expression neutral, though not without effort. The shape she had seen was a cross, life size, with wrist and ankle cuffs attached and dangling from it. Carly wasn't entirely sheltered enough to not know what it was for, but she had never seen one in person. Beyond the cross was a sawhorse that looked ready for its traditional purpose except for the black padding across the top and leather cuffs identical to the ones on the cross attached to each of the four legs.

Her eyes went to the trunk against the wall that used to hold old horse-grooming equipment; it didn't anymore. It was open, and Carly saw things that were becoming less surprising: whips, floggers, paddles and a number of contraptions she wasn't sure she knew how to label or identify.

Carly cleared her throat. "Did you have a yard sale with the horse and farm equipment?"

David smiled. "Thanks for not freaking out," he said quietly. His voice rose to normal level. "All the old equipment and storage is in the back room." He nodded toward the dark doorway to the room Carly imagined was rather crowded now. David's eyes roved around. "I...redecorated."

"Yes..."

David moved forward and ran his hand along the cross, his fingertips brushing the silver hardware of a wrist cuff. Carly was about to say more when a knock on the basement door that led outside made her jump.

"Come in." David raised his voice just enough to be heard outside the door. Carly looked at him. She didn't ever remember their using that door.

The door opened slowly. Carly's view was blocked by it, but from where he stood, David had a clear view of who was behind it.

"Hi, sweetheart," he said. "Thanks for coming."

Carly blushed. He was bringing a woman in there while she was there? Did he think he had to show her how this stuff was used? Did he think she was interested?

The heat intensified in her face. Was she interested?

David with another woman certainly wasn't something that had occurred to her she wanted to see when she came there, but an unexpected intrigue and a bit of arousal shot through her.

The door opened farther, and the one David had called "sweetheart" stepped into view. Carly stared.

The man was about six feet tall. He wore jeans, a white button-down shirt and battered brown cowboy boots. He was about ten years younger than they were, and very good-looking.

And he was the town preacher's son.

"Hi, Carly," he said quietly, glancing at the floor.

It took Carly a second to find her voice. When she did, she shook herself.

"Hello, Nate," she said, stepping forward to shake his hand. He appeared ill at ease, and despite her shock, Carly didn't want him to feel uncomfortable.

She smiled, albeit somewhat dazedly, and lifted her other hand to join it with the one already holding his. "How are you?"

Nate met her eyes and acknowledged the question with a nod. "Okay. You?"

Carly nodded. "I'm fine."

"So, it's probably obvious what I wanted to tell you," David said at her side.

Moving away, bondage, men...any of the three would have surprised her about David. To have them come in a cluster was something she had a feeling might not even hit her full force until later.

"How long has this been going on?" she asked.

"Four months."

Carly nodded slowly. "Impressive that you haven't been found out yet."

"Yes. I would rather not be, obviously. But for Nate...." Nate looked up at them with a tight smile before dropping his eyes back at the floor. David didn't have to continue—he didn't have to explain how much Nate didn't want to be caught. "Nate's been helping out at the farm, so there's been an excuse for his being here."

Carly nodded. That would be helpful, yes.

"So I wondered if you'd like to see it," David said.

"See it?" Carly echoed. She wondered if she understood what he meant.

"See what we do."

David kept his gaze on her, and she didn't answer. Without a word, he gestured to the love seat behind her, inviting her to sit. Carly backed the few steps without breaking eye contact and lowered herself to the edge of the love seat.

David turned back to Nathan. Within seconds they were kissing, and Carly felt herself blush from the obvious heat between them. Like an abstract screen saver, clothing gave way and turned to skin before her eyes, and soon they were half naked before her, still standing, hands roaming like eels curling through water. Carly realized her lips were parted and closed them, glancing prudently at the floor.

The rest of Nate's clothes came off, and David, wearing only his jeans and boots, led him to the cross. He lifted Nate's strong arms and secured them into the wrist cuffs one at a time, and Carly caught her breath at the view of Nate's considerable biceps displayed below his bound wrists. The vision captivated her, actually, and Carly found herself almost panting as she stared, her eyes running eventually from the arms down the strong torso to the unambiguous hard-on protruding from Nate's body. Nate was in slightly better shape than David, which wasn't surprising given his age and the manual labor he did daily on the farm. David's body had looked similar a decade ago.

After fastening the ankle cuffs, David stood and ran his fingertips lightly up the underside of Nathan's cock. Carly heard Nate's breath change, but he made no movement save the involuntary flutter of his jaw muscle and slight dropping of his already hooded eyelids.

David backed up and went to the trunk. He pulled out a flogger. He ran it lightly up Nate's cock, the fringes sliding over Nate's erection with the gentleness of dandelion seeds blowing in the wind. Nate's face muscles twitched, his breath shifting to a pant.

Carly watched, mesmerized.

Abruptly David pulled his arm back and slapped Nate across the chest with the flogger. Carly blinked in surprise. Nate winced, and his hard-on seemed to surge forward and up.

David slashed the flogger across Nate's rigid cock, and Carly almost winced. As she watched, David worked the flogger around Nate's body before backing up and lifting from the trunk a narrow cane. The crack against Nate's skin this time did make Carly cringe, and she watched closely, unable to imagine how Nate could be enjoying what was happening.

But judging from the rampant rigidity of his cock, he seemed to be.

After a brief bout with the cane, David reached and unbuckled the silver hardware of the wrist cuffs holding Nathan in place. He trailed his fingertips down Nate's chest as he bent to undo the ankle cuffs. Despite the welts now covering his skin, Nate showed no reaction beyond his heavy breathing.

David gestured with his head, and the young man draped his body over the nearby sawhorse. David latched all four cuffs in place and stood in front of his partner.

Then he stepped back and unzipped his pants. Nate's head extended like a turtle's from a shell, reaching for the cock millimeters from his mouth. David touched Nate's lips with it then stood back, leaning forward to brush it against the younger man's skin occasionally.

Carly, entranced, suddenly realized she was looking at the cock of the man who used to be her husband. The cock that had been inside her countless times, that she had seen on a regular basis for almost a decade. It now hovered in front of another man's mouth, one it was a safe bet it had been in before. Carly felt something stir in her, but she wasn't sure what it was.

She wasn't sure what she felt at all.

Abruptly, David shoved his cock forward with such force and abruptness Carly was startled, and she almost gasped before Nate's mouth opened automatically to take it. David thrust forward rhythmically, gripping Nate's hair as he slammed his cock deep in his throat. Carly couldn't see the evidence of Nate's own arousal now, but she guessed from his muffled moans that it had changed little.

David yanked his cock away and took a step back, and Carly could feel the hunger emanating from Nate as his head lowered. It was a hunger she understood, as one who loved to suck cock herself.

David moved around behind the sawhorse, never glancing Carly's way. Neither of them had looked at her since the introduction had been made, and she wondered if they remembered she was there. She had a sense that the intensity in front of her was so acute it might leave no room to recall anything else. She certainly didn't have a feeling they were putting on a show.

David had procured a condom and rolled it down his rock-hard dick. Standing behind Nate, who was breathing heavily but who was otherwise completely still, he poured lube into his hand and ran it up his cock slowly, his slick fist sliding easily up and down the rubber. With his clean hand, he reached and palmed one of Nate's buttocks. Then he drew back and slapped hard, murmuring something Carly couldn't quite make out as Nate whimpered. The slapping and low monologue continued, words she couldn't hear but a tone that she could, a combination of taunting and reassurance, simultaneously warm and ominous. She wondered what David was saying and strained her ears as he delivered one final smack and pushed his way into Nathan's ass.

David's buttocks flexed and dented as he shoved his cock in and out of Nate—the latter helplessly bound to the sawhorse—

grunting, sweat showing now on his forehead. Carly watched
with unabashed fascination, alternating between incredulity
at her voyeuristic position and the surreal awareness that she
was watching someone she had been married to and known all
her life.

And something else had emerged in her, too. Carly crossed
her legs and shifted a bit as David pounded away at his submissive. She wasn't attracted to David personally anymore, but it
felt impossible not to be aroused by the simple carnal attrac-
tion exploding before her eyes. Her ex-husband slammed into
Nate, involuntary sounds emanating from Nate's throat as he
took David's sizeable cock. David fucked him with no apparent
restraint, reaching occasionally to smack the younger man's ass.

David leaned forward and grabbed his partner by the hair,
yanking his head up and back as Nate let out a groan. David
pumped more frenetically, tangling both hands in Nate's hair as
he came with a roar.

Carly was breathless, her chest moving perceptibly as she
pulled air in through her mouth. She did not remember when
her mouth had fallen open or when her breath had turned to
gasps. Her panting, though silent, mirrored David's as he backed
away from Nate. She watched as he disposed of the condom
and attended to undoing the restraints holding Nate's wrists.
She wondered if they were done.

They were not.

In hindsight, Carly realized she should have known that.
David had never been an inconsiderate lover. There might be an
obvious power play going on, but she saw shortly that it didn't
mean anyone was denied what he was obviously there for.

Nate followed David back to the cross, where David
recuffed him facing forward again. Carly noticed Nate's
cock seemed even harder than it had before, appearing almost

painfully purple and, she could only imagine, needing release. She wondered in what form it would come.

David leaned in and gripped Nate's throat, hissing low in his ear. Knowing she wouldn't be able to hear what was said, Carly just watched. David ran his fingers slowly over Nate's engorged cock as he murmured, his tone switching back to the gentle taunting she had heard him use earlier. Nate winced at the contact of David's fingers, and Carly wondered if it didn't feel more torturous than all of the beating Nate had endured so far.

David's voice seemed to rise in a question, and a breathless Nate nodded in desperation, as though his head was acting of its own accord to agree to whatever would result in his being allowed to come. The cock on which David's hand still rested seemed like a volcano ready to blow.

He let go of it and backed up, looking straight at Nate. When David turned his head to look at her, Carly jumped. His eye contact was like a sudden burn, the intensity of the scene reflected in—or perhaps emanating from—his eyes seeming to transfer to her with his gaze.

He smiled. She smiled back, baffled.

Raising his eyebrows, he gestured with his hand at Nathan's cock. It appeared to be an invitation. Carly blinked, her eyes widening.

There was a pause, and David said evenly, "Would you like to finish him off, Carly?"

Her mouth dropped open again, though this time she was aware of it. She looked at Nate, who continued to stare straight ahead, still breathless, his cock painfully swollen. Carly realized she felt no hesitation in wanting—she did indeed want to make that cock blow.

What was the hesitation, then? She looked back at David, who still held her gaze, his expression open and inviting as though he had just offered to get her a drink at a party. The whole of their lives together seemed to flash through her imagination: chasing each other as kids through the edges of the cornfields, playing on hay bales in the barn until the sun went down and they were called inside. Making out behind the grain bins at the back of his family's farm in high school, riding the horses out night after night to the deserted plot her family owned the summer after they graduated. Farming and living and working and sleeping side by side for seven years in the house where she now stood, after they had been married by the father of the man shackled to the cross feet away.

And here they were again in the same house, the man who had been her husband inviting her to suck another man's cock.

His lover's.

Carly stared into David's blue eyes, remembering the day they looked at each other and faced what they both knew and both knew the other knew: They didn't want to be married anymore. There was something else out there for both of them.

Carly blinked and broke her gaze. For David, that certainly seemed to be the case.

She looked back at him, and he smiled, a smile that was so familiar she almost gasped. At that moment, she would have sworn he had just watched the same movie of their lives together with her, some connection in their look allowing them to share the same memory.

She took a step forward. David backed up to allow her through, his hand gallantly brushing her lower back as she stepped forward to the cross.

Nate's breath was even now, though sweat still stood on his face. His eyes were downcast, and Carly stood in front of him until he raised his eyes to hers. She didn't know him well enough to read them, but she saw nothing in them to indicate fear or resistance to what she was about to do, which was what she was looking for. She trusted David, but she was in undeniably unfamiliar territory, and she didn't want to be a pawn in a power game in which Nate was unwitting.

She should have known better.

Nate gasped sharply as she knelt and touched her lips to his cock. She had planned to go slowly, to tease a little bit, but the obvious hunger of the cock in front of her combined with the arousal in herself she hadn't known the degree of until that moment propelled her forward without restraint, and she sucked Nate's cock with the same vigor and aggression with which David had fucked his ass.

Predictably, the young man came in seconds, the vocal accompaniment sounding both the desperation and the euphoria of the release. He spurted into her mouth repeatedly as she kept sucking, letting his warm come run out her lips and down her chin as she took his cock all the way to the back of her throat, feeling it continue to shoot there. Eventually she pulled back, her mouth, lips and face a warm, sticky mess. She glanced up at the man shackled to the cross. His eyes were closed, his head thrown back. His body hung limply, the restraints almost appearing to hold him up.

Carly backed up on her knees and stood, wiping her mouth with the back of her hand. Her heart was still pounding, her knees slightly shaky as she moved out of the way to give David room to undo Nate's bindings. The charge was such that she had almost come herself, and she imagined it wouldn't take much to do so once she was back in her car alone with her fingers. Her climax would come, she suspected, before she reached the end of the driveway.

\* \* \*

"I wanted you to see it. See it that way," David said. His voice was low, and Carly remembered the rumbling sound of it when he had spoken to Nate and she hadn't been able to hear what he'd said. She nodded.

"I didn't know what you'd say, what you'd think. I didn't know how to tell you. I felt like there was no way to tell you." His blue eyes pierced into hers. He shrugged. "So I thought I'd show you."

Carly nodded again. The conversation they were having almost seemed more surreal than the experience itself, as it was devoid of the adrenaline charges of sexual arousal and surprise. She was left having what would seem a mundane conversation with her ex-husband, punctuated with intermittent flashbacks to the scene they had undergone the day before.

"I understand." She paused. "I'm curious, though—did you plan to...have me...?"

David shook his head. "No, I didn't plan on your being involved." He shrugged, giving her a rakish smile. "I just went with my instinct. I've trusted them before when it came to you. They've never seemed wrong yet."

Carly smiled and dropped her eyes. It was quiet for a few moments as she studied the floor.

"Well, I'd better get going. My flight leaves in a few hours." Carly stood up. She paused and looked back down at David, recalling why he had called her there in the first place. "You said you're leaving. Are the two of you leaving together?" She didn't say, but it seemed to her such evidence would be almost as damning in this small town as if they were discovered here.

He shook his head. "No. I'm going first. I'll be taking off in about three weeks. I'm going to the Omaha area—I left the address for you to take with you on the counter." David nodded at a sheet of paper on the counter to Carly's left. "Nate's going to wait until the end of the summer. He's going to go to grad school at the University of Nebraska there. We're not going to live together right now. We'd still be too easily found out that way." David shrugged. "I don't know what will happen, to tell you the truth. I've been thinking about getting out of here for some time, though. Nate's wanted to for years."

"Would...would his parents finding out have the implications I imagine for Nate?"

"Yes." The answer came before the sentence was even finished.

Carly lowered her head. She felt tears forming and took a deep breath. "I wish you both the best," she said sincerely, stepping forward as David stood to meet her in a hug.

"I know," David whispered near her ear. "That's why I told you."

Carly stared out the airplane window, fingering the slip of paper with David's soon-to-be address written on it. It was funny. She had lamented the seeming lack of privacy in their lives, their relationship, while they were married. The complete support from their families was unquestioned and at times felt to her too much so. She couldn't imagine what the ominous specter of so much the opposite felt like to David now, and even more so to Nate.

How long would they wait? What if they were found out? Would they come out themselves? Did they really want to leave—or did they feel like they had to? Carly watched the green and yellow patchwork of Midwestern fields shrink below her, feeling like what she had learned spawned more questions than it answered.

But maybe they weren't for her to answer. Or maybe they were

part of something everyone had to answer, innumerable questions that took different forms but ultimately were all the same.
Questions asked of everyone, including not only David and Nate
but Nate's father, her parents, David's parents, every resident of
the tiny Nebraska town she had just left and everyone who lived
in the city toward which she now headed. And herself.

Carly glanced at the paper in her hand. She was returning to
a place where she had relative anonymity, a luxury neither David
nor Nate had—yet. Her eyes scanned the unfamiliar address
written in familiar handwriting. She folded the paper and leaned
forward to slip it into her purse, then settled back, watching the
receding fields below fade from sight.

Maybe they were questions that didn't have answers. Questions that somehow, by the very asking, allowed life itself.

# CLOSETED

## Emily Bingham

Just breathe in and out. Don't panic. Okay, maybe counting is a better idea.

*One one-thousand. Two one-thousand.*

Just keep track of the minutes and time will go by faster.

*Three one-thousand. Four one-thousand.*

Count and breathe. There is plenty of air in here.

*Five one-thousand. Six one-thousand.*

Keep shifting weight between knees. He can't leave me in here for long, can he? Oh, god, he wouldn't dare.

*Thirty one-thousand. Thirty-one one-thousand.*

This is officially boring. My knees hurt. I really have to pee. No, I'm supposed to be thinking about something important while I'm in here. Like the true nature of my submission. Screw that, I'm going to piss in his closet—that will show him.

*Fifty-eight one-thousand. Fifty-nine one-thousand. Sixty one-thousand.*

Breathing and counting, I've no clue how long I've knelt there, just that after the first several minutes I stopped thinking so hard and focused on the darkness. Even behind the effective fur-lined blindfold, I can sense the complete lack of light compared to the relative brightness of the bedroom before the closet doors were closed. The idea that there is a blacker place than behind the blindfold is disconcerting. I keep assuring myself that an ordinary closet has plenty of breathable air. That I won't run out anytime soon. That the vinyl cling tape around my mouth leaves me plenty of room for nose breathing.

I'm surprised that my arms have not yet started to fall asleep, secured as they are behind me in an arm binder fashioned out of rope. Obviously, he had known what he was doing back there to keep the blood flowing properly so I can stay in the darkness alone for as long as possible.

This is a vast improvement on spending the time rapidly feeling my fingers tingle and lose all sensation until finally both of my arms were entirely asleep. At that last very urgent moment I would have to throw myself against the swing-out doors and wildly make noises to convey that my arms were ready to fall off. I would then be left to deal with the consequences of "escaping."

This was a scene that played out nearly every time he bound my arms when we were first exploring rope. Thankfully we've moved past those days and into moments like this when I know all my limbs are safe, and I have nothing but the evil things he might do next to worry about. Thinking about other times I've escaped by whining about unpleasant pain, I wonder why I don't try the same method now to get out of the mind-numbing dullness of the closet. Simply brushing my hands against the door as I shift my weight, however, is met with a stern, "Hold still!" from the other side of the door. My body goes cold and I don't dare move again, knowing without seeing it that he is out there making "the face." The one that means business: head tilted down to glare over the rim of his glasses with stony impassible eyes and a firmly set jaw.

My behind begins to hurt all over again thinking about that look and the paddle, the evil broad-faced one with symmetrical holes bored into it to cut down on air resistance. The one that hits my skin with a frightening crack; me with my face shoved into the carpet, ass in the air, arms sharply tied behind—hoping not to earn any more smacks if I can just hold still. There's nothing pleasurable about the noise, the biting pain.

The worst of it is the look of disappointment in his usually kind eyes before the blindfold goes on, before the tape is pressed over my mouth to make sure my sarcasm—amusing in life, aggravating during play—doesn't get me into any more trouble. Immediately after my bum is paddled to a sore bright red, I'm placed in the darkness to contemplate how to behave properly.

But the smart-assery comes so easily and as soon as I'm alone, the running comedy routine starts in my head anew. Apparently I'm not very good at this redemption thing. Even with all my hopes of being a good girl and never incurring the wrath of the mean paddle again, my mind never quite focuses on reverence or apology. Instead discomfort, boredom and claustrophobia take center stage. After what seems like ages, I vaguely hear foot-steps getting closer and suddenly the closet doesn't seem so bad anymore. Scarier is the not knowing what comes next: leaving the safety of the darkness to learn what is in store for me thanks to his devious mind.

As the doors squeal open, I try hopelessly to make myself as small as I can. *Maybe he'll forget I'm in here and just change his shirt. Think invisible thoughts,* I tell myself. I know I couldn't possibly be more visible as he leans down to grab the generous finishing knot of the ropes and haul my body off the floor. My legs don't work properly after all the kneeling, and I hear the frustration in his slightly labored breathing as he does the majority of the work. He drags my weight across the room to guide me back to my knees somewhere in the vicinity of the bed.

I sense him moving around behind me, probably walking around to kill time and make me wonder what will happen for just that much longer. My heart barrels through my chest, so noisy I can't hear where he is in the room anymore, which forces me to jump when he tenderly touches my shoulders from behind. He kneads them, bringing more blood to my constricted hands. The kind touches are more painful and unexpected given my words earlier in the evening. I would gladly take more of the paddle to apologize for breaking the no-bratty-attitude clause of our relationship, but every stroke of his soft hands across my sore arms compounds the guilt. How can he still be kind when I keep forgetting the simplest things? When I can't even use the closet time properly to think about not repeating the mistake? I know he can tell just by looking at me that I was in the closet being insolent rather than industrious. Some things never change.

Soon he moves in front of me to sit on the bed, his lap level with my face. I tilt my head, wishing I could see his expression. One knee on either side of my head, he leans in to kiss the part of my hair as he unbuckles the blindfold, whispering a reminder to keep my eyes closed for a moment. In a hurry to see his face, however, I open my eyes a bit too soon and squint into the light, blinking until I can see more than blurs of color to finally recognize him in front of me. He gives me a small friendly smile as if to ask, "Well, what now?" And I wish I knew.

He strokes my hair and face so gently it is painful, as if he's the one who needs to apologize. I wish my mouth were free so I could smile back; instead I make purring noises to convey my gratitude. The petting morphs into his hand gradually bringing my head into his lap, and I awkwardly nuzzle my face against the heat of his crotch, enjoying the knowledge that he is growing harder in his pants. After several frustrating minutes, he pulls me away from him and shakes his head, *tsking* at me, and I know the torture hasn't even begun.

All I want is to be released from the rope and the gag so I can show him I understand my error by using my mouth for something worthwhile. If I could just get the tape off my face I could put my mouth around his cock, and we could move on to the pleasant part of the evening and forget about all my earlier silliness, which is of course exactly what he isn't going to allow to happen. First he has to tease me to the point of near madness, then we'll be even again.

Being practically unable to move without his help, I'm left to totter on my knees in front of him as he grins and stands, adjusting his erection to a more comfortable position. That this elicits a longing sigh from me only makes him grin further while he walks behind me to reach around and grab my nipples. No amount of moaning or rocking back and forth on my knees to get away can convince him to stop; instead it gives him an excuse to squeeze and twist harder. Just when it feels as if I can't take another second of the pain, he takes hold of the arm binding and dangles me over the floor for a cruelly long moment before adding carpet burn to the pain on my nipples by releasing me so that I fall on my chest.

Squirming without the use of my arms, I feel him walk into the space between my legs until he is able to use his ankles to hold my thighs open, reaching up to grab the rope harness with one arm. With the other, he roughly gropes between my legs. Feeling how wet his attention to my breasts has made me, he pulls me a bit farther off the floor so they can dangle, nipples brushing against the Berber carpet—me squealing, him laughing at the situation while forcing two fingers into me. He fucks me violently, knowing very well that doing so causes my nipples to graze the carpet in a more intense rhythm. Just as the pleasure of his fingers is beginning to outweigh the pain of my chest, he very abruptly stops, dropping me back to the floor. *Damn him.*

Still holding my thighs open, he reaches somewhere outside my line of sight for a stinging instrument to hit my wet lower lips with. I don't recognize the sensation—a crop perhaps—but am thankful that at least it isn't the horrible paddle making a reappearance. After a handful of slaps, I am no longer willing to hold still and take the pain, but my attempt to wiggle away is met with much harder strokes of the crop against my labia. I give myself a pep talk to convince my body to hold relatively still. When the spanking becomes too much to bear, he is forced to gently step on my behind to help keep me still. He slaps my inner thighs intermittently to remind me to keep them open and I growl in frustration.

"Oh, poor baby," he coos, continuing without missing a beat. "You like it and you know it. Look how wet you are, whore." The final sharp hit of the crop and the word hit me at the same time, and I'm not sure which one hurts more coming from him. And yet the warm feeling of arousal is unabated. Apparently, I am a whore and loving it.

He tosses the crop away and kneels beside me to begin the task of untying my arms. As each loop of rope comes loose and he pulls them free of my arms, I feel the relief of my muscles being able to move again and the ache of them being motionless for so long. Rather than allowing me to enjoy regaining the freedom of my arms, he uses the same rope he has just removed to tie them in a different position.

With me still lying on the floor, he straddles my body, pulls my wrists behind my head to force my elbows to bend at a painful angle and ties them off to the rope harness still looped around my chest. He watches me gracelessly attempt to raise my chest off of the floor with my elbows while he half sits on my back, laughing at the struggle. *Glad I can be so amusing. Now get off, you're heavy.*

Done with my arms, he turns his attention to securing my thighs to my ankles in a sort of frog tie. With my feet tied tight up against my behind, my legs are forced awkwardly into the air. This leg binding severely complicates my attempt to protect my sore nipples from the rug. Thoroughly distracted by this dilemma, I don't notice until too late that he has heaved my dead weight up onto the edge of the bed.

I hear the telltale release of a zipper behind me while I'm busy groaning under the effort of taking the weight off my chest, which I soon realize is impossible with my legs dangling off the bed. Having no control over my legs also makes it impossible to keep him from between them. How convenient. Using this to his devious advantage, he takes an ankle in each hand and spreads my thighs. Even with the pain of the crop fresh on my cunt, I'm dripping wet, making it even easier for him to glide inside me.

He pushes in as far as possible with a grunt and then pulls out until we barely remain in contact for several long torturous moments. Holding my ankles tight, he then begins to buck wildly against me, his bare skin slapping rhythmically against mine. I can't decide which sensation to focus on for any length of time— the joy of having his cock finally inside me, or the gnawing pain of him purposely causing as much friction as possible on my just-spanked bits. Soon the pain becomes so intense it registers as pleasure, and I feel myself begin to tighten in readiness for release, wondering if he'll notice or allow it.

I should know better than to think he would let me off so

easily, but I'm still shocked when he stops midstroke just as I'm about to cross over to orgasm. Ignoring my moans of total frustration, he flips me over. The sadistic grin on his face only further aggravates me, which I try to convey with pleading, narrowed eyes. This only amuses him more and I glance down to notice he is stroking himself only millimeters from my cunt, which is totally exposed between my straining thighs. With my legs trapped under me and elbows straight in the air, I can't move far enough to force him to make contact with my clit.

My frustration reaches a frenzy just as he comes messily all over the front of me, marking his territory. Rubbing the remnants of his ejaculate off the head of his cock against me for one torturous moment, he says, while still breathing heavily, "That was fun, ready for bed."

I almost believe he's going to leave me tied up and unsatisfied and go to sleep, as he turns off the bedroom lights. There are several long minutes of silence as I'm left to wonder in the darkness if I should choose this moment to try to escape as my legs are going numb and I can't hear him moving around anywhere. Just as I start to wriggle around to find a loose point in the ropes, I hear an all-too-familiar mechanical hum. He's in the room again and has turned on a vibrator of some sort. As he gets closer, I realize a buzzing noise that loud could only mean one thing—he's gotten out the Magic Wand. *I'm in so much trouble.*

I realize the moment the vibrator makes contact with me that, being the wonderfully evil man that he is, he's placed it on the highest possible setting. This means that the orgasm that had been building is almost painfully ripped out of my body by the too-heavy vibrations within a couple of seconds. To add to the overwhelming nature of this moment, the tape is still over my mouth, so I'm unable to make any noise and am limited to little whimpering sounds. But in my head, I'm praising every deity I don't believe in as my body shakes uncontrollably and the warm bursts of orgasmic energy fill every inch of me.

He, however, doesn't relent by moving the vibrator as my happy orgasm noises become frustrated, overwhelmed groans. The next climax comes without me thinking about it, so intense it's as if my body has turned against me. That's the thing about the Magic Wand—it never stops and therefore the orgasms just keep coming whether I like them or not.

I come until I'm convinced I'll pass out if he leaves the vibrator on my clit for one more second. At about this time he must sense I'm having a hard time breathing between the uncontrollable orgasms because he lifts my head and finally begins to unwrap the bondage tape from around my mouth. I breathe in a huge gasp of air as yet another climax runs through me. This time I'm able to make all the unintelligible noises aloud that the gag had been holding back.

At last, he switches off the vibrator and I hear it drop to the floor. My heart is racing crazily, and I'm so breathless it feels like I've run a marathon, so I'm glad it's over with, thankful for the pleasure but hoping he's had enough of torturing me for one evening. He lifts himself onto the bed beside me so that we are able to kiss hungrily as he unties the ropes and frees my limbs. The moment my arms are free I wrap them around his sweaty body and enjoy the calm now that it's all over.

"What do you have to say for yourself now?"

"Thank you, Sir," I say, with a huge smile. Obviously pleased with this response, he resumes kissing me deeply. I pull away for just a second to add, "I love you."

He pets my hair softly, pulling me a bit closer to his warmth to kiss my forehead. "Good girl."

# VEGAS TREAT

Rachel Kramer Bussel

I fingered the metal clamps, my body already seizing up in reaction to them. "You want me to wear...all of them?" I asked softly. I'd been the one to volunteer for the bondage photo shoot, it was true. I'd never done anything quite like that before, but when he'd seen me strolling around Las Vegas while on vacation with the boyfriend I was pretty sure I wanted to break up with, Tyler had picked me out and approached me. I felt like a modern-day Lana Turner, but instead of a drugstore counter, I'd been approached at a slot machine where I was well on my way to losing many quarters.

I guess I'd looked the part of bad girl gone wrong: bright red hair, freshly dyed; eyeliner galore; black rubber bracelets circa Madonna 1984; dark, tight jeans and a white tank top with a flimsy black bra; hot pink platform sandals and an I-could-care-less look. Well, the look wasn't just an affectation; I wasn't really into the whole Vegas mystique, but Eric had offered to pay to get us out of Michigan for the weekend, flush from a win at Internet poker and eager to try his hand at the real thing. When I told him a stranger wanted to photograph me, maybe nude, he merely grunted and asked me to get him another soda from down the hall. I stalked off to get his soda and run some ice over my neck. The room was air-conditioned, but I was bored. So I pulled out my phone and hit DIAL after letting my finger hover over Tyler's number. We should've been celebrating my twenty-first birthday three months before, but Eric's not the type to notice anything like that; I'd been drinking with him for the last two years and had the fake ID to prove it. I didn't want a surprise party, but a little attention would've been nice. The slot machines were kind of fun, but not enough to make up for feeling like I was so undesirable my boyfriend was more inter-ested in money than me.

And that's how I wound up topless, wearing just my skimpy white panties with pink flowers on them, one of the most girly items I owned, while Tyler dangled a pair of nipple clamps in front of me. Actually, it wasn't a pair, it was a trio, because there was a clamp to go on my clit. I wasn't a virgin or anything, obvi-ously, but maybe I'd been meeting the wrong men because none had ever proposed so much as a threesome, let alone bondage and sex toys.

Here was Tyler, barefoot, in a ripped black Violet Femmes T-shirt and holey jeans, assessing me like I was a piece of meat—a very sexy, tender, juicy, delicious, lucky piece of meat. And just then, I wanted to be the rarest cut of all, the one whose taste lingers not just on your tongue but all through your insides long after it's been swallowed and discarded. I didn't want to fall in love with Tyler and live happily ever after, but I wanted to make my mark, wanted him to remember me not just as some random girl who spread her legs for his lens. I was sick of guys looking right through me, or seeing only what part of me they could grab, use and walk away from.

Tyler seemed to be hungry for a part of me that he couldn't get just by fucking me, as if he wanted something deeper, and I, full of youthful bravado, wanted to give it to him. "Now, Rina, you know this is going to hurt, right? It's going to hurt a lot... maybe not at first, but when I take them off, the blood's going to rush back to your nipples and clit. It's going to look so hot; trust me," he said, then flashed me the grin that had made me talk to him in the first place. "And I have a feeling you're going to like it. You have something about you that tells me you need a little pain to rile you up. Not to tame you, because nothing could do that, but to somehow give you back all the energy you bring to your life." That was deeper than I was expecting from a twenty-five-year-old UNLV dropout, but I liked it. I was sick of people treating me like a baby, assuming that I had nothing going for me simply because of my age or how I dressed. Even if Tyler was just bullshitting me, it made me feel good, like maybe this photo would catapult me out of my small-town, dead-end life and going-nowhere relationship.

"How'd you know I'd never done this before?" I asked. I could've been referring to the modeling or the clamps, but he went right ahead and answered.

"I just know. Girls who've done this before just roll right with it. They don't look at the clamps the way you are." Did I look scared? *Was* I scared? I was so used to being bored that scared never even entered into it. Maybe I looked scared and that was a good thing; maybe he wanted me to look scared, to make a better image. I didn't think about it too much; after all, he hadn't asked me to act, but to model. I wasn't sure if he was paying me, but I didn't really care. I was doing something I was sure no girls back home were doing.

"Relax," he said and touched my arm, sending sparks the

likes of which I'd never felt before shooting along my skin. I hated feeling young and naïve usually, and anyone who suggested I was either would get a scowl and the finger. But Tyler didn't sound like he was laughing at my inexperience. He was more like a teacher—a very sexy teacher. "You don't have to do anything you don't want to do, and if you don't like it, we'll stop and do something else. But something tells me you're going to like it, Rina," he finished, then stood and stared at me, his face so close and bold and open, I had to look away after a few seconds. No one had ever looked in my eyes like that, not even Eric. They looked at my body or my face or my hair; they looked long enough to know, maybe, that my eyes were a murky hazel, that I could win a staring contest, that I was tough on the outside, but not enough to see beneath that brash surface. Tyler saw and asked for me to peel it away to give him something else, something deeper. Tyler seemed to want to know everything, even though this was supposed to be a work thing for him, and all of a sudden my nipples were standing at attention, getting ready for their journey. I wasn't sure if I wanted him to see all of me, but it turned me on that he wanted to, so I decided to go with it.

His voice was so sensual, so smoky and intense, the aural equivalent of rich Texas barbecue, that I melted into it the way barbecue melts on my tongue. "Now this is a cute little outfit," he said, fingering my panties, "but I think we need to take these off. Maybe I can stuff them in your mouth later," he said. His voice was deadpan but it still sent shivers along my skin. He was so close I could smell the smoke lingering on his breath and I whimpered. "Can I take your panties off, Rina? Or do you want to do it?"

I had to answer now. I swallowed, then braved a look at him. "You can take them off." He didn't just pull them down the sides of my legs. He reached inside and felt that I was wet, felt that my juices had soaked the panties, before he singlehandedly pulled them slowly down my legs, making me aware of the sensation of the cotton tugging against my skin, exposing me. He dropped them on the bed and then I was just naked, bright red hair, big eyes, erect nipples. "Come over here for a minute," he said, then he showed me the biggest collection of handcuffs I've ever seen, even now, years later, and I've seen a lot. There must've been three dozen sets, from metal ones to padded leather to silk to fur-lined. Some had pink hearts, some had shiny black bows, some had Velcro. One pair said BRAT across them. I didn't even know that handcuffs came in such assortments; I'd truly never given it any thought. I'd barely had anyone even hold me down. I shivered.

"You like what you see, Rina?"

"Yes," I said softly. Already, he'd taken me down a notch; I wasn't vulnerable because I was naked, but because this was so new, and I suddenly wanted it so much. Seeing all those cuffs let me know that plenty of other people did these kinds of things too, otherwise there wouldn't be such an array; manufacturers wouldn't bother. Silently, that drawer full of restraints spoke to me and calmed my fears. "We're here for you," they said. "We want you, we welcome you. We'll take care of you, even when if feels like we're not. We need you." Maybe that was melodramatic, but I'd always felt more kinship with things than people, with the clothing I used to adorn myself, the books I lovingly read and reread, the bike I used to zip as far and fast down the street as I could. But these belongings came with an owner, a man who was quickly making me melt. He was the real force behind what I was experiencing.

I lifted a pair of black leather cuffs, admiring their heft. He reached for them and dangled them before me. "These are ankle cuffs," he said, "in case I really want to immobilize you. Let's stick with your wrists for now. I want you to spread those pretty legs wide for me." His words could've sounded dumb or cheesy, but they didn't. They made me wet.

I reached for a pair of purple padded cuffs; it's always been my favorite color. They were soft to the touch, nothing menacing about them...nothing except the look on Tyler's face, like he could read my every pervy thought. Was I that easy? Was every girl's first time like this? I'd prided myself on being so different for so long, but now, I wasn't so sure. My heart was pounding as I handed the cuffs over to Tyler.

"Good choice," he said, and I let out a breath I hadn't realized I'd been holding. He paused and just watched me, and I got the impression there was no right answer, but that each action of mine would trigger one of his, would let him know what I was up for—or thought I was up for. His trusting patience, his interest, his sexy eyes watching me, more than anything else, made me relax, even as I became more and more excited. My body was primed for almost anything, but my heart was calm. Tyler would take care of me. I pawed through his offerings, adding to the pile like we were shopping. Pink bondage tape, the cuffs, the clamps...

"What's this?" I asked, holding up a metal contraption with a wheel full of spikes attached to a silver handle.

"It's called a Wartenburg wheel. I'll show you," he said, then he took it and lightly ran the metal spikes along my arm. It didn't hurt, and he did it so lightly at first that I didn't think it could, but then he did it again, a little harder, before turning my arm over and tickling the underside of my wrist with it. "This can be used anywhere." He let the possibilities dangle in the air.

"I'll help you get ready." He hummed as if to himself as he bound my arms behind my back with the cuffs. The first thing

I did was tug on them to make sure they were tight enough. He noticed but just stood there, waiting. My breath came heavily as I realized that there was no turning back now. I stood upright, at attention, proudly looking back at him as I offered him my breasts, the nipples now harder than ever. Tyler took the clamps and fastened them one on each nipple. He knelt down before my clit and just stared for a moment, then spread the hood so it popped out. "Are you ready, Rina?" he asked.

"Yes," I whispered as he pressed the padded edges of the clamp against my clit, prodding it, teasing it. If such a thing was possible, I was ready. I breathed through my nose, tears aching to surface.

"Don't breathe through the pain, breathe into it," he told me. "Can I tape your mouth?" he asked, holding up the bondage tape.

I surprised myself by moaning. Yes, it all hurt, but even more, it felt wonderful to have my wrists warm and snug in the leather, the heat coursing through all three points of contact with the clamps. It made me focus on the parts of me I could move—my tongue, my head, my toes, my hips—before darting back to that heat, that pain with pleasure edging up underneath. I nodded, then sealed my lips. "You can make noise through the tape, but that won't be your safeword. Shake your head back and forth three times in a row if you want me to stop," he said. "Do you understand?" Tyler looked directly into my eyes. I nodded.

I should've been nervous and scared, but I wasn't. I was wet, remembering his promise to make me part my legs. The tape was almost gentle as it sealed my lips. I swallowed hard and without any warning he started shooting. I stared back at him, bold, direct, my green eyes fixed on him, hoping he liked what he saw. Tyler was so focused on whatever he saw through his lens I didn't know if he even realized all the emotions I was going through. I was wet, turned on, unsure if it was from being bound or because of him or both.

"I'm gonna zoom in, Rina. Show me what you're feeling. Show me everything." He made it sound so easy. I didn't focus too much on being a "good model" but rather thought about all the things the toys were making me feel, all the things my body had clearly been yearning for but would never experience with Eric. They made me want to cry and grin at the same time, to curl up into a ball and to roar like a lion (once the tape came off). Every time panic started to set in, I willed myself to be calm, knowing there was a great reward awaiting me at the end.

I became the brat who wanted to get her punishment, the girl whose body was blatantly exposed to not just Tyler, but the world. I thrust my chest out, pushing my bound wrists behind me and downward as best I could. I shook my hips, smiled, bit my lip. I stepped closer to the camera, wishing I could run my hands up and down my body, give Tyler a real show, but from the constant clicks, I knew he was getting what he needed.

That made me relax. He didn't want to see me in distress, just to see me. Maybe he was a pervert, but maybe pervert wasn't such a bad word. Tyler muttered things under his breath like, "Give it to me, Rina," and "Struggle against those cuffs," and "Snarl at me," then other words that rumbled together into a kind of sexy song, like background music. I realized that though he had been the one to physically tie me up and put the clamps on, I was the one bringing the real show. Amidst so much fake glamour, this was real.

I twisted and turned as much as I could, spreading my legs while he zoomed in. While the pain had plateaued after the first rush of intensity, now it was back and I longed to bite my lip, my favorite coping mechanism, but of course I couldn't. I focused on his mantra to breathe into the pain, and I did, every second of it. The tears came unbidden as I took deep breaths through my nose, walking close to Tyler's camera until I could toss my hair back, feel it tickle my bound wrists, and expose my clamped nipples right to the eye of his camera. His clicks came fast and furious until they stopped, and he put the camera down and took me in his arms.

First he undid the tape. "I have to do this fast," he said and tore it right off. My lips were a little numb, but I didn't mind. He traced a finger over them and then let me rest my head on his shoulder. I could tell he was hard, but he wasn't trying to simply screw me; our encounter had gone far beyond that. "Now I'm going to take off the clamps, but let's have you sit down right here on the couch first," he said softly. "You were amazing. I got so many good shots, and I'm going to send them to some bondage and fetish magazines. They're gonna love you."

Now I bit my lip, because I knew something big was coming. First the clit clamp came off. I let out a cry as the blood came rushing back. "Good girl," he said and lightly trailed his fingers over my wetness. I had barely realized it, but I was very, very wet. "You're beautiful," he said softly, with no trace of the tough guy I'd glimpsed previously. Then the nipple clamps came off. I watched as he eased the lever down on what I now know are tweezer clamps and saw my flattened nubs come to life again.

He dropped the clamp on the floor and leaned down to suck one bud, lightly tracing his tongue against it. The wetness made me squirm, in a good way. His fingers again found my wetness, plunging deep inside. Now I could talk, but I didn't have anything to say other than a series of insensible moans. There was too much to feel, and I was glad my wrists were still bound. Too much freedom all at once would've been a shock to my system.

I rocked against him as he gave me what I hadn't known I'd

been missing, his fingers going deep, his mouth switching from one tormented breast to the other. This was my initiation ritual, my belated birthday present, my kinky debutante ball featuring just the two of us. I gave myself to him as I'd done before and in return, Tyler gave me the best orgasm of my life, one that rocked me from the inside out, spiraling through my body like a tornado. I cried when I came, and he kissed my neck, then my lips, placing his over mine so he could take my breath from me too.

Tyler made me come I don't know how many times, then he showed me some of the photos he'd taken. Only much later, after I'd had some water and fruit and cheese, after he'd removed the cuffs and shown me another pair, did he even show me his cock. Then it was my turn to select a pair of cuffs for him. I fumbled a little putting them on, but when I got them secured behind his back, I sank to my knees and toyed with his cock, savoring every second of his stern, stiff heat as I discovered that blow jobs could be a lot more fun when I was in charge.

Tyler gave me so many gifts on that first trip, and the photos were, indeed, a hit, necessitating many more trips back to Vegas. It was easier to get there once I moved to L.A. and started a new life, far from Eric and Michigan and the innocent girl I'd once been. Every time I slip into a cage or offer myself up to a lover to bind, there's still a part of me that remembers the treat Tyler gave me, and what he saw in me before I could see it in myself. I hope every girl is lucky enough to have a Tyler in her life.

# THE CARTOGRAPHER

Angela Caperton

**M**y body is a map.

The continents are accurate and bold, the oceans pale peach. Arching shoals rise in the curves of flesh, and muscles cradle the gentle bend of bay shores. Cliffs rise on subtle scars, the physical reminders of pleasures and pains borne during my lifetime. I own this unyielding truth, that as I age, I do not heal as I did in my twenties. The scars and darkened lines from play and life do not fade so quickly, but remain, like ghost ships on a living sea.

I relish these marks, each fathom, each swell; I see them in the mirror as I towel myself after a shower and smile as I remember Paul's instructions, his control, his steady, calm hand.

But the chart, the glorious, detailed canvas of coastline and island chains, brings my body to life. My breath trips, my belly tightens and between my legs, a river flows. The precise ink that outlines points and coves, battered shores and smooth golden beaches, wraps around my ribs and over the soft flesh of my breast. Dark dots mark ports and cities, their names immortalized in an archaic scrawl so precise I gasp to think of the wondrous pain of each dark needle bite that etched my nerves and bones and now is as delicate as a web upon my skin.

I reach behind me and trace the inked skin on my right shoulder, the first of Paul's gifts. We'd shared so few words on meeting. Maybe it was true—tops know bottoms by smell. Before long, I had come with Paul's cock hard and thick in my pussy, his bite claiming me above my collarbone, my breasts and ass red from the crop he'd used. For weeks, we tested and tasted and enjoyed each other in the new frenzy of our relationship, and then, on our three-month anniversary, Paul showed me his shining silver teeth.

"I want to give you a gift."

My heart ballooned in my chest. Completely aware of time and place, of every whispered breath upon my skin, the quiet buzz of aging fluorescent lighting, I nodded and gave myself to him completely.

I'd been so scared that first time, my orgasm shattering flesh and bone, mind and spirit. There were hours of sexual denial and exquisite, tingling pain as I lay on the table, coupled with true gratitude for the pleasure I found with this extraordinary man after he had drawn my blood and marked me forever his with the biting puncture of merciless needles and ink.

I had come, screaming, my pussy clenching, gripping, as if I could bind him to me, my fingers curled into the sweaty sheets of his bed and crumbling the glossy brochure for the ABC islands— the intense ache of being given the Leewards pushing my nerves and my need to dizzying heights I had never imagined.

Exhausted, collapsed on the bed, Paul covered me, sticky and panting, the pulse of my cunt drawing one long satisfied groan from him as he slipped out, dripping, spent. His most tender kisses circled the bandage covering the islands he'd given me. Six weeks later we swam the waters of Aruba, Bonaire and Curaçao.

"What did it feel like?" Paul asked me the next morning as we sat across from each other, cups of dark roast in our fists.

What? What did he want? My shoulder throbbed with the reminder of the needles, my pussy flooded anew with the memory, but my ears and my mind registered the tone and careful question. I silently screamed for filling, even as I ached from Paul's rides, and my skin flushed with a reverie of his strokes and kisses, but I knew, I knew that wasn't what Paul had asked for.

"It hurt," I said, staring into my cup. Silence covered the table like a cheap tablecloth for several moments, no sound but the uneven tock of the water filter in the refrigerator.

Those invasions of metal and ink—fast, precise, purposed—and my reaction to them seemed as foreign as ancient mosaic art. The distance of hours and his simple question helped me put the pieces in place.

"It hurt, but the pain, it was true and focused." I looked up from my cup into Paul's depthless gray eyes. "I had to believe in you in those minutes. What you did, what I could not see, would mark me forever. What you put on me, in me, is still not mine to see, but as I squeezed my eyes shut, as I felt each piercing, each smear of your cloth over my skin, blessing the pain and taking my blood, I trusted you and took you into me."

I reached behind me and touched the bandage, the tender flesh beneath pulsing seductively beneath my fingers.

Paul reached across the table and took my other hand.

"I have never known such uncharted beauty," he whispered, his voice succulent and rich, the timbre shivering my spine and shocking the thousand pin pricks that mapped my desire upon my skin.

That was the beginning.

Over the years, he added to the map—the Bahamas, the Maldives, the Canary Islands, Greece—each beautiful stamp accompanied by an extended vacation to the location. The last had been a year ago. He'd spent six hours working over my right hip, accurately embellishing the Aleutians. Over the remainder of the weekend, he exhausted me with his hand, his mouth and his cock. I never got more than a couple of hours' reprieve before he spanked, licked, fingered or fucked me. Three months later, we'd spent two weeks on a luxury cruise to the Alaskan islands, my pussy dripping with every coastline I saw that had been immortalized on my skin.

I always savored the slap of his hand across my ass; I whimpered when the thin rattan cane turned my inner thighs zebra red, thanked him with every begging cry for him to fuck me after hours of denial, but I knew I loved him the most when he laid out the ink and displayed the needles like shining, sharp silver promises.

Each time I stared at my body in the mirror, at the thin dark lines that harbored such grand memories, I knew that all too soon, there would be no more oceans to cross, no new lands to chart. He never considered tattooing my arms or legs, but the map of inlets and capes covered nearly all of my torso and upper thighs.

The world, his world, as laid upon my skin, was finite. All that was left was the plain of my left belly stretching over my hip to the base of my back. Once it was marked, Paul would find the canvas full. I knew soon Paul would have no more horizons to chart.

We lived, loved, fucked. I kissed his knees through tears of welcome humiliation minutes before I donned eight-hundred-dollar dresses to stand beside him and greet his business clients and friends, my thighs and ribs raw and chaffing from his measured attentions. He liked it when I wore backless dresses and I did often, displaying paradise to men and women who examined the landscapes and the creamy sea between them. Paul only smiled, his hand straying to the shores, thumbs stroking me to wetness.

I knew the moment he walked through the door. His eyes, blue as the ocean at noon, did not smile, did not storm. They were still, cool, studied. After so many crashing waves and surf-kissed beaches, I recognized Paul's need. *Where? Where this time?* was my first thought.

Right before my pussy soaked my thong.

He didn't speak, didn't move, just stood in the threshold and stared at me, his gaze roiling like reef-churned foam. Then, wordless, he put his laptop case just inside the apartment and retreated, the soft fall of the latch blasting in my ears like the dying chord of a requiem choral. I couldn't move from where I stood in the living room. I stared at the solid stained Georgian door, cold dread in my belly as I waited for him to come back through it.

He returned, well past midnight, walked to me where I sat curled defensively in a chair in the living room, kissed the top of my head and headed straight to the bedroom.

"Come to sleep, Sabrina," he said, his voice heavy with fatigue and scented with whiskey.

That was it. No explanation, no apology. I didn't expect one, and I didn't ask, but I couldn't deny the black ache in my heart as I rose from my chair and followed him to bed, where I knew he would do exactly what he'd commanded me—sleep—and where I would try, though fear turned my stomach hot with acid.

We shared space, spoke little and barely touched for nearly two months. One night, as I undressed for bed, he just stared at me, at my unmarked waist, his gaze reflecting such conflict, the punishing clash of water and earth. I saw exactly what he saw—the end. One more, and the world would be his, the goal complete to sit a pretty prize, no longer a journey, but a memory. He slept that night, his arm around me as if I were the most fragile, handblown glass vase, fingers tracing like airy mist the outlying islands that bordered the last mysterious sea. My eyes stayed closed, my body tense, his strokes on the tattoos a living flame to my need, and I wept, eyes and pussy, wanting him, needing his touch and his will. My pride screamed for me to turn up my face and force him to acknowledge my desire, but I knew as surely as the tears fell from my eyes that what Paul struggled with demanded my respect, not useless dramatics.

The next morning he came to the kitchen, a small suitcase and his laptop in hand. "I have to go out of town for a few days," he mumbled as he put the bags down and approached me.

Blood didn't soak my blouse from the wound. That, at least, was something. I nodded, busying my hands with coffee cups. "Will you be back in time for Reggie's party?"

He covered my hand with his as I went to pour him coffee. He leaned in and kissed me, a distracted pressing of warmth and uncertainty. He cupped my face and gave me a small smile. "I don't know. Make my apologies if I'm not back. I'll call." He stroked my hair and kissed me again on the forehead before he returned to his bags, picked them up. His footsteps echoed in the hall. The door opened and I heard him, his voice muffled by walls. "I'll be back soon, Sabrina."

The door closed behind him and for the first time since I'd met Paul, I struggled to believe him.

He called once, nearly a day after he'd left, to tell me he had arrived at his destination, and that he'd be home soon.

In that moment, I hated the word "soon."

Three days: work, go home, fret, toss, turn, rise, repeat. Reggie's party, a stuttered phone call of regret, and the kernel of doubt became a stone of concern, then a ball of anger and uncertainty. I managed my accounts at work with nearly neurotic ferocity, to the point of driving my assistant home early with red-rimmed eyes on day five of Paul's absence. I hated myself for that. The local flower shop reaped the benefits of my guilt.

If I didn't get a grip during Paul's absence, a whole host of businesses along Lakeview Avenue would fatten their wallets with the weight of my angst—if my assistant didn't walk out first.

I turned the knob of our apartment at nine and dropped my purse along with the completely self-indulgent fast-food tacos I'd picked up on my commute home from work.

Paul stood in the living room, his expression carved of caramel marble, his eyes blue as summer heaven and calm, still and...determined.

My gut tightened, the lips of my pussy puckered and moistened, even as my throat burned with the bitter heat of a thousand accusations, condemnations and general fuck-yous. Over a week without a word! He could have been dead in an Amsterdam alley or bent over getting his ass fucked by a New York bouncer named Mikey, and I wouldn't have had a clue. My world had revolved around an unheard ring tone on my cell, a never-received text or email. Nothing.

And now he stood in his living room, watching me walk through the door like the days hadn't passed, stared at me with a gaze still as a frozen lake, flat as the doldrums.

We waited, each in our slips. I shut the door, but didn't move.

"I'm sorry I didn't phone. I didn't plan on returning so soon." Paul clasped his hands before him as he leaned against the back of the couch.

My mind exploded with all the replies I wanted to give. *Fuck*

*you, Paul! Where the fuck have you been?* registered as the clear
winner among all the possibilities, but I beat the impulse into the
ground. "Are you hungry?" Was he? In spite of my emotional
desire to throw heavy objects at him, I was. I was ravenous.

I glanced at the fast-food bag. "I can make something."

"Starving. And dinner is in the oven."

We went to the kitchen, my purse and the rejected tacos left at
the door. We ate delicious take-out Thai, barely spoke, but now
Paul watched me with the intensity I had come to love through
the years. Hunger and resolve burned bright in the blue, and the
muscles of my shoulders relaxed just a little. We both knew a
gulf lay between us.

He rose, chopsticks placed neatly across his half-full plate.
"Come with me, Sabrina."

A warm shiver slid down my spine. His tone allowed no
disobedience, and in that moment, he put our future firmly
in my lap. I could submit without question, go to him as he
commanded, or rail, resist and pick up my purse and soggy tacos
on the way out of his life. The choice was mine.

I mirrored his movements, placed the chopsticks across the
plate, and rose, following his retreating back into the bedroom.

Candles flickered on the nightstands and dresser, the table he
used when he tattooed me at the center of a pool of lamplight,
and on a smaller, enameled table beside it, the glittering treasure
of needles and ink.

He pulled me into his arms and kissed me, his tongue
demanding, hot, invading, punishing my lips, dominating my
tongue, his hard body pressed so tightly against me, his belt
buckle bit into my stomach, and the pulse of his cock shot sparks
through my thigh to shock my pussy to aching life.

He worshipped me with his mouth as we shed our clothes.
His teeth teased my nipples and his fingers stroked my wet cunt

until I came in a grinding orgasm that trembled my legs. While I was still panting, my feeble kisses on his chest, he picked me up and placed me on the table, my back nipped by the cool padded vinyl.

He stood by the table and ran his hands over my body, cupping my breasts, tracing each hollow of my ribs, splaying his fingers wide over the center of my belly. My blood rushed to heat beneath his touch, my nerves alert to the pressure and possession. He traced the outline of the small tuft of hair that crowned my pussy, and when his fingers again slipped inside me, I gripped the sides of the table and arched against his hand. My clit, already sensitive from his previous manipulations, bloomed anew as he circled and teased it. Orgasm floated nearby, bobbing like a cork just beyond my grasp.

"This is the last, Sabrina," Paul whispered as he kissed me tenderly and continued to explore my wet pussy.

"Yes," I breathed, my heart stabbed with a dark ache even as my body sang at the edges of ecstasy. The last, and as Paul slid his long index finger into my pussy, pumping and grinding, adding another, then a third, I knew he'd make this last one something I would never forget. I came hard, sweat tacking me to the table, the muscles of my stomach vibrating with the force of it.

He prepped me in silence, my eyes squeezed shut by his command. My stomach and left side were cleaned and stenciled, and soon the hum of the gun echoed in the room and in my blood.

The first cool touch of his gloved hand on my belly balled anticipation in my whole body, and with the first glorious bite of the needles, a flood of relief ran down my spine to flow out of my pussy.

His breath caressed the abraded skin, blew comfort over

the hot lacerations, each vibrating puncture another eternal branding of him on my soul. The dull, pressured pain radiated through my skin, into my veins. It sailed across my chest to ache in my nipples and turned my cunt hot with the pounding pulse of expectation. Suspended in time and in the skin of desire, the mechanical whine of the gun became an anthem, the stroke of gauze over the new marks, a prayer. When Paul's lips and tongue ravaged my breasts, the blast of arousal nearly bowed my back to breaking. He pushed me back down.

"Be still," he commanded, and with considerable effort, I complied. He licked each nipple again, cruel in the challenge, and my pussy watered, my heart thudded.

I floated in darkness, clamped my teeth against groans and pants. I sweated, the vinyl greasy with the slick heat of the trial, my hair sticking to my neck. He shut off the gun, the song dying in the grip of my disappointment. He covered my belly with a sterile bandage and rolled me over gently. His deep chuckle surprised me.

He smeared my juices over my ass, his fingers sliding into my pussy, toying, teasing. I bit my lip and squirmed against his touch. I wanted his cock, needed it more than ever before, and I knew he knew it. The crack of flesh against flesh shocked me before my right cheek burned with an outline of his hand. Again and again, he struck my round ass, the glorious cadence of the strokes driving me hard into the table. The deliciously familiar shock of the spanking rocketed jagged pleasure to my cunt and nipples. I ground against the table, letting the padded top stroke my clit, climax just a few blows away. I clenched the muscles of my ass, anticipating the next blow, hoping it would be the one to toss me from the impossibly high cliff of my arousal.

Then came the snap of fresh gloves and the whine of the gun. The bite near my spine drew out my frustration in a cry.

"Be still!" he growled, the tattoo gun humming above my skin.

My heartbeat rocked my whole body, but I willed my muscles slack, squeezed my eyes shut and focused on the buzzing and the swipe of gauze over newly minted skin.

The nerves at the base of my back and my side flared outrage as the needles assaulted, the controlled invasion of metal and ink burning and razing as my skin submitted to change. Change: each pulsing edge of pain brought me closer to it, pushed me toward a door I had to walk through. I had no vision of what lay beyond it and could only see the swirling black emptiness that my closed eyes now knew.

Fatigue weighed on my muscles. Hours of exquisite pain and ratcheted sexual tension began to hollow me out. I wanted it to end even while I fought time to stop. More than once, Paul had given me that wild juxtaposition of desire and dread. Would I know it again?

He shut off the gun, and for a moment silence crashed against the walls. I heard Paul remove his gloves, then with tender attention, he smoothed over the fresh tattoo with gauze.

"It's beautiful, Sabrina. You're beautiful."

His words broke over my heart, closing my throat with the sincerity and finality of his tone.

He gripped me at my ribs, pulling me back toward him. The table scuffed against the floor, the clatter of the gun hitting tile adding to the blast of sound that ricocheted off the walls. Rough, urgent, he folded me over the edge of the table, pulling my wrists together in the wide expanse of his long, strong fingers. My shoulders screamed, and the fresh tattoo on my back raged at the pressure of my trapped wrists rubbing against it. He kicked my legs apart, and in one long, graceless penetration, filled my denied pussy with his rock-hard cock.

Nothing tender, nothing given—he simply took. He held me prone, fucked me, pounding my body with a fury beyond even his usual assault. The raw, new skin on my belly and back trilled sharp arias of pain as he ground me against the table. My pussy clenched around his cock, hungry, devouring each selfish invasion, and as he fucked me, my clit bounced against the table's edge, tortured and poised, as our bodies slapped together in harmony, the music ours alone. Tingling dots of shock radiated off my stomach and back, the hard slide of his cock in and out of me; the musk of blood and ink, sweat and sex, swirled around us, cloaking and binding as the wave within me rose higher, higher, and with another shattering thrust, the crest curled and I fell, bliss and oblivion mine, his, ours; the world ours in ecstatic perfection.

His howl echoed my scream. He came, grinding into me three more times, my channel flooded by his semen and my own release. His harsh panting branded my shoulder as he rested his head between the blades. His cock slipped out of me and a part of me broke.

The end had come at last.

Yet he never stopped touching me, never let my skin cool, my body rest. The night stretched to the following day, and that evening, exhausted and momentarily sated, he held me against him, my back to his chest. My mind, no longer cottoned by ecstatic sensation, coldly rushed to the fore.

"What now?" I whispered into the faint light offered by the few remaining guttering candles.

He didn't move, but his breath had lost its calm rhythm. He rolled away from me, and I cursed my impetuous question.

He rose from the bed and went to where his suitcase sat against the far wall. He picked it up and carried it to the bed. I sat up, pulling my knees to my chest, the sheet a useless shield against despair. He reached into the side pouch and pulled out a small ring with a key on it, then tossed it to me.

I picked it up. I didn't want it, wanted to hurl it back at him, but all I could do was stare at it in my hand. The end.

"We live."

A flutter of paper landed next to me, what looked like a neatly folded chart and a glossy photo of a large sailboat. I put the key down and looked at the boat a moment, before picking up the map. The slight gray font at the edge of it read *Oceania*. An outline had been drawn around a section and written above it in Paul's neat hand, a single name: *Polynesia*. From Hawaii to the north and Rapa Nui in the distant east, thousands of square miles of ocean and islands stared back at me. The journey would take a lifetime.

My belly and back tingled as I looked up into Paul's face. He picked up the picture of the boat and took the key from where I had dropped it.

"I've already given her a name," he said. "She's called *Legend*."

# THE APIARY

## Megan Butcher

This is the last story Miranda tells me about the chair:

*It was abandoned. I saw it on the sidewalk, beside a run-down church, abandoned buildings on either side, windows boarded up like eyes. There were cracked, full-length mirrors, a fridge without its doors, filing cabinets with drawers gaping. The chair's spine finned up above the trash. The sun hit it and the grain glowed.*

The room is stuffy, west facing, with the sun pouring in. I can feel the sweat running in channels through the hair on my calves. It soaks the sides of my camisole as it runs in rivulets from my pits. The smell is acrid, fireworks just burst.

She pauses; absently orders me to move forward, to press the fronts of my thighs against the back of the chair. to keep my hands tight behind me.

*I swam into the garbage. Grabbed the top rung and pulled. It hardly moved. That just made me want it more.*

Her voice loses its dreamy quality, slices through the dust

motes and cat hair in the sunbeams. I squint.

*What, do you want more?*

I clench. I want to tell her. I want to spin her a story, a fairy tale of our time together, not this story with no happy ending.

The first time she told me about the chair she told me in the cab on the way home from the bar. We were leaving the monthly women's dance at the Eagle. I usually didn't go, not my crowd, but the April air was stirring my hormones and making my pussy ache. I'd been single the whole winter, hibernating in a small, drafty room under piles of blankets. The night of the dance, my body had had enough solitude and woolen weight, wanted swaying hips and loud music moving through it.

Even if the bar hadn't been near empty when I got there, Miranda would have stood out. Her cropped hair—a dashing black shot through with silver—was in need of a trim. She was a head taller than the next tallest woman in the room, with severe features: a blunt chin and large hooked nose. She was leaning back against the long bar in front and watched me walk slowly across the room.

I ordered my beer and she turned toward me, placed her left arm on the bar, leaned down. She opened her mouth and looked surprised at herself when she spoke.

*You smell like honey.*

Her voice was a smooth contralto and I was immediately taken. I looked up into gunmetal eyes laughing at the edges, dead serious at the center. I smiled and put my hand on her forearm, took a long drink of the beer that had appeared in front of me.

We made out on the dance floor; we made out in the bathroom. We finally decided to go. She found us a cab, opened the door for me, went around the other side to let herself in. She

gave the cabbie an address twenty blocks away and then directions, slid her hand between my knees, tiny strokes on the back
of my thigh making all my skin come alive.

*I want you to see this chair I have. I found it after a storm
one day. One of those storms where it looks like the clouds are
eating themselves, rolling over and over on top of each other. I
left work early, took the long way home to pass the community
garden. It was August, full summer heat, the sun just appearing,
brassy at this late hour. At the back of the garden there was a
small path overgrown so badly I'd never noticed it before. It
led around the back of the shed, through a copse of trees and
up a bit to the crest of a hill where they kept the hives—hardly
buzzing after the rain. The river opened up below, caught the last
of the sun and hurt my eyes. I turned and saw a long shadow.
This chair, a wooden chair, was nearly covered in ivy, practically forgotten near the trees, like it was growing out of them. I
wanted it. I tore the vines off and its heft felt good in my hand,
the whole way home through the still-heavy air.*

We went upstairs when we got to her house, her in the lead,
me watching her hard ass work through tight jeans. She turned
in at the first room on her left. I hovered in the doorway. The
room was empty except for the chair. It was unremarkable, not
at all what I expected after the story she'd spun out over the long
rain-slicked streets.

She beckoned me in.

*Keep your eyes open. No matter what.*

I stepped carefully a few feet into the room, like I was looking
for a hidden secret, or something to ooze from the bare walls
perhaps, since the only place to hide anything was a small chest
of drawers near the tall narrow window. She stood with square
shoulders on the other side of the chair from me.

*Say "Miranda, no," and I'll stop. That's a promise.*

She waited for a response from me. I looked at her closely for a moment, her strong posture, her left arm loose and relaxed, the calm of her gaze. I nodded.

*Take your clothes off. Start with your shirt.*

The shirt was a complicated affair, with buttons and ties, hooks and crossing loose pieces. I fumbled at first, then my fingers found the right rhythm and I played it for her, the material revealing my olive skin in random geometries, sliding slowly down my sloped shoulders, making my nipples hard and darker red as it brushed them. My breasts felt fuller for her gaze on them. I dropped the shirt, finally, to the subtlest intake of her breath.

*Grab your tits and squeeze them. Tilt your head forward, too. Keep your eyes on the floor.*

The pressure of my hands on my breasts made my vulva grow between my legs, like it might blossom out obscenely.

She opened drawers and closed them. I heard wood on wood, metal on wood, clinks, a few quiet slaps of leather on flesh. I felt her in front of me but didn't raise my head, just kept squeezing and pulling and twisting until I thought I might come just from waiting.

The collar looked narrow but felt wide on my short neck as she put it around me and pulled it tight, a feeling I would come to crave in short order. It was leather, supple, old and well cared for, a plain matte black with one large ring fixed to the front, directly over my Adam's apple.

She moved me to stand behind the chair, told me to move closer till my legs made contact. The wood seemed to vibrate against my thighs.

I felt a hand on the back of my neck, and I bent over till my forehead nearly touched the seat. She had both wrists grabbed up quick in her meaty left hand.

*Stay there, like that. So pretty.*

Over at the dresser, I heard metal on metal. Then, one end of a chain was clipped to a ring on one leg of a chair and fed through the ring in my collar, the other end clipped to the other leg. I could move my head freely side to side, but only two inches farther down, two inches farther up. The top rail of the chair bit into my hips.

She took my wrists back, pushed my arms as far as my shoulders would let her. I could feel the heat from her cunt; it matched my own and I wanted it, wanted in. I started to squirm, wanted to pull myself around to get at her with my face.

*Not yet, honey girl.*

The back struts of the chair quivered and frayed, grew tendrils at the edges that shimmered and hovered like a glimmering of hummingbirds. Then they stopped and wavered out in grasping prehensile threads. They twined into thick, blind ropes reaching suckers for my legs. I tried to shift away but she had moved to stand right behind me; pressed me in, into the chair. A high-pitched hiss swirled in my larynx.

*Do you see those?*

The first one touched my leg and the hiss gathered force, moved up and started to move out, from between clenched teeth.

*I thought you might.*

She drew her nails hard across my thighs in random crossing lines, leaving red welts rising. The tendrils followed the heat and wove their mesh around me. I was immobilized from the hips down, merged with the chair.

*It's not everyone who will, you know.*

The heat from her cunt against my ass was nearly unbearable.

The hiss receded partway; I swallowed the rest. She let go of my hands, placed them one at a time on the edge of the chair, caressing and smoothing them into place. She stepped back a few paces, told me to lift my head, to look at her.

Miranda was bigger than life. She caught all the light in the room, breathed with all the force of it. Or it breathed through her. She was tall, wide, well padded, with a waist cinched in practically under her breasts. The hunch and twist of her upper spine was just apparent over a right shoulder that sloped severely and curled forward. Her right hand was a soft cup near her cunt. She had long haunches and delicate ankles.

For sex, for fucking, for bossing people around, she had told me, sometime between the mess of the bar and this clean space, she prefers being naked, for her body to move as it would and does without the binding seams of clothes not built for her shape, to let the animal grace of her body appear unsheathed.

She let me stare for a few moments, take as much of her in as I could with just my eyes. She turned slightly this way first, then that, then padded toward me. I bowed my head, but she hooked a finger under my chin and lifted my gaze back up, pressing my nose into her full bush. I closed my eyes and breathed my lungs full.

*Put your tongue out. You want to taste me.*

And I did. I stretched my short, blunt tongue as far as I could make it go. I lifted my head, stretched farther, caught the edge of her clit hood and pushed as much as I could underneath it. Her body twitched; she leaned into me lightly.

More, though, than my tongue around her swelling clit, I wanted her sweaty dancing smell to cover my face and be the only thing possible for me to breathe. I tried to lift my hands to grab her ass and push her farther into my mouth. They moved a half inch off the surface before a magnetic tension pulled them back down with a hard smack. I fell farther forward instead, putting less pussy where I wanted it. The tendrils pulled tight

and rasped my skin raw. I grunted in irritation and discomfort.
She laughed.

*I like you.*

Her voice was a thick liquid coating the inside of my head. I
lifted my mouth again to drink.


I stayed drunk for months, barely lifting my head, hardly eating,
just breathing in the air she breathed out, working intermittently
and walking aimless circles around the rooms till she got back
again. I didn't give up my apartment so much as not answer
the phone when my roommates called for the rent. There was
no need to go back for my things. I'd been living like a nomad,
moving from room to room, from city to city for three years,
following my ex as he moved, too. My books were like bread-
crumbs on friends' coffee tables, at the foot of other lovers' beds.
I never tried to find my way back, but knowing it was there was
a comfort.

Her space became mine, too, with surprising ease—it wasn't
even a few months before it felt like I'd been there forever, had
no life before this one with her. She made enough at her job
that I could work part time from home and so spent more time
there than she did. My clothes looked comfortable tossed over
the cedar chest at the end of her—our—bed. My smell started to
combine with hers to permeate the space.

And the smell of our fucking quickly sunk into the plaster
and wood of the structure around us. We fucked in every room,
on any surface that afforded us purchase, at random times, after
not talking for hours, or in the middle of chores, sometimes after
long hours of teasing messages over the phone and through our
email inboxes.

She took me one morning over the kitchen table. I'd been
clearing the dishes, my robe loosely tied and falling partway

down one shoulder. I was stiff and sore from the night before, cranky with impending migraine. As I was leaning over to get the last mug, I felt her soft right hand pressed in an arc between my shoulder blades, pushing me down till my breasts were flattened against the table amongst the detritus of breakfast.

My body started to respond as it always did. The heat emanating out from her hands softened me all over, and in turn my hands automatically clasped above my head the way she liked to see them. My hair fell across my eyes and face, tickling my nose and falling inside my mouth. My face was pressed hard to the table. Her hand pressed into my lower back.

She pulled my asscheeks open.

*Such a nice hole.*

I felt the spit drip down, her finger on my pucker. I clenched.

"Miranda," I said. "No." The cat behind the vines on her favorite mug grinned and swallowed my words.

She didn't stop. I couldn't open my mouth again, too full. Too full. Hair and the sawdust of useless words. It took hours, seconds, one decade off my life as I disappeared.

Then I was back; I was on the floor; I was curled up; I was crying choking sobs that started just north of my pubic bone and came from a place that never ends. She stroked my hair but it felt like nothing at all.

I was barely a whisper. "Miranda, I said no."

*Honey girl, I'm sorry. I didn't hear you. I'm so sorry.*

I just shook my head and squeezed my eyes shut. Let the crying come.

It was weeks before my body responded to her again at all. Weeks after that before she would trust herself to touch me. Even when we touched, we started again slower than we had started at first, with her asking for permission for any touch, then using only her soft hand—my favorite one—to do so. Then we progressed to her other hand, then both, then her mouth, too.

The door of the room with the chair stayed closed.

We were gentle, learning each other all over again, new patterns and rhythms, how our bodies might fit together this time. We started and stopped, her voice slow and low every time she asked permission to do something that was suddenly new.

One morning, I opened the door to the room. It smelled dusty and sweet. She came home and went upstairs to change. I heard the squeak of the floor, the scrape of the chair on the hardwood floor. When I went up, I found her standing naked in front of the chair, the collar in her hand. I went to her when she beckoned.

The silence has gone too long. I thought I was supposed to stay quiet. Her voice sounds like it's been rasped.

*I said. What do you want. More.*

I bend over till my forehead nearly touches the seat. My shoulders tremble with my palms pressed together between the blades, elbows like sharp wings. The back struts of the chair quiver and fray. Grow still. She moves quiet across the room on her bare feet, draws her nails across my thighs in *x*'s, red welts rising.

Her voice is quiet now.

*More.*

I stare at the seat, the grain glowing in the sun, I drop my tears into the crevices where the sun doesn't catch. Unclasp my hands. Stretch them wide, fan the fingers over the back of my rib cage. I collect all my breath under them; they move like sated bees through golden air until they come to rest on the cheeks of my ass for a splintered second; they pull, gently. I'm open. The sun is warm on my asshole.

# WIRED

## Lisabet Sarai

P ay dirt!

I stared at the images arrayed in Krishna's browser, my heart-beat accelerating each time I clicked on a new tab. Here was a tanned surfer type lashed to a cross of wood, his cock straining against the tight leather thong that pulled it against his belly. A masked woman clad in latex posed behind the cross with a wicked-looking paddle. I swallowed the lump that had formed in my throat.

In the next tab, a muscular black man knelt before a pair of shiny high-heeled boots, his wrists cuffed to his ankles, a red ball-gag strapped into his mouth. His penis jutted up between his bulging thighs, the bulb shiny with precome. My eyes caressed the gleaming ebony skin, sweaty from his effort at keeping his balance. The man's eyes were wide with fear. A riding crop dangled from the unseen mistress's hand, just at the edge of the picture. My pussy grew damper.

Tab after tab, image after image, there were men in every

sort of bondage: with chains looped across hairy chests, silver duct tape wrapping contorted limbs, strands of leather biting into tender flesh and intricate rope patterns whose beauty only heightened their perversity; men cocooned in plastic wrap or latex. I squeezed my thighs together. My clit throbbed, hungry, angry with me for my neglect. Soon, I promised myself, I'd attend to my needy cunt. I wanted to understand the full extent of Krishna's depravity.

Most pictures focused on the immobilized victims. They merely hinted at the presence of the dominant. The image on the last tab was an exception. A naked man bent over the footboard of a double bed. His legs were sprawled wide, ankles encircled a dozen times with rough-looking rope and then fastened to a spreader bar. His arms stretched out parallel to the edge of the bed, lashed to the rail at the wrist and above the elbow. His chest, looped with more rope, lay on a pillow. He had turned his head away from the camera, but the tension in his body was obvious.

A blonde wearing heels and little else stood in the triangle formed by his legs. Black straps circled her upper thighs, contrasting with the creamy skin of her full ass. She gripped his hips. Her back was to the camera, so her face was hidden. Her strap-on dildo was invisible, too, but there was no doubt at all that it was buried deep in her bound companion's butt.

I nearly came just from looking.

It wasn't just the pose, the power of the woman and the helplessness of her victim. My rear hole twitched as I imagined the bulk of her cock stretching my rectum, but that wasn't what really got to me, either. What turned me on the most was the indisputable fact that the man was a willing collaborator. His elaborate binding could never have been accomplished without his cooperation. Being bound, being fucked: that's what he had wanted.

That's what Krishna wanted. My mouth watered at the realization. When I'd broken into Krishna's system, I had been looking for some key, some way of getting past his reserve. I hadn't quite been expecting—this.

I glanced at my watch: seven fifteen. No one else on the team ever arrived before eight, and except on Mondays when we had a staff meeting, Krishna rarely got to work before eleven. I had time for a quick jill, if I dared.

I could have gone off to the ladies', of course. But I wanted to gaze at the picture as I came.

I rucked my skirt up around my waist and pushed my right hand under the elastic of my panties. The cotton was soaked. I stroked one finger across my swollen clit. Pleasure shuddered through me. This wouldn't take long at all.

I rocked back and forth on Krishna's ergonomic chair, two fingers probing my wet folds and my thumb wriggling my clit. With my other hand, I plucked at my nipples. Vibration shimmered down internal strings to my core. My pussy clenched around my fingers. Everything tightened as I frigged myself hard, staring at the monitor.

What would it feel like to be that woman? I'd never worn a strap-on, but sometimes I browsed the online toy stores, just out of curiosity. Some dildos offered bases designed to stimulate the clit. I'd even seen double-headed dildos, intended to penetrate both the fucker and the fucked. My hands busy, I imagined being filled by the fat base of my strap-on while I plunged into the ass of my helpless victim. I pictured Krishna splayed underneath me, his lean body straining against the bonds, the sand-colored ropes biting into his smooth, nut brown skin. His black curls were plastered against his slender neck. His round butt tensed each time I entered him. I could hear him moan, cry, call my name, begging to be released, begging my pardon for making me wait so very long. I just fucked him harder. I knew that despite his protestations, that was what he wanted.

A sharp climax ripped through me and pleasure exploded between my legs, sending fragments spinning to my extremities. My eyes screwed shut, I rocked with the force of my come.

The orgasm left me trembling and weak, slumped against the chair back. When I had recovered enough to look around, I discovered that Krishna's screen saver had kicked in, hiding the outrageous photos. I pulled down my skirt, wiped my sticky hands on his seat—it served him right for frustrating me—and typed in the password again so I could close his browser. I didn't want him to know that I'd discovered his secret. Not yet.

I glanced around his cubicle one more time, making sure that I hadn't left any telltale clues other than a faint odor of pussy. The doe-eyed, jet-haired beauty framed on his desk gave me a reproachful look. "Come on," I said to her. "Lighten up. You're just his sister. I'm not stealing him from you." I refused to feel guilty for hacking Krishna's machine. It was, after all, for his own good.

I'd been in lust with Krishna ever since he joined the company six months earlier. He looked like the hero from some Bolly-wood extravaganza: lush black hair that curled around his ears, eyes like molten chocolate, unblemished skin the color of varnished wood. His arched nose gave him a regal air. His ripe lips screamed to be kissed.

The other engineers wore polos and jeans. Krishna came to work every day in pressed slacks and a white dress shirt. As the day warmed, he might unbutton the collar and roll up the sleeves. I'd think of excuses to walk by his cubicle, just to admire the contrast of the snowy fabric against the smooth, dark-furred skin of his forearms.

I'm the only woman in our twenty-person development group.

I've fended off advances from several of my teammates as well as from a manager or two over the years. I know better than to get involved with a coworker. I've seen where that can lead.

But in Krishna's case, I couldn't help myself. Every night when I went home, I'd lecture myself about being professional, not letting my feelings undermine my future. Then I'd dig out my vibrator and pretend it was Krishna, telling myself that a little fantasy couldn't hurt.

The next day I'd be back, trying to get Krishna's attention.

Not that it did any good. He acted shy with everyone, but to me he barely said a word, though I put myself in his path as often as I could. I'd drop by, pretending to need his advice about some algorithm or asking about the status of his code. I'd gossip about the latest upper management pronouncements. I'd drop hints, telling him I was going away for the weekend, sighing about the fact that I had to do it alone. I invited him for coffee, for lunch—he was always too busy, or so he told me.

"Are you married?" I asked him finally, determined to be rude if I had to. "Do you have a girlfriend?"

"Oh, no," he replied, looking flustered. "Not yet. I don't have enough money to marry. That's why I'm here in the States."

"Who's that, then?" I pointed to the photo on his neat desk, a voluptuous woman wearing a sari and a sweet expression.

"That's Sita, my younger sister. Actually, I'm trying to earn enough for her dowry, as well." He glanced down at his long-fingered hands, spread across his keyboard, then back at me, seeming confused. "Excuse me, but I've got to get back to work, Liz. Sorry."

What the hell was wrong? I'm no movie star, but I'm attractive enough, if you like the slender, athletic type rather than busty cheesecake. I'm the smartest person on the team—I'm not bragging, ask anyone—and I've got a decent personality.

I'm creative, helpful, sociable and occasionally even funny. I've also got a wicked imagination, though most of my mates don't know about that. Why was Krishna completely insensitive to my charm?

Now I knew. My Krishna's desires were just a bit...unusual. I was confident, though, that I could give him what he wanted. Especially considering my own reaction to his dirty pictures.

*I should put together a plan*, I thought, staring at the code on my own screen around lunchtime. The low-level hum between my legs made it difficult to concentrate. *I should do some research. Buy some equipment.* I'm usually the careful, methodical type. Self-discipline is my middle name. I'd waited six months; I could stand waiting a few days longer.

Something in me rebelled at the notion. My body screamed with impatience. Deep down, too, I was a bit worried that if I waited, I'd lose my nerve.

"Hey, Liz." I started and blushed, surprised in my reverie by the object of my machinations.

"Oh! Krishna!" I moved a pile of books off my extra chair. "Come on in. Sit down." Had he sensed my concentrated lust beaming in his direction? I brushed my hair out of my eyes. Lately, I'd been trying to let it grow. I wanted to look more feminine.

"Ah, no, that's okay. I just wanted to make sure that you check in all your work tonight before you leave. I'm doing a major backup of the repository." In addition to his development duties, Krishna also served as system administrator for our group.

"Um, of course. Definitely." I smoothed my skirt over my thighs, glad that I hadn't worn jeans.

"Good. I'll start the scripts around ten. You'll be finished by then, right?"

"You know me. I'm a morning person. I'm never here after six. But you should probably talk to Steve and Rob."

"Yes, I will. I'm going around letting everyone know." So he hadn't just come to see me. I was ridiculously disappointed. "See you later."

"Yeah. See you later, Krishna." I watched him make his graceful way down the aisle between the two rows of dividers.

Ten p.m. tonight: I digested this information as I chewed my chicken sandwich. Krishna would be, in all likelihood, alone in the office. Alone except for me, that is.

I forced myself to sit in front of my screen all afternoon, although there was no way I was going to get any work done. I resisted the urge to visit Babeland or Adam and Eve to check out some of the toys. I knew that was dangerous. The company might well have installed spy software to monitor our browsing.

A chill shot through me. If they did have snoop tools installed, they'd know about Krishna's kink. They'd fire him. Hell, he was H1-B—they'd send him back to India.

I calmed my racing heart. No use worrying. None of that was going to happen tonight. Tonight I was going to give Krishna what he wanted. What he deserved.

I left the office on the dot of five. Once home, I booted my laptop and searched for bondage information. I only had a few hours, but I was determined to learn as much as I could about tools and techniques. Wikipedia had a great article about Shibari, complete with amazing photos of rope-tangled flesh and links to primary sources. I found sites dedicated to duct tape and others specializing in handcuffs.

I couldn't eat. I drank a glass of orange juice as I paged through photos and skimmed blogs. Finally, around eight, I lay down in my darkened bedroom and closed my eyes. My head spun with kinky images and advice. My pussy was soaked and swollen. What was I going to do to Krishna? I really didn't know. I'd just have to trust my instincts.

The building was mostly dark when I drove into the parking lot. A motion sensor switched on an overhead light as I approached the door. I punched in my security code; a buzz, a click, and I was in the lobby. The guard's desk was unoccupied. The click of my heels echoed through the dim, empty corridors.

I slipped through the fire doors that led to my group's space. The glassed-in server room was lit, plus the ceiling fluorescents above Krishna's office. The floor was carpeted in this area; I moved without a sound.

Krishna sat with his back to me, focused on his screen. From where I stood, outside his cubicle, I couldn't see what he was gazing at so intently. But I could guess.

"Krishna," I murmured.

He swiveled around, simultaneously flicking the OFF switch on his monitor. I could tell that the move was well practiced. "Liz! What are you doing here?" He backed the chair toward the desk as I entered, trying to put more distance between us.

"I came to visit you. I thought you might be lonely." I took another step forward. He had nowhere to go. An embarrassed grin stretched his lush lips.

His shirt was open to the middle button. A gold chain nestled in the black curls on his breast. He was breathing hard; the rise and fall of his chest made the necklace glitter. I dropped my gaze to his lap. As I expected, I found a significant bulge.

"Um, no, I'm fine, just making sure the backups are all right. I was going to leave in a few minutes..."

I brushed a fingertip across the lump in his groin. He shivered. His nervous smile evaporated. "Don't go yet," I crooned. "I just got here."

I had changed out of my work clothes. I now wore a tight

purple jersey with a V-neck that flattered my modest breasts and a short denim skirt. I trailed a finger down my throat to my cleavage. Krishna's eyes followed in fascination. I retraced my path to my throat, the feathery touch making my nipples pebble, and removed the scarf I'd draped around my neck.

He gripped the curved arms of his desk chair, as though he were afraid he was going to faint. I slipped the scarf under the chair arm and wrapped it twice around his wrist, then tied a firm knot. He didn't move. The lavender silk was lovely against his brown skin.

"Is that too tight?" My voice was barely louder than a whisper. Krishna shook his head. His eyes were black pools of lust. I pulled a second scarf from my back pocket, this one turquoise, and secured his other arm. He trembled when I touched him.

I seated myself on his lap. His erection poked deliciously at my bottom, even through the heavy denim of my skirt. *He must be huge*, I thought. I'd know before long.

His beautiful face hovered inches from mine. He dropped his eyes, focusing on his bound wrist. "No," I protested, lifting his chin so that he could not look away. "Look at me, for once. I've been trying to get your attention for months. You're not getting away from me this time."

Krishna's lips parted, as though he was about to speak. I stopped him with a fierce kiss. At first he resisted, struggling against the scarves, his lips pressed tightly together to keep me out. I braced my palms against his chest and bore down on him, prying those lips apart with my tongue.

All at once he let go. His mouth was as lush and hot as it looked, tasting of coffee and anise. I fed on him, nibbling and sucking, pouring out my long-denied lust. He opened to me, not exactly passive, but giving me control.

My bare thighs grew damp with the heat of that kiss. My

nipples peaked into aching knots. His smell surrounded me, soap and sweat and the coconut oil he used on his hair. His rod prodded the crack between my legs. I burrowed deeper into his mouth, kissing him harder.

He arched up, grinding himself against my ass. I broke the kiss and hopped off his lap. "Oh, no, you don't! That belongs to me."

"Please, Liz…" Krishna looked miserable and needy.

"Oh, now you're begging!" I strutted back and forth in front of him on my high-heeled boots, giving him an eyeful of my slutty outfit. "Maybe I should just leave you here, tied up and frustrated. After all, you've frustrated me for an awfully long time."

"No, please…"

"What will Steve and Rob think when they come in tomorrow and find you tied to your chair? And when they turn on your monitor?"

I reached over his shoulder to click the switch. As I'd expected, the screen was full of kinky images, men hog-tied and suspended, secured in a hundred uncomfortable positions, all with huge, hungry erections.

Krishna looked terrified. "Don't tell anyone—please don't tell! They'll deport me if they find out…."

"Your secret is safe with me." I tangled my fingers in his opulent hair. "Provided that you cooperate, of course."

He didn't bother to ask me what I meant.

I took a moment to drink in the gorgeous picture he made. If his complexion had been lighter, I knew I would have seen the blood heating his cheeks. The festive scarves looked like they'd be pretty effective in keeping him where he was. But they weren't enough, I sensed. Not for him.

I scanned his office, seeking inspiration, kicking myself for not having brought some of the heavy twine that I used to tie up the bougainvillea on my balcony. On the other hand, the twine might be too coarse. It might seriously damage that flawless dark skin.

Krishna watched me, eyes wide; frightened and expectant. The weight of his need settled on me like a boulder. Suddenly I felt lost. What was I doing? What did I know about bondage? I paced around the office, trying to act confident and bossy. Playing for time.

*Don't screw things up now, Liz.* He squirmed a bit against the silk, testing the strength of the bonds. My pussy spasmed at the sight. *Think.*

I was getting desperate. Then my eyes lighted on the pile of Cat 5 Ethernet cables coiled neatly in the corner. Aha! Once again I gave thanks for Krishna's role as systems administrator.

I turned my back on him, bending from the waist to rummage through the collection. My skirt rode up, revealing the purple silk panties that clung to my ass. Krishna's gaze was a hot spotlight on my scarcely concealed flesh. Could he see the dampness of my inner thighs?

Each cable was labeled in my victim's precise handwriting. I selected one marked as ten meters. *Should be long enough.* As an afterthought, I grabbed a couple of short lengths as well. All three were an electric blue color, which I thought would harmonize nicely with the scarves.

I hadn't thought Krishna's eyes could open wider. I was wrong.

"No, Liz...don't..."

"I'll do what I want." I was already wrapping the longer cable around his torso. The plastic-sheathed wire circled under his arms and ran across the back of his chair. I made four or five loops across his chest, careful to align them nicely in parallel stripes across his snow white shirt. The vivid blue strands were tight enough to indent the fabric and to dig in slightly where they crossed his partially bared chest.

Krishna released a deep moan.

"Too tight?" I paused in my labors, brushing my hair away from my sweaty forehead. His eyes were closed, long lashes feathering his beautiful brown cheeks. I reached into his lap to squeeze his erection through his trousers. His eyes snapped open. He was harder than ever.

"No, no, it's just...I shouldn't...what if someone sees..."

"That's my problem, not yours. You don't have any choice anymore. In fact, I think I need to gag you to stop you from complaining."

"Gag me?" His face registered true terror, yet his solid cock leaped in my hand. I decided to believe his cock.

I dragged my skirt up to my waist and shimmied out of my panties. The ocean smell of my pussy filled the cubicle. "Open wide," I told him.

Shame, fear and desire battled in his elegant face. I laid a palm against his smooth cheek. "Open your mouth, Krishna," I murmured, trying to make my voice gentle. "I know you want to. It's okay."

Our eyes met. I saw him melt. I sensed his sudden trust. A bolt of lust sizzled through me. I held the drenched undergarment under his nose. His nostrils flared. Slowly his ripe lips parted. I stuffed the damp ball of crumpled silk into his mouth. He coughed.

"Breathe through your nose," I told him, remembering what I'd read. "That's a good boy."

I hurried to finish the binding I'd planned, eager to get to the next stage. After tying the long cables in a knot behind his chair, I bent to secure his legs with the shorter lengths of wire. It would have been easier if he'd been sitting in a normal chair. I rounded each ankle several times. Then I had to fasten the cable to one of the supports radiating from the star-shaped base. It looked messy, but I hoped that it was stable and tight enough to excite him.

I stood back to survey the result. It took my breath away.

Sturdy blue cables lashed Krishna's lean body to his chair. The muscles in his thighs tensed under his neat slacks as he strained against his bonds. His mouth was wadded with shocking purple. Damp jet curls tumbled over his brow, making him look boyish yet somehow dissolute. The naked V of chest exposed by his unbuttoned shirt gleamed with perspiration. Tendrils of black hair curled around the wires compressing his tawny flesh. His nipples poked out between two parallel strands like pink pearls.

The fact that he was mostly dressed, the shelf of technical books in the background, the computer monitor blinking behind his trussed form, only made the picture more lewd. There was only one thing missing.

I knelt between his thighs, spread wide by the cables around his ankles. Forcing myself to move slowly, to build the suspense, I reached for his fly.

He jumped at my first touch. My panties muffled his protest. "Don't you dare come," I told him, as I drew the zipper down. "Not until I give you permission."

His cock sprang up through the gap I made. Behind the gag he whimpered like a beaten dog. Saliva gathered in my mouth. Pussy juice trickled from my cleft.

*Patience, Liz. Give him what he needs. Then you can take your pleasure.*

Trying to ignore the pulse between my thighs, I rolled back onto my heels and stood upright, then pulled out my cell phone.

"Now you're ready, Krishna. Now that you're controlled, I'm going to capture this for posterity." I pointed the camera lens at his bound form.

He grunted, shaking his head violently, tugging against the cables and the scarves. For a moment I worried that he'd topple the chair.

"Hush! Don't worry. This will be our little secret—as long as you behave, that is. Don't you want to see what you look like?"

He calmed. He rested in his bonds, motionless and silent. Only his eyes spoke.

"You're beautiful," I whispered, framing his cable-wrapped form on the LCD screen and snapping the shutter. "Beautiful and perverse and unbelievably hot."

I stuffed the mobile back into my right pocket and pulled a condom from my left. I had waited long enough.

He trembled when I rolled the latex down his length. He moaned into his gag when I straddled his body, knees on the chair seat on either side of his hips, and lowered myself onto his jutting cock. I rocked back and forth, sinking him more deeply into my soaking cunt. I was filled with hot hard flesh—Krishna's flesh that I'd craved for so very long. He was mine.

The thought was as intoxicating as the sight of his restraints. Now I was the one who was moaning, pumping up and down, grinding my clit against his pubic bone as I rutted in his lap. He stayed mostly still, allowing me to use him however I liked. I plucked at the taut cables. I pinched the rosy nipples peeking out between them. He gasped and arched up, driving his cock into my wet, hungry depths. I wanted more, always more, his heat and hardness making me cruel as I impaled myself on him again and again. I clenched around him, reaching for the climax that shimmered just out of reach, and felt him surge in response.

He tensed and swelled inside me. He was coming. I looked

up at his face and saw such bliss that my scolding died on my lips. Instead, I came myself, pleasure welling up and spilling over, unexpected and effortless. Pure delight, golden and viscous as honey, flooded my senses. His cock blasted me with liquid fire and I came again, rich and smooth and full.

I collapsed on his cable-wrapped chest, breathing his odor of sweat and sandalwood. His cock nestled in my dripping pussy, still half hard. I pressed my lips to the brown hollow at the base of his throat. I wished, for a moment, that his arms were free so that he could embrace me.

All at once his computer emitted a loud beep.

We both jumped. I laughed and pulled the gag from his mouth. He sputtered a bit.

"The backup process," he said. "It's done."

"Oh. Should I untie you?" Now I felt oddly shy.

"Not quite yet." His eyes gleamed.

I felt it again, the thrill of knowing that it wasn't just my pervy mind directing this scene. He wanted what I had to give. He could have stopped me, at the start or later. I'm strong, but no match for a guy a head taller and forty pounds heavier than I am. He could have escaped, even turned the tables on me.

But he didn't. The thought made me dizzy with delight.

"Kiss me, Liz. Please."

His full mouth beckoned. I didn't see any reason to refuse him.

"Thank you," he said when I finally peeled my lips away from his. The naked gratitude in his voice actually embarrassed me. I clambered off him and started to unwind the cables.

"It's just—I've wanted you for so long, Krishna..." I bent to untie his ankles, not wanting him to see my blush.

"I wanted you, too. I just couldn't imagine that you'd be interested in—well, that sort of thing."

"I didn't know that I was." I concentrated on undoing the scarves.

Deliberately, I coiled the cables and piled them in their corner. Then I returned to sit on Krishna's lap once more, his hardening cock pressing against my still-bare bottom.

"And it didn't scare you or turn you off?" He looked uncertain again. His arms slipped around my waist. I leaned against his shoulder as I retrieved my phone and showed him the photo. "You know, the fact that I was so—deviant?"

The exquisitely obscene image—this work of art we'd created together—astonished us both. I smiled up into his worshipping eyes.

"I think that makes two of us."

# HOW THE LITTLE MERMAID GOT HER TAIL BACK

Andrea Dale

O nce upon a time there was a woman who, after consuming enough vodka gimlets to loosen her tongue, finally dared to confess to her husband all the dark, delicious, dirty things she wanted done to her.

Unfortunately, her husband thought her desires were disgusting and degrading and told her so in no uncertain terms. She stuffed those needs back into the dungeon of her subconscious and pretended it had all been a product of the gimlets; denied it was what she really wanted, who she really was.

Eventually, though, her husband left her for a perky and decidedly unkinky soccer-mom type, his parting words a sneer that his new wife wasn't some kind of perverted freak. Our heroine languished, alone and unfulfilled, seriously questioning whether what she wanted was normal and okay.

That really, really sucked.

Then she met Philip.

Philip wanted to hear about her fantasies. It was hard for

her to reveal them, though, after the betrayal, but he coaxed them out of her, bit by bit. He stroked her hair, held her close while she blushingly whispered her confessions. Then he fisted his hand in her hair at the base of her skull, held her immobile and watched her as she gasped and trembled and tried to duck her head away, only to be jerked back by the pain.

"No, look at me. Tell me more."

Helpless, she did.

Our heroine (whom we'll call Ella) still couldn't tell him everything. There were things too kinky, too out there, too perverted, that she still feared would drive anyone away, even Philip. But as their relationship progressed, he showed an exceptional capacity for tapping into her secret desires, for anticipating what she feared and craved in equal measures.

She teetered on the knife edge of honesty and terror, and that's what made her come so hard, time after time.

It should be mentioned, because it's important to the tale, that Ella and Philip met professionally. He was an entrepreneur with a focus on restaurants, and she was a brilliant marketing strategist who knew just how to coax the public into descending in droves on any new venture she put her mark on.

After several successful restaurant openings and many, many intense sexual encounters that pushed her to her limits (or so she thought), they joined forces on Philip's newest venture, an upscale sushi joint.

"I was thinking about a big fish tank in the middle of the room," he said. "Exotic fish. Frilly, rare, eye-catching ones." Ella shivered as he smiled his wicked smile and added, "Deadly fish, even. Puffers, that sort of thing."

Mouth dry, she shook her head. Personal and professional warred. "Mermaid."

His eyebrows rose, as if she'd foolishly asked for mercy. "Mermaid?"

"A woman in a mermaid costume, in the tank," she said. In her mind, she could see it, like a burlesque swimming show, only updated and trendy and modern. Perfect for his type of restaurant. "Risqué, but not distasteful. Think Dita von Teese, but maybe not quite so distracting, because you'll want people focusing on the food. The food, though…it'll be daring, sexy."

"Audacious," he agreed, and the way he said the word sent thrilling tremors through her. "Encouraging people to take chances, face their hang-ups about food…and, subconsciously, other things."

She couldn't argue with him about that. He always took her ideas and tweaked them ever so slightly (or sometimes blatantly) to be about kink and deviance. And that worked, whether his patrons realized it or not.

Some of them did realize it, she knew with a delicious shudder. Some of them looked at her, consideringly, or even enviously.

They made a very good team.

She designed the ad campaign, started a buzz, made sushi sound like the most desired and deviant thing on the planet. She gave her input on the mermaid tank, and Philip listened intently and then rewarded her for her ideas.

There were always hiccups and panics as things got down to the wire, of course.

"We have a problem," Philip said. "We can't find anyone to be the mermaid." He cocked his head, watched her. Even without him touching her, she felt his gaze like a caress—if a caress could be defined as something that bored into her soul. "I think you should do it."

She sucked in her breath. His request sounded innocuous enough—she'd been a competitive swimmer in high school and college, was no stranger to pool or surf—but for her it held more. She wanted to please him. He made it sound like a light request, but in truth it was a command.

A command to which she acceded. Because Ella still didn't realize the depth of Philip's depravities.

Or, for that matter, how neatly they dovetailed with her own.

He didn't show her the mermaid outfit until that night, not until after she'd had her hair piled artfully atop her head and threaded through with strands of gleaming pearls, after her waterproof makeup was applied, after they were in the empty restaurant and she was admiring the tank in the center of the room.

The tank contained a soft faux "rock" shaped to perfectly cushion a lounging woman with her head and upper torso out of the water. Some filmy green plants were spaced to float in the water, which would be added once Ella settled herself in.

A wave generator would add some ripples, and fresh air would be pumped in to counteract the fact that a lid would enclose her.

Ella's sole job was to sit there and smile and occasionally run her hands through the treasure chest of gold coins and bright gems.

In Philip's office at the back of the restaurant, she stripped. She rather hoped he'd do something to her—spank her, maybe, to refresh the pain of the caning he'd given her a few days earlier. Her ass still bore the fading stripes, which felt a bit sore rather than outright stinging.

Instead he just watched her, his dark eyes glittering. She knew that look. It meant he had plans for her. Plans that would entail making her cry, making her come, making her soar.

He brought out the mermaid outfit.

First, the scallop shells that would cover her champagne-glass breasts. She'd assumed they'd be some sort of halter top, but oh, no: just the shells themselves, with grooves on the insides that looked like they should hook to something. Her nipples weren't exactly the right shape…

That was when Philip produced the clamps.

Oh, sweet Poseidon.

Her breasts were sensitive, and once Philip had discovered that, he exploited the information at every given opportunity. Clamps, feathers, ice cubes, hot wax, and sometimes just sucking and tweaking until she came and couldn't stand being touched anymore and he didn't care and forced her to come again.

Ella loathed and craved breast play in equal measure.

That meant her nipples were already hard even before Philip tightened the clamps on them. She hissed against the pain as it transmuted to pleasure and back again.

"You will be beautiful tonight," Philip whispered in her ear. "You will be perfect. You will be mine."

Ella didn't have time to think about his words, because next he revealed her mermaid's tail.

She caught her breath. The scales shimmered and danced in emerald, sapphire and amethyst—not as bright jewel tones, but as muted undersea hues that flowed and sparkled like a prism.

When he helped her into it, she discovered how much more he had planned for her.

Thanks to the clamps and his very touch, she was already wet and open. She'd tried not to think about how aroused she was, about how she wished for his fingers or his cock or…well, if she'd wished for a dildo, she was certainly getting one now.

Built into the tail, the fake cock slipped into her, snugly filling her. She moaned and clamped down on it, and probably could have come right there if Philip's words hadn't penetrated her haze.

"Not yet, my sweet."

Not yet, but how long, how excruciatingly long would he make her wait?

The tail pressed her legs together, fitting firmly but comfortably around her waist. She couldn't touch herself, couldn't move her legs, couldn't thrust against the dildo.

If she concentrated, she could probably clench down rhythmically and bring herself off. Probably? Definitely, given her aroused state. But he'd told her not yet, and she'd already agreed that he was in charge of when she came. The problem was that the dildo, hard and pressed into her and undeniably *there*, would keep her stimulated the entire time.

She took a deep breath. She could get through this.

She repeated that to herself when Philip snicked the tail closed with a tiny lock. He'd release her when he was good and ready; she had no control.

Once the shells were hooked to the clamps—sending a fresh wave of pleasure through her—Philip rolled her out to the restaurant floor on a cart, and he and a waiter positioned her in the tank.

As the comfortably warm water rose, he kissed her forehead. "Do you trust me?"

She found the question strange. "Of course I do."

He covered the tank. She was left with the faint humming sound of the motor and the swishing ripples of the water. She languidly flipped her tail up and down, amused by the sensation and the waves she created. Of course, the motion also made the dildo rock inside her. She smiled. She'd enjoy this tease because later, their sex would be incredible.

The first guests arrived, peering into the tank before accepting champagne and mingling. She waved at them.

Then she caught her breath as her entire groin vibrated to

life. Eyes wide, she sought out Philip in the crowd. Saw him smiling. Saw him palming the remote control that operated the clit vibe and made the dildo squirm inside her.

Was he serious? Did he really think she could keep from coming if he manipulated her like that?

Then she heard his voice and realized there was a speaker in the tank.

"Sweet mermaid, I would never torture you by denying you pleasure tonight. You have my permission to come at will, as often as you wish."

Was he serious? Did he really think she could come here, now, surrounded by people and on display?

Did she really think she couldn't?

The vibrations weren't up to the max; in fact, he toyed with the remote, sometimes turning it up high, sometimes turning it off completely. Even as he chatted with guests, he watched her.

She was drenched, inside and out. Whenever she shifted, she felt her juices pooled and slippery inside the tail. Nobody else could tell; nobody else knew how aroused she was, what sweet torture she suffered.

Then, when the room was full, and the guests nibbled sushi, Philip cranked up the remote control and nodded at her.

No. Her mouth formed the word, a pursed *O,* but she didn't make a sound. It wouldn't have mattered anyway, because he couldn't hear her; the only thing that would make him stop was if she pushed the button near her right hand, which would release the top of the tank in case of emergency.

She didn't want to come in front of a roomful of people, but the choice wasn't hers, never had been hers. She was Philip's; she'd given herself to him. She hadn't lied when she'd said she trusted him.

The sensations were too much. The buzzing against her clit

and the writhing dildo inside her built the pressure to dizzying heights. She barely had time to press her hands against the sides of the tank before the orgasm slammed through her.

She thrashed as she came, her tail slapping against the water, her back arching, her shell-clad breasts thrusting up and out.

She opened her eyes and tried to compose herself as her climax subsided to gentle pulses. She managed a weak smile at the guests who stared at the tank, and she flipped her tail as if to say, "Just part of the act."

But Philip didn't turn down the remote, and she felt another orgasm building inexorably, and again she was helpless to stop it.

He made her come again and again, delighting (she was sure) at her wriggling and squirming and thrashing, her struggles to pretend she wasn't coming her brains out in front of a roomful of people.

"Everything okay, my sweet?" he asked during a reprieve.

Cheeks flaming, she nodded.

And he turned the remote to the max again.

Somewhere in the middle of an orgasm, or perhaps in one of the mindless moments between, Ella felt something inside her crack open. The words her husband had left her with—*dirty, disgusting, perverted*—had hardened and lodged deep in her psyche, blocking her acceptance of who she was, what she wanted. Philip had chipped away at her shame, but now fractures fissured through it.

Opening her eyes, she again sought Philip out in the crowd. As their eyes met, he asked again, "Do you trust me?"

She nodded.

And then she felt a fresh wave of fear and humiliation and arousal crash over her as she watched him hand the remote control to the woman standing beside him.

The original story of "The Little Mermaid," she remembered,

was that the mermaid had given up her tail for the love of a man, and he'd betrayed her and left her in constant pain.

Now, she understood. She trusted Philip to the point that he could share her with others. She was his prized, beloved possession, and he wouldn't share her unless it was with reverence and respect.

He'd given her back her belief that she wasn't wrong, or different, or broken.

He'd given her back her tail.

Another climax built, and Ella welcomed its freedom.

You can bet they lived happily ever after.

# THE LADY OR THE TIGER

## Bill Kte'pi

Nicholas Comus offered a little of everything. In friends' homes, he could light a candle from across the room, make watch chains or cuff links rise to the top of a pint glass turned upside down on the table, or fill an hour with the usual pick-a-card tricks. His stage show included the usual levitations, penetrations, vanishings and teleportations, performed with the assistance of the Beautiful Molly. The show progressed through a series of these tricks to those in which his assistant was the victim: he would levitate her as she reclined on a table beneath a thin bedsheet, make her vanish from inside the elaborately decorated wooden cabinet he had acquired on travels in far-off lands and saw her in half, after which her severed lower half would kick its shapely stockinged legs for the applause of the audience.

The act ended with the Lady or the Tiger. In tails and top hat, Comus addressed the audience beyond the footlights, as Molly drew back a curtain to reveal a specially made box the size of a small room, with gleaming mirrors set into the sides. "There's a story they tell about an unconquered king who ruled in Roman times," the magician explained. "One of those kingdoms that was eventually absorbed and civilized to create the world we know today. Like many of the ancients whose mysteries have passed down to me, this king followed traditions we may find alien, even barbaric, but nevertheless admire, and one such was the way he dealt justice in cases where the evidence was not sufficient to make obvious a verdict of guilt or innocence."

When the houselights came up, when the applause died down and they saw that there would be no encore and no bow, the audience filed out the doors. Comus and Molly soon found them-selves alone backstage, where their privacy from the venue's staff was ensured by his insistence on the magician's need for secrecy. As it always did, the act had enervated them both, and as they boxed this and secured that, they found excuses to touch each other, until they had the leisure to take to the dressing room. She was soon on top of him, pushing him down against the kneeling bench used in the Head of Medusa illusion, clamping handcuffs around his wrists as she'd done on stage. In the act, he would have been on the *crux decussata*. The leg shackles would have followed and showy but ultimately irrelevant straps across his thighs, waist, and chest. Instead, she now burdened him only with her body, with the distraction of her mouth on his, her breasts free under her thin top and pressing against his chest, the smell of her skin rising beneath the faded blossom of her perfume and the wafting scents of whiskey, tobacco and burnt flash powder that had accumulated in her hair. Her thighs gripped him strongly; indeed, several portions of Comus's act depended on Molly being stronger than she looked.

"Like those who studied the flights of birds to predict the future, or determined fortunes with a roll of the dice, this king believed that fate made known its wishes when events were released to chance—as a feather let loose will travel where the wind takes it." And here Comus released a feather from his hand, which followed the updrafts of the room, multiplying into two feathers as the breeze split it, then four feathers dancing, then sixteen, then abruptly, a dove, shaking loose from the cloud of feathers before soaring for the rafters, where it cooed to itself.

The way the unspoken game worked, he had only a few seconds to free himself, or Molly would walk away, her interest lost. It was not that getting out of the handcuffs was difficult. It was that she tried so ardently to distract him, to break his concentration, to make him lose focus. Her tongue would be in his mouth or her teeth in his throat, against the tender skin of his clavicle, biting his nipple through his silk shirt. She would stretch out against him, her hands on his arms, the weight of her breasts against his face, letting him feel the heat between her thighs, which alone had been enough for him to lose the game some nights, nights which ended with him alone in his hotel room.

"Creation wants to order itself. Like a still, blue lake, every moment of its surface is disrupted by our passage through it, wobbling, trembling. Our disruption ends only after we've left, but if we still ourselves, pause in our motions, we minimize the waves we make and can see ourselves reflected in the glassy surface." A velvet rope tumbled down from the ceiling, and as Comus pulled on it, the great box's platform rotated slowly, and when it came to a stop, the magician was reflected in the side exposed to the audience—a reflection which stepped out from the mirror as the "real" Comus disappeared.

She moved roughly against him, letting him feel the texture of her, of her clothes, of her skin, of her mouth as it grazed him, and he could feel the weight of her shift the way he could feel an audience's attention waver, as she began to lose patience and give up on him. But he was fast enough tonight, had already unlocked the cuffs and only waited for her to lean closer, so that he could encircle her with his arms, cuffing her wrists together behind her back. This always woke her up, quickened her breathing, especially as he forced her onto the kneeling bench and shoved the base of it with his foot, until her back was against the wall. Molly had large breasts she was self-conscious of, which she bound during the performance so as not to disrupt the lines of her figure. When she was trapped like this, when he would unbutton her top and open it, pushing the sleeves back over her shoulders to bare her breasts completely so that the lights were shining on them and she could look up at him and see him staring at her, see him seeing her, she hated it. She blushed, she chewed her lip, but she loved it, too, loved that he forced this on her. Her breasts were pale, making the marks from a long day and full evening of being strapped down stand out that much more vividly.

"The accused was instructed to choose one of two doors, and his choice would determine his fate—and the revelation of his fate would reflect creation's assessment of his guilt or innocence. Behind one door, a beautiful woman. Should the accused choose this door, the woman was his to marry; such was the will of creation." Comus spun the box again, opened a door on one side, and the Beautiful Molly stepped into it before he closed the door behind her.

He knew that when he slapped her across the face, there was a part of her that was relieved because it redirected their attentions. His wrists hurt not only from the way the metal had dug into them as he'd freed himself from the handcuffs, but from the escapes of the act, and the various illusions of production and vanishing that had required him to hold a heavy weight casually enough to suggest that he held nothing at all. But he still slapped her hard enough to leave a handprint across her face, because he wanted her to know that however much his hands hurt, the discomfort was faint compared to his desire to hurt her.

"But should the accused choose the other door, behind it lay a vicious tiger, starved—with the sort of cruel precision only barbarians could master—just to the point of greatest hunger but least loss of ferocity. Death was sure, if not always swift. I'm told the great beasts like it when their prey struggles." Another spin, another door opened, and this time the audience was shown the tiger from the Rajah's Challenge illusion earlier in the act. The great cat yawned, but seemed no less deadly for his boredom.

He fed her his cock, pushing it deep into her mouth as he rocked back and forth against her face, his hands pinning her throat to the wall. The theater was quiet, the doves cooing in their cages, the tiger making quiet noises as it chewed on its snack, Molly on her knees whimpering as she sucked him, pausing to gasp, to moan, each time taking him deeper down her throat. The near-silence, the pressure of his hands, the wall against her back, the movement of his hips toward her, all contributed to a growing panic that made her pulse drum, made her thighs squeeze together, made her feel as though the magician had made the world into a fist that now closed around her. She struggled, but every movement she made only pushed her closer to him.

Comus pulled the cord again, and the box spun and spun and spun, until no one was sure anymore which door led to what, at which point a volunteer from the audience chose for the magician, directing him in which door to enter. "You have been a generous audience, my friends, and I leave you with this thought. It is not always as clear to us as it was to the ancients, whether a door may lead to the lady or the tiger. Our only choice is to stride through the door with dignity." And with this, he opened the door the volunteer had indicated and stepped inside. The box collapsed the moment the door closed behind him, the mirrored sides falling away, crashing, the rope spiraling up to the ceiling, but just before the houselights came up, a sound was clearly heard which could have been the moans of a woman or the growl of the tiger.

# SEALED FOR FRESHNESS

## Jennifer Peters

With a small stable of submissives at my beck and call, there are few chores that I still do regularly, but grocery shopping is one of them. As I approached the aisle I was looking for, I was very glad to have kept this one task for myself.

Shelf after shelf was stacked with long, thin boxes, each promising to keep my food fresh or make cleanup easier, in hopes of convincing me to choose one brand over another. It took a full minute just to find the cling wrap, never mind sorting through the variety of offerings. Did I want colored Saran Wrap, or generic plastic wrap patterned with holiday prints? What about sticky-on-one-side waxed paper, the alternative to plastic wrap? I examined every package carefully, reading the detailed sales points printed on each cardboard container, but I knew what I wanted and it wasn't any of those fancy films. I wanted clear plastic cling wrap, the kind that sticks to itself when you unfurl it, forcing you to twist it this way and that until you've nicked yourself on the jagged metal cutting strip.

When I finally found what I wanted, I pulled a box off the top of the stack and placed it in my basket. And then I pulled nearly a dozen more boxes off the shelf, unceremoniously dumping them all into my basket with the first. I couldn't wait to see the look on the cashier's pimply adolescent face when I paid. And that was just the beginning.

Back at home, I unloaded all the boxes of plastic wrap and stacked them neatly on a table in my playroom. I had big plans for the evening.

I changed into my leather catsuit and pulled my hair up into a high, severe ponytail. I stepped into my five-inch platform heels just as I heard the bell ring, and I took my time going down the stairs to answer the door. I wasn't going to rush for a submissive.

When I at last opened the door, I found Mitchell on the other side, head bowed and hands folded neatly in front of him. He was greeting me in the proper fashion, and he seemed to have dressed as I'd ordered, but he was still going to be punished. No amount of sucking up and playing nice was going to get him off the hook for his misbehavior the last time he was in my presence.

"Good evening, Mistress Claire," he greeted me, his eyes peeking up into mine though his head remained bowed.

I nodded and led him into the house, going straight to the playroom at the back. Once we were over the threshold, I ordered Mitchell to strip. He folded his clothes neatly in the corner and then stood, head still bowed and hands folded before him, in the center of the room, naked. Now it was time for my fun to begin.

Picking up the first box of cling wrap, I grabbed the tabbed end and ripped it open. I peeled the edge of the plastic from the roll and pulled it out over the serrated edge, being careful not to rip it. The plastic made a quiet crinkling sound as I peeled it, and

I felt a shiver run down my spine at the faint noise. The feel of the film between my fingers was equally arousing, and my juices pooled between my thighs as I unrolled a few more inches of it.

When I had about six inches of plastic stretched straight out from the box, I walked toward Mitchell and crouched down low. Starting at his ankles, I began to unfurl the film, wrapping it around his legs, from ankles to knees, until it was several layers thick. When his lower legs were bound tightly, I used the metal edge to cut the plastic, pressed the loose end firmly against Mitchell's legs to keep it in place and then started the process over, this time encasing him from knees to hips. I stopped just below his hanging cock, and when his upper legs were completely encased and the roll empty, I pressed the loose plastic edge into place and went to get another box.

I started the second roll at his shoulders and worked my way down. Mitchell held his arms straight at his sides as I mummified him, wrapping him tight from shoulders to wrists. I used up almost the entire roll of cling wrap on his torso, and when I was finished and had sliced the film free from the roll, the only things still uncovered were his hands, ass and cock. But they wouldn't be so easily accessible for long. Tossing aside the almost empty roll of plastic, I grabbed one final box and opened it. I teased the film free of the roll very slowly, making Mitchell sweat with anticipation and causing my pussy to drip copious amounts of juice into my leather-encased crotch. When I'd finally freed the end of the roll—and aroused myself and Mitchell more than enough—I began to wrap it around him, starting at the crack of his ass and working around and around, over his hands, over his cock and back to his behind. I pulled the film tight as I circled his body with the plastic, making sure he could do little more than futilely wiggle his fingers. Getting an erection would be no picnic for him either, considering how close I'd bound his cock to his body. But with each pass of the plastic wrap over his dick, Mitchell only moaned more. For a moment I contemplated berating him for the obvious show of pleasure, but I knew his punishment would teach him a lesson, even if he happened to enjoy parts of it a little too much.

With Mitchell encased practically from head to toe, I put away the plastic wrap and then circled his body, taking in his appearance from every angle. I had him trapped in layer upon layer of strong plastic film, but I could still make out his body's natural lines and curves through the thin sheets. It excited me immensely, and I paused long enough to rub my cunt through my leather, just to take the edge off. Then it was time to play.

Walking across the room, I picked up my favorite flogger and a red ball-gag. "Come here," I ordered, my voice stern but my eyes, I'm certain, giving away my amusement at his predicament. Mitchell blanched at the command, but he had no choice and so he attempted to obey, his feet wiggling and toes reaching as he tried to cross the room. The task was nearly impossible— we both knew it—but like any good submissive, he did his best, and he'd traveled almost a full yard before I ordered him to stop wasting my time with his snaillike pace and went to meet him instead.

My flogger in one hand, I traced the other over Mitchell's body, running it along his ass and over his cock, which was becoming erect and pushing against its plastic prison. I grinned and imagined just how hard his cock would become once I started his punishment—and how hard it would strain to break through the plastic. *Mmm*, I thought, *this will be fun!*

Satisfied with how tightly I'd wrapped my sub, I took one last moment to admire the beautiful package in front of me.

"You know what you did wrong, don't you, Mitchell?" I asked, checking.

"Yes, Mistress Claire," he responded. "And I know that I must never again disobey my Mistress's orders."

"Very good," I said. "But you must still pay for your misbehavior."

"Yes, Mistress."

Questions answered, I placed the ball-gag between his lips and waited for him to open his mouth to accept it. When it was properly in place, I tightened the strap at the back of his head, keeping the gag firmly in his mouth.

Then, still standing behind him, I raised my flogger. I dropped my shoulder, lifted the lashes until they were even with my elbow, and then I swung. My wrist snapped quickly as the heavy leather strands came into contact with Mitchell's ass, and the sound of the lashes on the plastic wrap was arousing. The usual *snap* and *thud* were replaced with a muffled *thwack* and the sound of ripping plastic. I paused long enough to check the damage on my submissive's behind, and I saw that the top layer of cling wrap had perforated where the flogger had landed. It delighted me immensely to know that my swing had been powerful enough to cut the plastic, and I raised my flogger for a second throw.

My pussy throbbed with each flick of my wrist, and every time the tails of my flogger landed on Mitchell's plastic-wrapped body, I shivered with arousal. I peppered his ass and thighs with strokes from my flogger, each time delighting in the sights and sounds. Mitchell was fairly well mummified, so he had no way of dodging a swat or twisting to make it land where he wanted. He couldn't even ask me to hit him where he wanted thanks to the gag—not that I would allow such behavior anyway. I laughed at his attempts to move, knowing it was impossible, and took several more swings. When I stopped, I moved closer to examine his ass, and I saw that the plastic was severely shredded, his behind accessible through several holes that had ripped clear through the layers of cling wrap. It was one of the most beautiful sights I've ever seen.

I caressed my sub's ass, feeling the warmth from his skin and the rough texture of the ripped plastic wrap. "Good boy," I told him, proud he'd taken his flogging and hadn't tried to resist his punishment. I'm sure he thought that was the end of it, too, being bound in plastic and flogged, but I had a few more plans for him.

Hanging up my flogger, I took down my favorite crop. Since I'd already reddened his ass, I circled his body slowly, lightly swatting his arms, legs, back and chest as I went. I pinched his nipples, too, first through the layers of plastic and then by ripping holes in it to get direct contact. His cock was straining against the plastic, and I could see precome already smeared on the cling wrap. My cunt spasmed at the sight, and I decided I needed pleasure more than Mitchell needed further flogging.

"On the floor," I commanded him, and his eyes went wide instantly. I knew he was trying to figure out how to get down there, considering his current bound state, and I let him struggle for a moment before helping him.

Crouching low, I ripped the plastic along the backs of his legs up to his thighs then stood and helped him down to his knees and onto his back. When he was lying on the floor, I got another roll of cling wrap and re-bound his legs. I unzipped the Y-shaped fly over my pussy and bared only that small part of my body to Mitchell. Then I straddled him, lowering myself over his head, stopping almost six inches above him to remove his ball-gag. With that out of the way, I lowered myself the rest of the way until my pussy rested on his mouth and commanded: "Eat me!"

Mitchell is usually allowed to use his fingers when he pleasures my pussy, if not in me then to hold me and guide my cunt to his lips. Without that added tool, it was much harder for him, and it took him much longer to set his pace and really delve deep into my pussy. When he finally figured out what he was doing, though, he really devoured my cunt. His lips and tongue worked together to tease as much of my pussy as possible, with my labia getting licked and nibbled while my clit was sucked and laved. It was possibly the best head he'd ever given me, and I wondered if his being bound in plastic wrap had somehow helped egg him on orally while the rest of his body was forced to remain still. If that was the case, I had a feeling Mitchell was going to be wrapped up in plastic quite often—and I'd be spending a lot of time at the grocery store.

He was doing a fantastic job eating me, and I started to shake in my heels, my legs feeling unsteady and my pussy starting to throb uncontrollably. I was going to come. I reached down to the floor to keep my balance, and then I relaxed and waited for it to happen. I climaxed much sooner than usual, and my orgasm was stronger than it had been in any of my recent sessions with any of my submissives. Mitchell seemed to work well under the pressure of plastic wrap.

I filled his mouth with my juices and listened to the muffled sounds of him slurping them down, which aroused me further. When he didn't stop licking—I hadn't told him to stop, so he had no reason to—I felt myself building up to a second climax, and in minutes I came again. None of my submissives had ever given me multiple orgasms in such a short time, and I started to believe it was all due to the way I'd bound Mitchell. I couldn't help but moan when I came the second time, filling his mouth with more of my juices. My climax was so strong that I had to grab my sub's cling-wrapped arms to keep myself steady or I would have dropped to the floor, my weak legs unable to support me.

Finally sated—at least for the time being—I rose, unsteadily, from Mitchell's face and moved next to him, crouching low by his waist. The plastic covering his cock was cloudy with precome, and I stroked his encased erection for a few moments, causing him to wriggle and sigh with excitement.

When I sensed he was getting close, I asked him if he wanted his reward. He'd certainly earned it.

"Yes, Mistress," he pleaded.

I stopped stroking him for a moment so I could rip through the plastic, pulling it apart layer by layer until his cock popped out through the jagged hole. The sight of his cock bobbing above his plastic-encased body was more of a turn-on than I'd thought it would be, and I felt a faint tingle in my cunt when I started to stroke him. I ignored my desire for a moment, though, wanting to reward Mitchell for his good work. I jerked his cock only a dozen times before giving him permission to come, and he did so immediately. I aimed his shooting cock at his stomach and watched as his come splattered on the cling wrap, creating abstract patterns as it streaked over the crinkly plastic. It looked delicious!

After bringing Mitchell to climax, I tucked his softening cock back into the plastic wrap and went to get a glass of wine while he rested. On the way back into the playroom, I grabbed a wet washcloth. I unwrapped Mitchell and cleaned him up, gave him a minute to get a glass of water for himself and then directed him to the middle of the room. I pulled a few more rolls of plastic wrap from the pile and started to swathe him in the clear film once more, this time starting with his cock. I intended to ride him later that night, if he was good, and like the box said, I wanted to keep him all wrapped up, sealed for optimal freshness.

# STOCKS
# AND BONDS

## Rita Winchester

"Shh, you're going to get us caught!" I race ahead of Tad and shriek at the sound of his heavy boots falling in the packed dirt behind me. He is so close, any moment he could catch me!

"I'm not the one screaming like a girl," he laughs, and I feel his fingers brush the back of my sweatshirt. He misses and I put on speed, even though I really want him to catch me. But the thrill and the foreplay are in the chase.

I round the corner by the torture chamber and dart behind a stack of skulls. "Foiled again!" I laugh. I hear him take the stack out in a clatter of plastic body parts—and his dark chuckling laughter.

"You'll pay for that."

"Oh, yeah?"

Dead silence. All I can hear is my heart pounding: in my chest, my ears, my temples—my pussy.

Nothing.

"Tad?" I turn in a circle, searching him out. It's dark out here in the woods. The Renaissance Festival where we work summers only has a few scattered spotlights because the fair closes at dusk. I see nothing but the fat white coin of the full moon in the sky.

Then big arms close around me and a mighty roar worthy of a pirate fills my head. "There you are! Now we make you pay, you cheeky wench!"

We are the final crew tonight, just us and three acres of old-world charm. I scream at the moon, laughing and kicking and so turned on I can't stand myself. His big arms are wrapped around me, and he's thumbing my nipple through my tank top. I've changed out of costume and I'm in nothing but yellow terry cloth shorts and a navy blue tank top. I push and kick but feel the perfect rod of his cock against my lower back. Oh, I want him too much for words.

"Tad!"

"That's *Pirate* Tad to you, you little whore."

My heart beats harder. He knows I love the dirty words. *Whore* and *slut* and *trollop*: all of them, they make me crazy and wet. They make me come. "Please, no!" But I shiver in his arms as a cool breeze floats by.

"Loose women get the stocks," Tad growls, carrying me around the corner. Even as I thrash and protest, he sets my head and shoulders in the hollow half moons and sets the top down over me. I am trapped. Tad tugs at my tiny shorts and gets them around my knees. My panties join them and I am dizzy from want. I push my ass back at him, begging him to use me; whatever he wants, however he wants. I'm trapped and helpless and his. All his. His loose woman.

Tad's big handsome face pops up in front of me and he says, "Stocks and bonds, baby. Bound up with your own shorts, trapped in the stocks. You can't get away. I can do whatever I want. I could leave you here for everyone to see in the morning.

Naked and pried open, your little red cunt exposed for anybody to come by.

I pant and moan and toss my head. "Please, Tad. Please, baby. Don't leave me this way."

"Hmm." He looks around and finds a crate. Stepping up so that he can be closer, he unzips his jeans and unbuckles his belt. His cock runs over my lips, warm and smooth. "I think I won't leave you here if we take it out in trade. Open your mouth, Kerri. Like a good little cock slut." He pushes his hands in my hair and sinks into my mouth. I hum, running my tongue over his cock and sucking him in.

He fucks my mouth and I inhale the perfect dark scents of him. "Do you like that, baby? Do you like being at my mercy?"

I nod, stiff as it is in the stocks, sucking and licking. In my mind, he is fucking me. Fucking me from behind, fucking my mouth, fucking my ass. Anything and everything he wants.

"You know they also used to spank the loose women, don't you, Kerri?"

I shake my head but moan around his dick. Tad pulls free of me and I chase after him with my tongue. I'm not ready to be done with the feel of the plump head of his cock slipping over my lips again and again. "Tad, please," I beg.

"Don't. Shh, you pretty little whore. I think we'll go with eight. One for each year we've been together."

For eight years, we've been together and for eight years we've worked the RenFest together. We never tire of it or each other. It's like a personal playground three months a year. At least after dark.

The blows are sharp and hard, and my ass flames with pain and pleasure. My pussy fills with the hot feel of my spanking. He takes pity on me and makes it a fast but severe spanking. Tad tests me with his fingers, pushing them deep in my cunt and then running them in slippery circles over my clit. He teases me by running the head of his hard cock along my asscrack and below, pushing at my holes but never going in. "Please! Please, Tad!"

We've worked all day long in the hot sun in full costume. We've dealt with rowdy kids and cranky adults and drunken sailors. I need this. Badly.

"Say you're a slutty little wench." He pushes the head of his cock into my cunt and freezes there.

"I'm a slutty little wench!"

"Who deserves the stocks and to be bound with her pretty little yellow shorts."

"Yes!" I yell, because already I cannot remember what he's said.

"Beg me."

"Please, baby. Please fuck me. Please!"

"Spread your legs for Daddy, Ker."

I moan when he says that. A fat bundle of his fingers pushes into my pussy and he flexes, stretching me for his cock. "Say you want Daddy, Kerri."

"Fuck me, I want you, Daddy. Fuck me."

He pushes into me, his cock filling and stretching me in that nearly spiritual way. It is a holy experience to me when Tad and I fuck. It's love and life and communion, Heaven and Hell and the most perfect place on earth. The stocks bite at my wrists, splintery bits of wood rubbing the skin raw. He smacks my ass hard and drives into me, angling my hips so that he bangs my G-spot like a war drum.

"Oh, god, baby."

He spanks me harder, the bonds of my little yellow shorts allowing my legs far enough apart for him to enter yet keeping them close enough that the friction is higher than it would normally be. The effect is maddening, and I struggle both to get away and get closer, for him to let up and for him to be rougher with me.

"Tomorrow will you be such a slutty little wench?"

"No, I'll be good."

"You won't let the visitors stare at your tits and your ass?" He pushes his thick middle finger into my ass as he says it, rubs in tandem with his slippery cock driving in and out of me. I would throw my head back but I can't. I would sob but I don't. I like it. I like the pinching bite of pain that makes the friction that much better.

"I won't."

"You will. We both know it."

"It's how I'm made to dress," I cry.

"But you like it when they stare at you and then run off behind the trees and masturbate. You like that when they come they're thinking of your pretty pink tits and your rose-colored nipples." Tad slams into me harder. The finger in my ass slips deeper, his free hand clutching me to him as he fucks me. "You like it that they come all over the forest floor thinking of you sucking their cocks. Or thinking of fucking your tight little pussy. Or worse, the dirty boys who want to stick it in your back door. Fuck you in the dirty place."

I come then, around his long, hard cock that I love so much, with the hands I love so much touching me and the voice that makes my pulse go up and my heart grow big whispering filthy things in my ears. "Yes," I say, coming in long, slow waves, coming and then coming again. "I do. I like it."

Tad clutches at me, grabs my hair that's trapped behind me by the antique stocks and jerks hard, coming with a growl, his body slapping against mine, driving me into the old wood. "Me, too, baby. Me, fucking, too."

When we leave, everything is locked up tight. The stocks

are back to normal. The fair is done for another night. As we leave, we pass the puppet stage. Tad catches hold of me, grins. "Tomorrow night you want to put on a dirty puppet show?"

I take his hand. "You know it."

# HELEN LAY BOUND

## Suzanne V. Slate

I wake Helen early on tight-lacing days. Blinking and rubbing her eyes, she follows me into the bathroom. I gently lay her down on the cold tile floor. I administer an enema while she lies quiet. Helen does not particularly enjoy her morning enema, but she insists upon it, for it empties and flattens her belly, allowing us to lace her corset just a little tighter than the day before.

While she showers, I prepare her usual spartan breakfast of an espresso and biscotti. As she nibbles and sips, she casts furtive glances as I devour my cereal, fruit, yogurt and multiple cups of coffee, but she utters not one word of complaint. This is her choice.

When she finishes eating, we begin. In the bedroom, she lets her robe fall to the floor while I warm lotion in the palms of my hands. Slowly, I work the lotion into the skin of her midsection in long, firm strokes, worshipping her shape as I do so. My hands travel freely over her beautiful breasts, lingering for a few seconds on her dark red nipples, which flush and stiffen at

my touch, responding even at this ungodly hour. I massage the
lotion into her belly and her back, spanning my hands nearly
all the way around her tiny waist, then stroking firmly down to
her magnificent buttocks—full and rounded like a goddess in
a Rubens painting. I knead and squeeze her flesh, cupping her
asscheeks and gently pulling them apart. Her breath quickens,
but she remains silent.

While the lotion dries, I open the top drawer of her bureau.
There, wrapped in pink tissue, lies Helen's corset. It is simple
and classic, heavy boning under softly glowing black silk. I
remove it from its wrappings. Helen watches my every move,
her eyes fixated on the corset as I cross the room to her. I lay
it on the bed, and Helen bends forward to loosen the laces. As
she does this, I powder her skin, preparing her body for a day
of tight-lacing. Naked, bent over the bed, Helen is irresistible to
me, and she knows it. Sleepy as she is, she cannot resist teasing
me a little, arching her ass up and tossing her thick mane of hair.
I respond by circling the powder puff over her breasts, petting
and tickling them until she laughs and begs me to stop. At last I
finish my task and gently wipe the excess powder off her body
with a towel.

Standing, Helen wraps the corset around her nude body and
fastens the steel basque in front, wriggling her body until the
corset is properly positioned. She nods her head and we begin
to lace.

While she holds the laces taut at the waist, I position myself
behind her and work from top to bottom, pulling the laces to
reduce the gap between the two halves of the corset. As I create
slack in the laces, Helen removes it by pulling the laces at her
waist tighter and tighter. After a few rounds of this we have gone
as tight as we can, so we take it up a notch. Sometimes Helen
reaches up and grabs a horizontal bar, hanging slack from it as

I continue to tighten. With her body stretched long and relaxed, we are able to bind her a little more closely.

Other times she sinks to the floor on her knees and stretches her torso prone on the bed. This is my favorite part of the morning. I tie her wrists to the bedposts and she pulls back, lengthening her spine as I cinch her corset a few millimeters tighter. At these times she is too much for me, her bare ass pressed against my pelvis as I jerk the laces, her knees parted, revealing the swollen red lips of her pussy. She is aroused, enjoying her helplessness. With each pull of the laces, she gasps sharply.

Sometimes as I draw the laces tight, I wring a drop of moisture out of her—a tear, a bead of sweat in the valley of her spine, a few drops of juice dripping from her warm pussy into my cupped hand. At these times I know she has surrendered to the corset; it has taken her over.

At last we can go no further. I tie the laces into a bow and tuck them neatly beneath the corset. Helen pants as her ribs and lungs adjust to the newly confined space inside her corset. I pant as well, from exertion and arousal. I want to take her right there while she is helpless on her knees, but we have to go to work. My pussy lips slide together as I stand and untie her wrists. This is only the beginning; I intend to spend the entire day in Helen's orbit, in her thrall. I help her stand and we dress.

Helen is a junior professor in the English department, specializing in medieval lit. I'm a grad student, finishing up my PhD in Victorian lit. Helen and I often talk about how we wish we lived in different times, at least for some purposes. I think that's why we study literature: it lets us spend a lot of time with our heads in the past.

For school we dress in what we call our "academic drag": jeans, boots, thick baggy sweaters. The corset is our secret. Helen wrestles her gorgeous, wild mane of hair into a ponytail, taming it. The only outward clue to her true nature is her makeup: mascara, black eyeliner, and glossy red lips, which she somehow manages to keep meticulously painted at all times. Other than that, we look exactly like every other teacher and student in the department.

The English department is pretty liberal, but the powers that be would certainly not approve of a new professor carrying on with a student, so while we are on campus, we keep our relationship under wraps.

Helen leaves the apartment first. Bound as she is, it takes her a while to walk the few blocks to campus. She moves slowly, with small steps, taking care not to get winded or sweaty. She smiles, reveling in her secret self-imposed prison. I watch from the window, smiling when I see her smile. Her careful steps, her rigid posture, her delicate movements, all remind me of the corset underneath. It binds her beautiful body and dictates the course of her entire day.

After Helen disappears from view, I head out the door. I catch up to her quickly, but as I draw close I slow my pace for a couple minutes just to watch her walk. As I pass her, I catch her eye and say hello before overtaking her and continuing on to campus. It is a game we play.

Helen holds office hours in the student union at lunchtime, from eleven to one. At a little before eleven, I grab a table in the corner of the cafeteria and open my computer, pretending to work on my dissertation. But really I am there to watch Helen and to get myself off. At five minutes to eleven, she appears. She selects a seat halfway across the room, facing me. Our eyes meet briefly and we smile. Promptly at eleven, her first student arrives. Helen is a stickler for punctuality. For the next two hours, fresh-faced undergrads appear like clockwork every fifteen minutes, nervous and smiling, offering their term papers for her comments and corrections. All of them are in love with her. Some of them offer to share their greasy bags of fries or giant cups of sodas, but she smiles and waves them off, claiming she just ate. She sips tea and nibbles a scone, relishing her self-imposed restraint.

The students bend over their papers, leaning in as close to Helen as they dare. They are dazzled by her, yet they are trying so hard to pay attention to her comments, wanting to impress her. I know the feeling. She sits rigid, leaning slightly forward, every gesture restrained and elegant as she marks their papers. Sometimes she will laugh at something, tossing her head back and baring her smooth throat. When she laughs, her ribs press against the corset's unyielding bindings, and she stops short, struggling for breath, panting a little.

Her students are transfixed, and so am I. As I watch her move and think about her tightly bound body straining against the corset, I feel a familiar quickening in my lower belly and between my legs. I cross them tightly and sit up a bit straighter, feeling the thick seam of my jeans pressing up against my clit. I have been wet all morning, anticipating this moment, and now the juices flow out of me and dampen the seat of my jeans. With a slight movement, I am able to shift back and forth in my chair while my jeans' inseam glides back and forth across my clit. Of course Helen knows I do this. From time to time she darts a glance in my direction, egging me on, loving the way she makes me lose control. She tilts her head, touches her neck, plays with her ponytail. Usually I am able to hold off and just enjoy the ride, but sometimes, like today, she is too much for me.

I come quietly, leaning my head back and closing my eyes, looking to the world as if I am taking a study break. I press my thighs together and arch my back slightly, keeping my clit in contact with my jeans. Behind my closed eyelids, I see Helen bound on the bed, or hanging from the bar, urging me to draw the corset tighter and tighter. Sometimes, when I come, the image of Helen and her corset blur in my mind so they become one and the same. Underneath that delicious, delicate exterior lies a solid steel foundation. You must follow its rules, pay attention, take your time with it, even worship it. And it is worth every sacrifice. So is Helen.

Gradually my strange, swirling thoughts subside and I open my eyes. Office hours are over. Helen stands and gathers her things, shoots me a glance and a smile, and heads to her next class. I do the same.

Often on tight-lacing days, Helen's body will adjust to the strictures of her corset, and she will be able to lace a little tighter as the day goes by. So I need to stay near her, ready to relace her whenever she summons me. Usually she calls or texts me.

Helen shares an office with a visiting professor who is rarely on campus. Usually we meet there. We lock the door. Helen takes down her jeans, pulls up her sweater, and bends over the desk. She grips the sides of the desk as I jerk the laces tighter. Sometimes she teases me a little, arching her ass up and pressing it against my pelvis, throwing her head back and moaning. Sometimes I tease her right back, slipping a finger inside her panties and sliding it in and out of her, just once. Of course she is dripping wet, hungry for me, but I make her wait. Ignoring her moans of desire and her wriggling hips, I withdraw my finger and lick it clean while she stands and zips up.

Sometimes if there's no other choice, we meet in a dingy out-of-the-way faculty restroom. We duck into a tiny stall. Helen drops her jeans and presses forward against the closed door while I pull her laces tighter, my hip against her ass for leverage. Here in this cramped little restroom, the danger of discovery checks our desire. How would it look if someone walked in on a faculty member and grad student in the same restroom stall? As soon as I secure her laces I bolt, not lingering for a kiss or caress. Scurrying down the hall, heart pounding, I sigh with relief at having escaped discovery.

Yet even at that moment of relief, I am already eager for my next fix, waiting for the moment when Helen again summons me to her side. Each time my phone goes off, I feel it like an electric shock all the way from my throat to my pussy. I laugh to think I'm no better than one of Pavlov's dogs salivating for its reward, but it's true. No doubt about it: I am besotted. Helen is my drug, and her corset is our delivery device.

4:00 p.m. The Friday Afternoon English Department Tea is about to begin. Faculty, grad students and a few ambitious undergrads gather in the lounge. Each week, one of us has to give a talk about our current research project, and today it's Helen's turn. Ever punctual, she is already standing erect at the podium, shuffling papers and smiling as people take their seats. Her eyes scan the room, looking for me. Of course I arrived early and found a choice seat at the back of the room. Here I can stare at Helen to my heart's content, and she can look to me when she needs reassurance.

For even though she hides it well, I know Helen is nervous. I can see it in her flushed cheeks, the fine dewdrops of perspiration on her upper lip and hairline. I can see her chest rise and fall as she draws rapid, shallow breaths, chest straining against the strictures of her corset. Though her bulky sweater hides the evidence, I know her breasts are swelling out over the top of her corset with each inhalation. I also know that a fine coating of sweat is forming between her breasts. My tongue flicks involuntarily; I wish I could lick it off. I envision her nipples, flushed and erect with anticipation and fear, and I feel my own start to grow the same.

This is getting dangerous. I snap out of my reverie and catch

Helen's eye, calming her with my gaze. She grins at me, sweeps her eyes around the room, and begins:

> *Adam lay ybounden,*
> *Bounden in a bond...*

Helen is talking about one of her favorite medieval English poems, "Adam Lay in Bondage." As she works through the poem, she discusses what it means to be bound. If we have chosen our own bondage, are we actually free? And can we choose bondage as a way to find our freedom?

She has practiced her talk on me a million times and I know it is brilliant, a fine piece of scholarship. But seeing her up there at the podium, voluntarily in bondage to her own corset, I start relating her words to our own situation.

On tight-lacing days, my role is to tend to Helen; I am bound to serve her like a worker bee serves its queen. And both of us serve the corset. It binds Helen, of course, but it also dictates the rhythms of our day, everything we do from the time we get up in the morning until we fall into bed at night. Yet we undertake our mutual bondage so willingly, even eagerly. Helen loves the discipline, the rituals and small sacrifices she must constantly undergo in order to make it through the day. And I love to serve Helen, to take care of her, to help her along on this path that brings us both so much pleasure.

Helen finishes her talk and the room erupts in applause. All the grad students and junior faculty hang back until the senior faculty have finished congratulating her. Then we swarm around her like a million stars orbiting the sun. Once again, Helen has dazzled us all.

Tonight we go out to celebrate with a few close friends. With them, and away from campus, we finally are able to dress to express our true natures. Tonight Helen is pure pinup, a glossy and shiny symphony of pink, black and red. She has removed her bulky sweater and from the waist up her corset is exposed. She has tossed a little bolero jacket over her shoulders, but the top half of her breasts are plumped up and on full view. Most people can't get past them, but I do, appreciating the entire delicious display she is putting on for all of us—but mostly for me. She wears long black opera gloves and a tight black pencil skirt that shows off her delicate waist and luscious ass to full advantage. Her skirt is slit high up the back, revealing seamed stockings with Cuban heels. A little farther up, for my eyes only, are black silk garters that hold the stockings up. I helped her fasten them half an hour ago. The finishing touch is a new pair of pink satin stiletto pumps that cost me nearly half my last month's teaching stipend. Helen's hair tumbles loose over her shoulders. Her dark eyes flash, her shiny red lips and white teeth gleam as she laughs. She looks like a bonbon in the center of a candy box.

I settle into my chair, sipping my glass of port, completely content. For tonight, among Helen and our good friends, I am free to express my true self, clad head to toe in the clothing of my beloved Victorians. I spend my days with their stories and poems in my head and my nights summoning their spirits by donning a stodgy three-piece man's suit, a pocket watch and a white shirt with stiff cuffs and a masher collar, fastened high and tight on my throat. As Helen helped me dress tonight, I channeled George Sand and my other Victorian heroines, dressing as men and moving in a man's world, breaking convention and taking life on their own terms.

The collar is the best part. It is my small taste of being bound, my attempt to share a little of what Helen experiences all day. When we dress, she tilts my head back and buttons my collar high and tight. She ties my necktie in a perfect knot, tugging

aggressively until I gasp for air. This way, I am always conscious
of the collar and spend the evening in self-imposed discipline:
eating slowly, moving carefully and sitting ramrod straight.
Helen can't take her eyes off me. She worships my self-imposed
restraint nearly as much as her own, and we both love the shared
sacrifice that binds us together.

At last we are home, alone. The entire day has been one long
foreplay session and it's time for release. Helen leads me into
the bedroom and undresses me slowly, tormenting me with her
graceful, deliberate movements. I am frantic, but my urgency
only makes her slow down all the more. I feel her hot breath on
my face as she moves in close, jerking my necktie tight one last
time before loosening it and freeing me from my constricting
collar. When I am finally naked, she pushes me down on the
mattress and begins to undress for me. She shrugs off her bolero
and wriggles out of her tight skirt, making quite a show of it.
At my direction, she leaves on her stockings and shoes—and her
corset.

Helen kneels on the floor at my feet. She parts my thighs and
I lean back, giving her room to maneuver. Her hand gently trails
down my lower belly and strokes the sensitive skin on the insides
of my thighs. I moan with frustration; it has been a long day, and
I've been on the cusp of orgasm for hours. In my mind, our love-
making blurs with our tight-lacing session early this morning; it
seems as though we have been making love all day long.

Helen looks up at me and grins. Very lightly, her fingers
graze over my mound. Each time her fingers touch even a single
hair, shock waves of pleasure shoot through my core and my
pussy contracts hard. I open my legs wider and thrust my pelvis
forward, begging her to hurry. Helen gathers her hair to one side
and bends down, concentrating her full attention on my pussy.
She slides her fingers up and down my swollen labia, dipping

inside me every now and then to gather more juice, which she spreads on my inner lips and thighs in slow circular motions. Even though she is deliberately avoiding my clit, it throbs; one touch from her and I will surely explode. All the while, I watch her on her knees, her full round ass emerging below the corset, just out of my reach. I lean forward to pluck the laces, playing her like a harp, but she pushes me back and orders me to lie still.

At last Helen flicks her tongue over my clit, first slowly and deliberately but then faster, fluttering in a steady rhythm. I glance down and see her face buried in my lap, her thick eyelashes fluttering like butterfly wings, echoing the rhythm of her tongue. Keeping up the pace, she reaches up and finds one of my breasts, squeezing and working my stiff little nipple between her thumb and forefinger. With her other hand she presses hard into my lower belly, intensifying the pressure building inside me.

Both of us are breathing hard. I arch my back and press my breast up against her hand. She arches her back in return, thrusting her ass in the air, her deep and rapid breaths swelling her chest and straining the corset's bindings almost to the breaking point. Suddenly Helen pinches my nipple very hard, and I cry out loud. I come fast and hard, like a freight train. Helen keeps up the rhythm until my clit has had enough. Gently, I push her head away. I lean back, panting. Drops of sweat snake down my back. Helen kisses and strokes my breasts, belly and the insides of my thighs. The sheets are drenched; the smell of sex is everywhere. Eyes closed, I take it all in. My senses are on fire.

Finally I sit up and look down at Helen. She peers up at me through her thick curtain of hair. Almost shyly, she presses her wrists together and holds them out to me, presenting herself for binding. I oblige, tying each wrist to the bedposts as she lies prone on the mattress, kneeling on the floor just as she did this morning. Sometimes after I've bound her I slide a long, thin, black silk scarf into her mouth. I pull her head back gently so her head and ass arch toward each other. She moans with pleasure and a little protest, biting the scarf and tossing her head as I use the silken reins to steady and control her. When she bucks her ass back against me, I am prepared with a dildo, which I've strapped tightly against me with a leather harness. For some reason, Helen is always shocked to feel herself suddenly impaled on a big, stiff phallus. She howls into the silken gag, shuddering and struggling.

I hold tight to the reins, plunging deeply into her cunt, riding her like a horse at full gallop. Suddenly an image from *Madame Bovary* springs to mind—the carriage careening out of control, hurtling through the French countryside as Madame B. and her lover fuck within. This sends me over the edge. Taking the reins in one hand, I pull up hard on Helen's laces with the other, jerking her back toward me like a marionette. I use the laces to draw her to me, and me into her.

As soon as I touch her corset lacings, Helen stiffens and grows still for a moment before exploding in orgasm. I quickly let loose of the reins so she can toss her head freely. The corset binds her too tightly to permit a full breath, so she is forced to come in quick panting gasps, whimpering with each exhalation. I release her, letting her set the pace as she rides the dildo, first quickly and violently, then slower. I encircle my hands around her waist to steady myself as she rocks back against me. The rhythmic pressure of the dildo against my mound causes me to come yet again, with a deep intensity that is almost painful—but not quite.

Finally she goes limp. I collapse on top of her. Beneath my breasts, I feel her back swelling and sinking as she struggles to breathe. The corset feels hot and stiff beneath me; the laces dig into my sensitive flesh, and I am reminded of what Helen has experienced all day.

I rise and begin to unlace her corset. As I loosen the bindings, Helen begins to breathe deeply, taking in great whooshes of air. While she adapts to her new freedom, I gently wipe the juices from her hot, swollen cunt and inner thighs, tenderly stroking the skin I had handled so roughly just a few minutes ago. Then I unbind her wrists, gently sit her on the bed and unfasten the front of the corset. She raises her arms compliantly, like a child, smiling sleepily at me.

At last, she is naked. I carefully examine every inch of her flesh, stroking and kissing the red indentations made by the laces and fastenings. I cup her breasts in my hands and lift them gently, peering around and beneath them. As I do this, I stroke my thumb over her swollen nipples, evoking moans from her and still another electric jolt between my legs.

Today the corset has left no abrasions, no bruises. I massage her skin to bring circulation back to the constricted areas. The reddened latticework of flesh trailing down her spine drives me wild, even in my sated state. I trace my finger gently over the X marks and kiss each one, all the way down.

But Helen is already in another world. After her long day with all its physical and mental challenges, she is exhausted. I pull the sheets back to help her into bed, but she frowns a little and shakes her head in protest. Ah, yes, the makeup. Helen refuses to go to bed with her makeup on. I grab one of those towelettes and carefully remove her mascara, eyeliner and what's left of her lipstick. As I wipe her face clean, I lean in close and whisper a little song: "Helen lay ybounden, bounden in a bond..." She grins and giggles, throwing her arms about my neck and kissing me.

When at last I tuck her into bed, she falls asleep instantly.

A small grin graces the corners of her pillowy lips. Sometimes she even snores a little, which always makes me smile. A few minutes later, I climb in beside her and she nestles into the crook of my arm, one hand cradled on my breast. I kiss the top of her head and stroke her hair. Soon we are fast asleep.

Tomorrow is Saturday, Helen's day off from tight-lacing. We will sleep in late, maybe do some yoga or go for a run. She will cook us an enormous brunch, and we will devour every last bit of it. We will breathe deeply and laugh loudly. We will make love, uncorseted and unconstrained. But in the midst of all this freedom, we will find ourselves wondering: why is it we both felt so much more free when Helen lay bound?

# THE RAINMAKER

## Elizabeth Daniels

H ope brought Amy to her knees, head bowed, cuffed hands
outstretched. The position felt less like a token of submission
and more like a twisted form of worship to a lesser sex deity. As
long as the being would answer her prayers, Amy would gladly
let it claim her devotion. After five months of sexual drought,
there wasn't anything she wouldn't do for an orgasm.

"Beautiful." Robert played an arpeggio along her vertebrae
and added the dimpled hollow at her tailbone as a grace note.
"I love your skin. Seeing you like this makes me wish I were a
painter instead of an architect."

Though the compliment pleased her, Amy did not respond.
Instead, she breathed lightly through the hole in her soft ball-gag
and tried to ignore the drool gathering around the seam where
her lips met the silicone. His touch, reverent and loving, made
it easier to think about being beautiful instead of about feeling
awkward. For months, their contact had been limited to the
brush of fingers as they passed the butter or brief collisions at

corners. Her frigidity, or more precisely, her sexual performance anxiety, had not only blighted their sex life, but also frostbitten the tenderness between them.

Her pussy had changed from a cornucopia to the Dust Bowl so suddenly she sometimes wondered if there were kernels of truth in the legends about evil fairy godmothers. If it was a magical curse, it was worse than anything the Brothers Grimm could imagine. At least Sleeping Beauty was awakened by a kiss after she pricked her finger. One night, Amy fingered a prick and thereafter, kisses failed to rouse her. Nor did spiced-up lubricants, spine-cracking sex positions or raunchy porn. Robert was supportive, endlessly patient and inventive, but for the first time in their five-year marriage, his efforts failed to ignite so much as a wet spark.

Furtively, she tried masturbation. Out went the gentle fingertip vibrator, replaced by the high-powered model she mentally dubbed the crotch rocket. But the B.O.B. was even less successful than Robert. The best Amy could manage were a few joyless, rubbery spasms, as satisfying as a muscle twitch. Although her pussy had the world's worst case of stage fright, it refused to be fooled by her finger or a vibrator. It wanted cock. Good cock. Robert's cock. And Amy wanted her husband, not a molded piece of improbably pink plastic.

Robert knelt in front of her, his crotch at eye level, presenting bare torso, loose sweatpants capable of hiding any erection. Her sigh whistled through the hole in the gag.

"Do you remember what I told you?"

Amy fingered the release strap on the soft bonds, tongued the ball loosely strapped in her mouth, and nodded. She'd insisted on the strap. She'd read one too many horror stories about wives left hanging like butchered deer after their husbands dropped dead during bondage play. She wondered why he had bothered with the gag; it was so small and strapped so loosely around her head that it was at best a token silencer.

"It's not to keep you quiet. It's to remind you who you are for now," he said as he fastened a long silver chain to the center of her cuffs. "No questions. No helpful suggestions. Above all, no directions. You're not in your office on Two Wall Street, and I'm not one of your middle management subordinates. You're here to obey me. I'm in charge. You're not."

Amy sank her teeth into the ball-gag. But what the hell, it was cheaper than couples therapy and the closest thing they'd had to sexual contact in a month. She raised her head to inspect the chain he had fastened to her bonds and had just time to catch a glimpse of her padded velvet sleep mask before he slipped it over her head and imprisoned her in darkness. Amy grunted in protest and then again in startled pain as a slap stung her bare ass.

"No," he said, and without the visual of his pleasant round face to contradict it, she could hear the firmness in his voice.

Like the pleasure of being caressed, she had forgotten he could be so decisive, had forgotten who he was when sex was only a satisfying aspect of their relationship and not a thousand-pound anvil hanging over their bed. She remembered what it was like to want him without fear of adding to her already vast reservoir of sexual frustration. The memory brought a welcome whisper of desire.

So she did not protest the discipline. When the chain ratcheted upward, she allowed herself to be drawn to her feet. His hand splayed over her back, pushing her forward so her ass was outthrust and her breasts dangled like fat bunches of grapes. She wasn't uncomfortable, but she felt exposed, her sexuality emphasized. And, though she did not like to admit it even to herself, she was scared. She was a creature of routine. Some had even called her a prisoner of her habits, a charge she couldn't deny. Knowing what was next comforted her, and her comfort line was cut.

His fingertips sketched her cheekbones, her chin. Against her forehead, his lips pressed a soft benediction.

"Trust me," he said, and Amy did. This was Robert, who knew her fears, Robert of the midnight confessions. Robert, who occasionally annoyed her but never betrayed her.

Yet when she first felt the rope, she still had to crush the ball between her teeth to keep from squealing with fear. Robert knew the thought of being completely immobilized terrified her. Although she couldn't imagine what else he could bind, he'd promised he wouldn't tie her feet or limit her movement other than her wrists. She had her safeword and the release catch. She forced herself to relax into the bonds and wait.

Slowly, he wound the ropes around her torso, running soft cottony lines above, below and between her breasts, like a rudimentary bra, but much tighter. Like a boy stealing a treat, he paused to tug at her tightening nipples before returning to his task. As he added more rope, the layers above and below her breasts thickened and squeezed like a constrictor flexing its coils around its prey. A final sharp tug almost pulled her off her feet. Then, nothing.

Darkness and the ropes enfolded Amy like a chrysalis. Her mind was clear, finally at peace. After months of agonizing over every step of foreplay, after sex that consisted of checklists and flow charts compiled from hours of research, for once, she did not need to think or plan. Like extradark chocolate, such dependence was not something she would want every day, but for the moment, it was a bite of bitter bliss.

Like a strangely discordant lullaby, the pain lulled her into a trance. Her world narrowed to the bite of rope into her flesh.

Like a foot squeezed into a fashionable shoe a half size too small, the pain was hot and compacted. Yet she found peace in pain, even pride that she possessed such endurance. As with the shoe, the benefits outweighed the suffering. She found herself wondering just how strong she really was, even wishing he'd given her more of a challenge.

Wet warmth gathered along the banks of her labia, ready to overflow. Yet she experienced her own arousal as if from a distance, without the all-too-familiar anxiety about completion. The complex savor of pain was all that mattered. When light cracked in through the bottom of her sleep mask and pressed against her closed eyelids, she was vaguely annoyed.

"Look," he ordered, his voice thick with lust. Reluctantly, she obeyed. He had adjusted the sleep mask to give her a blinkered field of vision, enough so she could look down, see her breasts and what he had done to them but nothing else.

Other than medical examinations, lingerie shopping and bathing, Amy had paid no more attention to her breasts than she had her arms or legs. Once she caught sight of herself, she couldn't stop staring. Her breasts, ordinary, soft and a little slack, jutted between the intricately twined white ropes like offerings on an altar, their round, forced symmetry an exotic fruit cultivated only for temple feasts. The skin was rich rose madder, thin and shiny as stretched satin. Her areolas and nipples had almost disappeared, the first camouflaged by the blood flush, the second flattened and stretched to the merest suggestion of a stem. Her mouth flooded as she thought of Robert biting into the bursting ripeness as he slid into her, of the two of them locked in climax.

But at the thought of orgasm, the familiar fright froze her. What if she still couldn't—what if he couldn't—how would he feel if she failed after all this?

Robert dangled a wide strap of shiny leatherette cloth in front of her face, interrupting her view.

"Amazing how expressive you can be, love, even with your face half covered. You're thinking again, aren't you? Bad girl."

The material popped as he flicked it across her breast. The slap was light, but burned as if she'd briefly touched the skin to a hot stove. The shock jolted her thoughts out of the rutted circle of worry. Greedily, she watched how her breast quivered at the blow, stared at the brief afterimage of the lash against her blood-dark skin. The pain was salt, adding sharp flavor to her pleasure. The lashes continued, painstakingly licking each inch of skin.

She rolled her safeword around in her mouth like a hot cinnamon candy. At any time, she could spit it out and the burn would end. She waited, savoring the intensity as long as she could.

When he stopped, she wept. She had gone so far beyond herself that she was startled when he touched her. Her pussy was succulent, dripping with readiness. He scooped its juice with two fingers and spread it over her clit in slow, hard circles.

"What I wouldn't give to fuck your tits right now," he whispered. "Cover them with lube until they dripped like your pussy, press them together around my cock and pump you."

Her mind flashed a montage: the meaty bell of his cock pushing up between her compressed tits, shining sleek purple and burgundy skin, the leathery slap of his balls against the underside of her breasts...

Five months of glacial repression melted in a flash flood. Drowning, she spat out her gag so she could suck in enough air. Dizzy from anoxia, she screamed her release, screamed for more, screamed that she wasn't going to survive what she had, screamed for his cock.

Most of her outburst he ignored, but the cock he provided, plowing into her warm open wetness and forcing out the last of the frozen lake in another climactic aftershock. Six, seven thrusts, each forcing out smaller washes of release, and he stiffened, going still against her, and groaned.

A warm salt rain of their mingled fluids trickled down Amy's thighs. She closed her eyes and smiled. The drought had ended.

# DO YOU SEE WHAT I FEEL?

## Teresa Noelle Roberts

I took a deep breath and felt the silky constriction, both comforting and arousing, of the ropes—chest harness, corset and teasing crotch binding—I wore under my red turtleneck sweater dress. Erik had suggested the dress for its relative innocence; it was calf length and it skimmed my body loosely enough that you'd have to look twice to make out I wore something unusual underneath. Erik had made sure the ropes weren't screamingly obvious, just as he'd made sure the shibari was neat and elegant, and that the crotch ropes were tight enough to tantalize me but not enough to either irritate that most sensitive skin or let me get off before he was good and ready. (Dammit.)

I'd laughed about his precision with the ropes and the way he chose the outfit so carefully to suggest and yet conceal them. "Ryo's blind, right? That's the point of this game. So what does it matter?"

Erik said, "Ryo's definitely blind. As for the point of this game…" He gave me one of those secretive, naughty smiles of his, the kind that reaches out and tickles my clit. "Other than turning us both on? You'll figure it out soon enough."

Then he grabbed a strategic knot through the soft knit of the dress and twisted.

The ropes tugged at my labia, pulling them open.

My husband is evil and perverted and I love him for it.

God, I was wet already, slicker than I'd realized. Slick with the caress of ropes and with the knowledge that I was going to be shown off, albeit to someone who might not be aware of it.

I'd probably end up naked save for ropes at some point, naked in front of someone who'd just go on talking with me like nothing was different because he wouldn't know anything was, wouldn't know I was bare and bound and by that point most likely dripping in front of him, trying to carry on a conversation while aching for him to leave so Erik could spank me or fuck me or whatever he had in mind as a final round to the game. Erik's games were always worthwhile in the end.

And always came with an unexpected twist.

I should have known that whatever assumptions I'd made were slightly off.

For instance, I'd imagined Ryo as one of those quietly brilliant Asian American science majors who was now grown up and making big biotech bucks but was still slightly geeky. Probably because, except for the Asian American part, that's what Erik's like. He may be wonderfully kinky, but what can I say? When he's not tying me up and having his wicked way with me, he plays Dungeons and Dragons with a gaggle of other thirtysomething geniuses with similar cases of arrested development. (Including me. Yeah, we have more than a few things in common besides hot sex.)

But the man who came to our door, guided by a golden retriever so well groomed she practically gleamed...if he'd been in a Japanese movie, he'd have been evil, doomed to a tragic death, or possibly both, because the beautiful men always are. He had sleek, shoulder-length blue-black hair; a body to die for, not much taller than I am, but perfectly proportioned; golden skin, killer cheekbones and a smile that would have melted my panties if I'd been wearing any. He was dressed all in shades of gray, from his topcoat to his shoes, and just a little too well for a dinner at a friend's house; I guessed the monotone might be less a fashion statement than a practicality for someone who couldn't see, but it looked yummy.

There were a few formalities—introductions, taking Ryo's coat, Ryo taking his guide dog out of harness. (The dog promptly fell asleep—I guess getting Ryo out here on the commuter rail from Boston was quite an adventure.) When that was settled but before we sat down, I repeated, "Hi, I'm Carla," and hesitantly extended my hand. I was surprised by how readily Ryo followed my voice and clasped it.

And even more surprised when he said, "May I? I like to see who I'm talking to." I caught Erik's eye, saw him nod, and muttered "Yes." Ryo's strong arms drew me in.

He ran his hands up my arms to my shoulders.

Paused where the ropes crossed over, giving a slight grin and nod.

Ran his hands through my hair and down my back, swiftly and lightly, but there was no way he could have missed the ropes under the soft knit.

Or, I suspected, the way I was trembling.

Finally, he raised his hands to my face. Gentle fingertips explored my features: traced my eyelids, feathered over my eyebrows, highlighted the shape of my cheekbones, got to know my nose, cupped my cheeks, outlined my chin.

It was one of the most incredibly intimate things anyone had ever done to me (and believe me, Erik has done a lot of

incredibly intimate things to me, including some that are illegal
in several Southern states and the District of Columbia).

The ropes seemed tighter, as if my entire body had grown
more sensitive, as if my breasts and pussy had swollen from
Ryo's touch on my face.

I closed my eyes and surrendered to the sensation, fighting
not to moan. It was just Ryo's way of seeing, right?

Ryo chuckled deep in his throat. "Erik, you dog," he said.
"You didn't tell me Carla's beautiful."

"Liar. I told you…"

"You told me she was hot, and I agree. But she's also beautiful. Some women are one and not the other, but she's both.
And I bet she has a very sensual mouth."

I froze. As he traced the shape of my lips, I struggled not to
kiss that sure finger, not to lick at it.

It was all too easy to imagine it circling my nipple with the
same delicate precision, or—oh, my god, on my clit.

I couldn't help it. I moaned.

Ryo slipped his finger between my parted lips.

My instincts had all sorts of ideas, but I am married, even
if ours is a slightly unusual marriage. I opened my eyes, looked
toward Erik as best I could.

He smiled and nodded. Yes. All part of the game, or at least
something he was comfortable to make part of the game.

License to play!

I intended to suck that finger like it was a mini-cock, to give
Ryo back some of his own teasing medicine.

Instead, his finger caressed my tongue, sending shivers
through my body and straight to my already aching pussy. I
sucked, and he caressed, and I leaned into Ryo's body, just a
bit and felt delicious hardness adjusting the lines of his elegant
charcoal pants.

Ryo slipped his finger from my mouth, pulled me closer, ran both hands down my back again. This time, they weren't light but firm and bold, exploring. And this time, he didn't stop politely at the small of my back but followed the ropes down, feeling how they dipped between my buttocks. He chuckled again, approvingly, and gave the ropes a little tug.

My lips swelled under the caress of the ropes, and my head swam.

This wasn't what I expected. He wasn't what I expected.

But he was making me melt, and it wasn't just a handsome man's hands on me, although I wasn't about to complain about that. I'm more than a little bit of an exhibitionist, and this wasn't the first time Erik had found a way to show me off to an appreciative audience, but the way Ryo was seeing me with his hands was something new. It was far more intimate than simply being watched and yet curiously impersonal in some ways. I got the feeling he'd explore anything new and interesting with as much delicacy and curiosity.

Although probably without a tempting hard-on.

Erik stood there watching (and probably getting hard himself) as his friend and I drove each other crazy.

And then, when my body was turning to liquid fire and Ryo bent his head down as if he was thinking about kissing me, Erik—damn him and his games!—said something studiedly innocuous about predinner drinks.

I'm not sure how to describe the noise I made. I'm afraid whining was involved as well as some more appealing elements like moaning.

Ryo laughed and said, "I'd love a scotch." He gave my butt a light squeeze before pulling away. "Carla, would you help me find a seat?"

He took my arm innocently, as if he hadn't just been driving me wild—then touched the bare skin of my wrist so lightly and yet so deliciously that I shivered.

I was so going to get Erik for not warning me that his blind friend wasn't going to be an innocent pawn in our game, that he was apparently just as toppy and arousingly evil as Erik.

On the other hand, would it have been nearly as much fun if I'd known?

Cocktails and dinner passed with excruciating slowness. I barely tasted my wine, although I might have sipped more of it than I meant to and couldn't be sure what I was eating even though I'd helped cook it. The guys kept up a stream of light, suggestive banter the whole time that kept me distracted, focused on the ropes and the throbbing, aching territory between my thighs rather than on food. That the banter was about me, but between them, just made it worse or maybe better. It was especially unnerving—and exciting—that while Erik kept smiling at me, touching my hand, including me in little ways, Ryo didn't even glance in my direction. The part of my brain that was still working logically realized that, blind since birth, he didn't bother pretending he could see who he was talking to.

The part of my brain that was playing in the gutter, and that was most of it, relished feeling like an object—a beautiful, fascinating object, sure, but an object—for the guys' amusement. Sometimes in our games I showed myself off and felt powerful, but this time I was being shown off and that was hot too: wrapped up and tied with a bow, like a special present, I was being shown off to Erik's friend.

Or offered to him.

How far would it go? We'd never involved others in our games beyond watching and being watched and some mild teasing caresses, but we were both open to the idea under the right circumstances.

Even though I'd just met Ryo, my body thought this was the right circumstances. My mind? Well, I trust my husband, and he'd known this guy since they were undergraduates.

And even if that wasn't what Erik had in mind, I knew we weren't done. The conversation had layers, and I had a feeling that the guys had something planned, something they were talking around just enough to make me crazy with curiosity and lust.

After we ate, I offered to make coffee. Not that I wanted coffee—I wanted Erik, or Ryo, or ideally, both of them—but I figured if I stepped out of the room, they could finish their plotting without having to be all cryptic.

As soon as I stood, though, Erik said, "No. Stay here. Ryo, would you like to check my work? It's been a long time."

"Hate to think you'd forgotten anything." He turned his face to where he figured I was—I was unnerved by how close he got, when he'd been talking around me for so long. "Carla," he said with exaggerated politeness, "would you take off your dress, please?"

His voice was almost as caressing as his hands had been and I had to grab a chair because my knees went wobbly. Trembling, I reached for the hem of my dress, but, "No, let me help you," Erik said. He crouched down, grabbed the hem, and lifted it.

I expected him to go slowly, to tease me further even if Ryo couldn't appreciate it, but instead he had it to my shoulders in a flash. I raised my arms over my head so he could pull it off.

He did. And then he grabbed my wrists and lifted me up until my tiptoes just brushed the floor. Erik is about six-five, with big, powerful hands (he works on it just so he can pull off tricks like this) so it was like suspension bondage without the suspension, a lovely strain that pulled the ropes tighter against my oversensitive lips, arched my breasts forward and made me even more aware of being helplessly, deliciously on display.

"She's ready for you, Ryo," he said. "Come see what I've done."

And of course, there was only one way for him to see.

With his hands.

He started at the top, caressed my face again, followed the lines of my throat to my collarbone and followed that line to the ropes.

He traced those down to where they started wrapping my chest; three wrappings of rope there, and he followed all of them across my body, checked where they went between my breasts. His fingers barely grazed the sensitive valley, concentrating instead on the ropes, but that was enough to make me squirm and moan. He reached the band of ropes underneath, traced those as well. This time his touch, by accident or design, was less precise, stroking the plump bottom curve of my breasts. He was nowhere near the nipple, but that flesh was almost as sensitive now as my nipples normally were. I bit my lip, but the "Oh, god," was still audible.

Ryo chuckled, and the appreciation in the chuckle was like another caress. He liked my reactions, and I liked that he liked them.

Liked it enough that moisture was trickling down my legs.

Ryo's hands moved lower, to the ropes corseting my waist. "You changed ropes here," he said, stroking one area repeatedly. He wasn't touching skin, except through rope, but it still set the skin there on fire and sent the flames traveling to my clit.

"Yeah. I'm surprised you can tell. They're the same kind of rope."

"Close, but not quite. I'd like to see how you handled the transition. It felt pretty smooth through her dress."

Erik turned me around like the thing I felt myself to be.

Ryo examined the knot work where the two ropes joined. "Very neat. A lot of people don't bother to make the back so tidy."

"You taught me well."

When I could string two coherent sentences together, I was going to ask for that story. A good story is the next best thing to being there, and since I couldn't go back in time and watch Ryo teaching Erik, I'd like to hear all the juicy details. But for now I could only relax and enjoy the sensations as Ryo examined all the knots and transitions on my back. It took a long time, and before he was done, Erik was letting me lean on him because I was shaking so much.

Or maybe it was just because he wanted me there. He kept kissing me, sending me soaring even higher. His sweater and jeans felt wonderfully rough against my bare skin and the wool of his sweater was almost painful, but in a good way, on my nipples. He pressed his crotch against my thigh and ground, and I could feel how hard he was, how much he was enjoying the show and the act of showing me off. I kept trying to move so he'd rub it between my legs, but he was having none of that. He wanted to keep the long tease going, and maybe—at least I liked to think so—he might have found that a little too much himself.

Finally Ryo said, his voice husky, "Great work, Erik. At least as good as mine. Turn her around. There's one last thing I want to check."

Erik whispered in my ear, "Are you ready?"

I had a pretty good idea of what was coming, and all I could possibly say was "God, yes. Please!"

Erik neatly turned me around and lifted me up again, using only one hand, arching me back against his body. He reached around me with the other, simultaneously hugging me close and pinching my nipple. I clenched and nearly came.

I was perversely glad I didn't quite make it, though. Ryo had something in mind and I was waiting for that.

Ryo put his hands on my waist.

Ran them down over the rope-covered curve of my belly.

Found where the ends of the crotch ropes were neatly woven into the waist wrap.

Then, excruciatingly slowly, Ryo traced the two ropes down, following them to where they were holding my pussy lips open.

"So wet," he said. "So very wet. You'll have to wash the rope." As he spoke, he stroked the damp, slippery rope, barely touching my flesh, not touching my clit at all. I needed to come so badly it hurt, but even the ache felt good.

I cocked my hips toward him, said, "Please. Please. Oh, god, please," or at least something like that.

"One last thing to check," Ryo said, and flicked my clit.

The guide dog started awake as I screamed and then screamed some more. His touch was as sure and delicate there as it had been everywhere else, but at this point he could have been clumsy as a teenage boy still trying to figure out female anatomy and I'd have gone off like a rocket.

"And that's the final test," he said, clearly talking to Erik, not to me. "The prettiest rope work in the world is useless unless the result's a wet, screaming woman."

Erik eased me down and I slumped between the two men, feeling like I'd just run a very special kind of marathon.

Only then did Ryo kiss me.

He kissed as deliciously as he did everything else, but when his watch quietly intoned the hour, he pulled away. "I should get going," he said. "If I catch the next train, I'll get home about when Jessie does—and the deal was I could come play without her today as long as I saved most of my energy for home. She was so pissed she got called into work today, but she's too new at the job to get away with saying no."

"Bring her next time," I said, surprised at my boldness coming back so quickly; surprised, in fact, that I could talk again. "That is...there'll be a next time?"

"I hope so," both men said at once.

"Jessie likes to show off about as much as you do," Ryo said, "and she likes to watch, too."

"And you have to show me that tortoiseshell pattern again," Erik said. "I thought I remembered it, but I don't think it's right."

"Be glad to, my friend," Ryo said, and called for his dog. "If the ladies are up for it, I'll show you on Carla and let you practice on Jessie. That way Carla can see what you're doing. Never know when an extra pair of hands could be useful. Does that sound good?"

I managed to stammer out "Yes," but it wasn't easy, because my mind was already flooding with images of Ryo tying me up while Erik and Jessie watched, Erik tying Jessie up while I watched, and Ryo "supervising" in his own special way that was sure to drive both Jessie and me crazy.

Fortunately Erik was thinking more clearly than I and managed to see Ryo off safely. He offered a ride to the train, but Ryo laughed and said, "It's not like walking in the dark bothers me, man, and I think you have something to do."

Which he did, bending me over the arm of the couch as soon as Ryo left and driving his cock deep inside me.

It wasn't until we were boneless, sated, and curled up on the couch together that I managed to ask something that had been plaguing me. "How did the blind guy master rope bondage anyway?"

"How he learned is a long story and you'd better ask him. As to how he does it, how do you think? By touch...and very, very slowly."

And just thinking about that was enough to get us started on the next round.

# TRUSS ISSUES

## Lux Zakari

E my didn't want to be tied up. One could say she didn't have much confidence in others.

Samir found this all very interesting. "Why not?"

A quick glance around the crowded outdoor patio of the restaurant revealed it was far too dark to see if anyone was listening in, but Emy decided the conversation had taken a turn too intriguing to care about eavesdroppers. She turned back to Samir, who sat opposite her, the light from a hurricane lamp flickering between them and dancing shadowy, suggestive patterns across their faces. His dark-eyed gaze studied her with an intensity that made her fidget. "I guess I've seen too many instances where people have put their faith in the wrong lovers."

"Really?" He arched an eyebrow and rubbed at the facial hair running the length of his jaw. "Like when?"

"Like I don't know." She flicked her wrist in indication there were too many times to count, but the way he watched her had ways of making her forget. "I saw a movie once where the guy tied a naked girl to his bed, duct-taped her eyes and mouth shut and just left her there. Then, because he'd done so much meth, he forgot she was there until three days later."

He granted her a reprieve from his stare by rolling his eyes. "I thought you meant something happened to you personally."

"It doesn't matter, it was still traumatizing. In any case, it's a prime example of why I don't sleep with meth addicts."

"That's a good code to live by. It doesn't explain why you won't let someone who's not a drug-addled psychopath tie you up."

A man worth consuming her with desire, tying her up—she'd never entertained that secret Option B before, which, now presented by Samir, sounded inexplicably sexy. Emy shook the foreign, fascinating thoughts from her head, tucking a strand of her curly red hair behind her ear and reaching for the bread basket. "Because it still seems quite fucking terrifying." She selected a fat round roll and cut it in half with her butter knife to give her suddenly nervous fingers something to do. "I don't want to have to worry about all the horrific things some guy could do to me when I'm at my most vulnerable." She shuddered. "What's erotic and fun about that?"

"Hmm..." was his only reply. He plucked a roll from the basket and pulled it apart like a man engrossed with his appetizer, but Emy knew better. They'd been seeing each other for three weeks, and she was already familiar with that look in his dark brown eyes, the telltale glimmer hinting at a scheme and a need to prove someone wrong.

Etiquette be damned; she pointed at him with her knife. "Don't try to persuade me otherwise."

The corners of his mouth twisted upward. "What do you mean?"

"You know exactly what I mean. You're sitting over there, trying to think up ways to con me into bondage."

Samir choked on a laugh and lifted his wineglass to his lips, as if in an attempt to recover his perpetually cool composure. "You think you know me so well."

"I do."

"There's something you might not have realized, though."

"And what's that?"

"I know you, too," he said. "Perhaps better than you know yourself."

"That's very audacious of you."

He smiled, an act that made his frequently stoic features look benevolent, even sensual, in the candlelight. "We'll see."

After dinner and a walk around the illuminated city, they arrived at Emy's building, a multifloor, white-brick affair stretching upward and disappearing into the dusky film of clouds overhead. She gave her date a wink. "Come up for a nightcap?"

"How can I refuse?" He opened the silver-handled door and placed a hand on her lower back, guiding her gently through the entranceway. Her heels pricked the silence of the lobby as they crossed to the elevator, which slid open with a *ding* as soon as Samir pressed the button.

They leaned against the mirrored wall as the doors closed, and the elevator gave a start as it ascended. A silence thick with anticipation hung between them, their conversation from earlier resonating through Emy like a struck tuning fork. She forced her attention on the climbing floor numbers. Two, three, four... She suddenly regretted living on the twentieth floor.

"Nervous?" He watched her with a contented, bemused smile, the kind a predator might wear as it toyed with its prey, biding its time.

"Why would I be nervous?" Part of her hoped he would actually know the answer.

"Because you know when we get to your apartment, I'm tying you up."

She drew in a swift breath and pursed her lips, trying to will the warring feelings of both fear and sexual thrill away. "Is that what you think?"

"No." Unabashed, his gaze swept over her body. "It is what I know."

"Someone's crystal ball has a crack in it." She frosted her tone as she again attempted to concentrate on the rising numbers, hoping he wouldn't notice how the intensity of his words affected her. Fourteen, fifteen…

He breathed a laugh. "If you say so."

They again lapsed into a silence, and just when Emy thought she couldn't take it anymore, the doors opened and she forced herself not to flee from the mirror-and-chrome cubicle clogged with sexual tension. Instead, she kept her chin high and back straight as she strode toward her apartment and slid her key in the lock. Once the door swung open, she gestured Samir inside with a sweep of her arms in a way that would make Vanna White proud. He gave a gentlemanly nod of his head in response as he forged ahead into the dark living space.

Emy followed him, tossing her key ring in the direction of a nearby table and missing completely. "Can you get the light?"

Her answer came in the form of Samir kicking the door shut and walking her backward until her shoulder blades pressed against the painted wood. "I could, but what fun would that be?" His lips trailed a path from her earlobe down her neck, then to her collarbone, as his body pushed against hers.

The darkness hid her smile. "You have a point." She tilted her head, giving him unbarred access to the sensitive skin of her throat, and her knees weakened at the feel of his cock against her thigh, nudging her through the fabric of their clothes.

Samir's kisses moved to her mouth and her lips parted, allowing his tongue to sweep against hers and leaving her lightheaded. Her legs parted, granting him permission to slide his hands up her thighs, touch her in a place most of her exes didn't get to explore until after several months, let alone weeks. She wondered what it was about Samir that permitted her to feel so wanton, uninhibited, unafraid, so much so that she'd slept with him after the first date. Where had the usual guarded feeling gone?

His teeth nipped at her lips, drawing a moan from her as he pinned her to the door using the strength of his legs. Her clit throbbed in anticipation as her dress skirted up her thighs and he slowly tugged her panties down until they puddled around her knees. Her breath hitched as her heart hammered away. She felt her whole body buzzing, awaiting his explorative touch.

Instead, his kisses grew slower, indolent, and his fingers rose, curling around her wrists and raising them over her head. A jolt ripped through her as she realized what a captive position she was in. "Emy," he murmured against her mouth, "I want to tie you up."

"I already told you. I'm not into that." To her surprise, her body didn't sync up to her beliefs. She felt a warm liquid rush flood her cunt.

"Is that so?" Samir captured both her wrists in one hand, his grasp firm, gentle and easily escapable—she didn't understand why she didn't break away. His other hand moved between her legs, eliciting from her a gasp as his finger dipped inside her weeping cunt. "It feels like you're into it. Admit it. You're turned on."

Cursing her body for its betrayal, Emy nestled her teeth in

her lower lip and forced her breathing to remain calm, to not come out as a needy whimper.

"Just your wrists." He punctuated the sentence with a lingering kiss. "I'll use my tie. You can slip free whenever you want to, or I'll untie you whenever you say." His tongue teased her, darting in and out of her mouth and mimicking the light, feathery motions of his finger, still flickering over her cunt. "Just think. You, with your hands bound behind your back, and me, licking you until you come."

The air building in Emy's lungs left in a groan as she pictured Samir's tongue in place of his finger. The visual he'd described— even her, trussed up—was too good to deny. She drew away from his kiss and gave him a brief, nervous nod. "Okay." She swallowed, her mouth dry, and looked between them at his hand between her legs, fighting off another moan. "But hurry."

Samir drew away from her and her panties completed their journey to the floor. She'd just enough time to kick them aside before he'd turned her around, her breasts against the door. Emy could feel his cock, thick and hard, nudging her skin as he ground against her backside, working at the knot of his tie with one hand while his other snaked around her body to pop free the buttons on her shirt. She felt grateful for the door and Samir— they were the only things keeping her upright at this point.

Emy sucked in a gulp of air as he collected her wrists at the small of her back and looped the thin, silky strip of fabric around them, linking them with a loose knot. She squeezed her eyes shut, not knowing whether to moan with pleasure or cry out in fright.

Samir turned her again, slanting his mouth over hers, and he placed his hands on her waist and took a few steps back- ward, guiding their path into the unlit living room and directing her into an armchair. She sank into a sitting position with some trepidation, her hands trapped between the cushioned seat and her spine. The words *untie me* were on her tongue until her gaze met Samir's. In the weak moonlight beaming through the half-closed blinds and casting bars of light over his face, she could see his dark eyes, watching her with a hunger that made her whole body swell. Stunned, she realized from his look that despite her bound situation, she felt very much in control and felt powerful at having a man look at her in such a way. The thrill caused her legs to part, granting him an unobstructed view. She enjoyed the way his Adam's apple bobbed in response.

He lowered himself to his knees and parted her open shirt, revealing her breasts encased in lace. Knowing she couldn't touch him in return sent another ripple of bliss through Emy and she licked her dry lips, her fingers turning to fists behind her back. Samir cupped both her breasts in his hands, kneading the globes gently until her puckered nipples leapt from the bunching, delicate fabric. With one hand still circling her left breast, his mouth descended upon her right, trapping one of the rosy nubs and lapping at it with his tongue.

Emy's head dropped backward and she didn't bother to fight off the moan that had been building inside her for what seemed like the entire evening. Samir gave a soft groan in response to the noise, a sound increasing her pleasure. Realizing he enjoyed this moment—this unfamiliar experience—as much as she did dampened her aching cunt further.

His mouth left her breast on a journey down her stomach, his tongue dipping into her belly button as his hands slid down the sides of her torso. She watched from beneath heavy lids how he observed her body like a man enthralled and on the verge of losing control. His worshipful expression blurred the distinction of who was the submissive one. She'd never felt more in control in her life. Her fear evaporated, replaced by pure desire.

Samir took a deep, trembling breath as he gently pushed her skirt up around her waist, completely exposing her. They both watched as his hands smoothed down then up her inner thighs and he traced the outline of her dripping cunt, eliciting from her a high-pitched sigh. He rubbed a slow, teasing circle over her clit with a wet fingertip, bringing about more gasps and breathy urges for him to continue before replacing his finger with his tongue.

Emy squeezed her eyes shut, straining against her loose binds as she cried out toward the ceiling. His languid ministrations sought and found a rhythm that made her legs shake and widen farther. He slipped a finger inside her slick, tight opening and she clamped down on her lip, fighting back a scream. She already teetered on the brink on climax and knew it wouldn't take much more to push her over the edge.

The need to touch him was deliciously excruciating and not being able to invoked a divine conflict where she both wanted to be free yet never wanted to be let go. "Fuck, Samir." The sense deprivation made her palms damp as her fists alternated between clenching and unclenching. Her head spun as she lay wonderfully trapped beneath his blissful torment. "I want you to fuck me."

One of his hands left her body and she heard the jangle of a belt buckle and the descent of a zipper, but never once did Samir's actions halt. Then he drew away from her and, placing both hands on her hips, pulled her to the edge of the chair, all but dragging her off the furniture entirely. With her hands pinned beneath her and Samir suspending her legs in the air, she'd never felt so helpless yet so excited.

Samir freed his cock from his pants, once carefully pressed, now wrinkled from passion, positioned himself at her entrance and pushed himself inside her with abandon. A scream tore from

Emy's throat as her hips rose to meet his thrusts. Her nipples, still peeping over the tops of their lacy confines, strained against the fabric as her breasts bounced in time to their age-old rhythm.

He pushed against her with every motion, providing her clit with maximum contact every time he drove into her. Incoherent, fragmented sentences tumbled from Emy's lips. She couldn't even comprehend what she tried to say, knew only that the desperation to touch him, rake her nails down his back and pull him close intoxicated her, pushed her farther toward the edge.

Samir remained silent, his whole body and his motions tight, coiled, anticipating release. His face creased with an expression of pain, but Emy knew he felt anything but. His gaze traveled over her body, completely at his mercy, and the look in his eyes made the muscles in her cunt tense. She closed her eyes, concentrating on the feel of him slamming into her, the perpetual friction against her clit and how he could do anything to her right now but remained devoted to her pleasure. The thought prompted another, final scream from her, her muscles contracting around his cock, and he came inside her, succumbing to a shudder enveloping his entire body.

He tugged her into a sitting position and they both tumbled onto the carpet, panting toward the still rotary fan overhead. "I told you being tied up wasn't so bad."

She glanced over at the man she'd come to inexplicably and wholeheartedly trust in such a short time, and it was all she could do not to grin like a fool. "Now I've done something for you, you have to do something for me."

"Anything." She knew he meant it.

Emy rolled to the side and wriggled free of the tangled tie's generous loop. She tossed the fabric in his direction. "Make it tighter next time."

# ABOUT THE AUTHORS

**JACQUELINE APPLEBEE** (writing-in-shadows.co.uk) breaks down barriers with smut. Jacqueline's stories have appeared in various anthologies and websites, including Cleansheets, *Best Women's Erotica, Best Lesbian Erotica, Where the Girls Are* and *Girl Crazy*.

**JANINE ASHBLESS** is the author of five Black Lace erotica books of paranormal and fantasy erotica. Her short stories have been published by Cleis Press in the anthologies *I Is for Indecent, Playing with Fire, Frenzy, Best Women's Erotica 2009, Sweet Love* and *Fairy Tale Lust*. She blogs at janineashbless.blogspot.com.

**EMILY BINGHAM** is a writer, coffee addict, sock fetishist, bookworm, pervert, word junkie, and lover of puns, poetry and red wine. She hopes to never grow up and pick a "real" job. When she isn't writing she can be found cooking esoteric baked goods and crazy multicourse meals.

**TENILLE BROWN** is a Southern writer whose stories can be found online and in such print anthologies as: *Do Not Disturb*, *Iridescence*, *Tasting Him*, *A Is for Amour*, *Dirty Girls*, *Making the Hook-Up* and the forthcoming *Fast Girls*. Tenille keeps a blog at thesteppingstone.blogspot.com.

**MEGAN BUTCHER** is a librarian and sex educator living in Ottawa, Ontario. Her writing has appeared in newspapers and magazines like *Capital Xtra*, *Herizons* and *Dharma Arts*. Every Sunday night, she posts some dirty micro-fiction to Your Weekly Dose (meganbutcher.com/weeklydose), her smut blog.

**ANGELA CAPERTON** writes eclectic erotica that breaks genre rules. She won the EPIC award for Best Erotica in 2008 with *Woman of the Mountain*. Look for her stories published with Cleis, Circlet Press, Drollerie Press, eXtasy Books and in the indie magazine, *Out of the Gutter*. Visit Angela at blog.angelacaperton.com.

**ELIZABETH COLDWELL** lives and writes in London. Her stories have appeared in numerous anthologies including *Spanked*, *Bottoms Up*, *Yes, Sir* and *Please, Sir*. "The Long Way Home" is dedicated to Cinturones, queen of the seat belt.

**ANDREA DALE's** stories appear in *Fairy Tale Lust*, *Alison's Wonderland*, *Sweet Love* and *The Sweetest Kiss*. With coauthors, she has sold novels *A Little Night Music* (Sarah Dale) and *Cat Scratch Fever* (Sophie Mouette). She believes all fairy tales are really for adults. Share her fantasies at cyvarwydd.com.

**ELIZABETH DANIELS** is a former reporter and teacher. Her erotic short fiction has appeared in several e-zines and in the

Erotica Readers & Writers Association anthology *Cream*. She is
a member of the RWA and the ERWA.

**EMERALD's** erotic fiction has been published in anthologies
edited by Violet Blue, Rachel Kramer Bussel, Jolie du Pre and
Alison Tyler, as well as at various erotic websites. She lives in
Maryland and serves as an activist for reproductive freedom and
sex workers' rights. Find her online at thegreenlightdistrict.org.

**DUSTY HORN** is the Smartest Ass in Show Business. A queer
porn performer, sex educator, social worker, diehard rock 'n'
roller and practitioner of professional BDSM, her culture writing
has appeared in *McSweeney's* and *Aorta*. She pens and distrib-
utes a nominal sex work memoir/critical theory zine and lives in
Oakland, California.

**BILL KTE'PI** is a full-time freelance writer with a variety of
credits. He currently lives in New Hampshire while planning
a move to the Southwest. He maintains a web presence at
ktepi.com.

**EVAN MORA** is a recovering corporate banker living in
Toronto. Her work can be found in *Best Lesbian Erotica 2009;
Best Lesbian Romance 2009 & 2010; Where the Girls Are; The
Sweetest Kiss: Ravishing Vampire Erotica; Girl Crush; Please,
Sir: Erotic Stories of Female Submission* and *Spank!*

**JENNIFER PETERS** works as the associate editor of *Penthouse
Forum* and *Girls of Penthouse* and is a contributing editor to
*Penthouse*, where she writes the "Pet Projects" column. You can
read more of her stories in anthologies such as *Peep Show* and
*Fast Girls*.

**TERESA NOELLE ROBERTS** writes romantic erotica and erotic romance for horny people who believe in love. Her short fiction has appeared in *Best of Best Women's Erotica 2*, *Orgasmic*, *Spanked, Playing with Fire* and other anthologies with similarly provocative titles. Her newest paranormal ménage romance is *Foxes' Den*.

**LISABET SARAI** has published six erotic novels, two short-story collections and dozens of individual tales. She also edits the single-author charity series "Coming Together Presents" and reviews erotica for Erotica Readers and Writers Association and Erotica Revealed. Visit Lisabet online at Lisabet's Fantasy Factory (lisabetsarai.com).

**SUZANNE V. SLATE** is a librarian who lives in the Boston area with her longtime lover. She has published a variety of nonfiction articles and a book, and has recently begun writing fiction.

**RITA WINCHESTER's** work has appeared in various online zines such as The Erotic Woman, For the Girls and Ruthie's Club. Her work has also appeared in print anthologies such as *Frenzy*, *Afternoon Delight*, *I Is for Indecent*, *Tasting Her* and *Mammoth Lesbian Erotica*. Visit her at myspace.com/ritawinchester.

**LUX ZAKARI's** stories, poetry and reviews have appeared in *Best Women's Erotica 2009* and *Girl Crazy*, as well as on the websites Clean Sheets, Oysters and Chocolate, The Erotic Woman and For the Girls. Her first novel is *Coercion*. For details, visit luxzakari.com.

# ABOUT
# THE EDITOR

**RACHEL KRAMER BUSSEL** (rachelkramerbussel.com) is a New York–based author, editor and blogger. She has edited over thirty books of erotica, including *Orgasmic; Bottoms Up: Spanking Good Stories; Spanked; Naughty Spanking Stories from A to Z 1* and *2; Fast Girls; Smooth; Passion; The Mile High Club; Do Not Disturb; Tasting Him; Tasting Her; Please, Sir; Please, Ma'am; He's on Top; She's on Top; Caught Looking; Hide and Seek; Crossdressing; Rubber Sex* and *Bedding Down.* She is the author of the forthcoming novel, *Everything But...,* *Best Sex Writing* series editor, and winner of 3 IPPY (Independent Publisher) Awards. Her work has been published in over one hundred anthologies, and she serves as senior editor at *Penthouse Variations* and wrote the popular "Lusty Lady" column for the *Village Voice.*

Rachel is a sex columnist for SexIsMagazine.com and has written for *AVN, Bust,* Cleansheets.com, *Cosmopolitan, Curve,* the Daily Beast, Fresh Yarn, TheFrisky.com, Gothamist,

Huffington Post, Mediabistro, *Newsday, New York Post, Penthouse, Playgirl, Radar, San Francisco Chronicle, Time Out New York* and *Zink*, among others. She has appeared on "The Martha Stewart Show," "The Berman and Berman Show," NY1, and Showtime's "Family Business." She has hosted In the Flesh Erotic Reading Series (inthefleshreadingseries.com) since October 2005, featuring readers from Susie Bright to Zane, about which the *New York Times's* UrbanEye newsletter said, she "welcomes eroticism of all stripes, spots and textures." She blogs at lustylady.blogspot.com. Read more about *Best Bondage Erotica 2011* at bestbondage.wordpress.com.

# More from Rachel Kramer Bussel

# Erotica for Every Kink

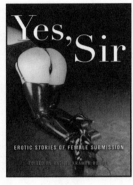

**Yes, Sir**
*Erotic Stories of Female Submission*
Edited by Rachel Kramer Bussel

The lucky women in *Yes, Sir* give up control to irresistibly powerful men who understand that dominance is about exulting in power that is freely yielded.
ISBN 978-1-57344-310-4  $15.95

---

**Best Bondage Erotica**
Edited by Alison Tyler

Always playful and dangerously explicit, these arresting fantasies grab you, tie you down, and never let you go.
ISBN 978-1-57344-173-5  $15.95

**Best Bondage Erotica 2**
Edited by Alison Tyler

From start to finish, these stories of women and men in the throes of pleasurable restraint will have you bound to your chair and begging for more!
ISBN 978-1-57344-214-5  $16.95

**Spanked**
*Red Cheeked Erotica*
Edited by Rachel Kramer Bussel

"Editrix extraordinaire Rachel Kramer Bussel has rounded up twenty brisk and stinging tales that reveal the many sides of spanking, from playful erotic accent to punishing payback for a long ago wrong."—Clean Sheets
ISBN 978-1-57344-319-7  $14.95

**Rubber Sex**
Edited by Rachel Kramer Bussel

Rachel Kramer Bussel showcases a world where skin gets slipped on tightly, then polished, stroked, and caressed—while the bodies inside heat up with lust.
ISBN 978-1-57344-313-5  $14.95

# Read the Very Best in Erotica

**Fairy Tale Lust**
*Erotic Fantasies for Women*
Edited by Kristina Wright
Foreword by Angela Knight

Award-winning novelist and top erotica writer Kristina Wright goes over the river and through the woods to find the sexiest fairy tales ever written.
ISBN 978-1-57344-397-5 $14.95

**In Sleeping Beauty's Bed**
*Erotic Fairy Tales*
By Mitzi Szereto

"Classic fairy tale characters like Rapunzel, Little Red Riding Hood, Cinderella, and Sleeping Beauty, just to name a few, are brought back to life in Mitzi Szereto's delightful collection of erotica fairy tales." —Nancy Madore, author of *Enchanted: Erotic Bedtime Stories for Women*
ISBN 978-1-57344-376-8 $16.95

**Frenzy**
*60 Stories of Sudden Sex*
Edited by Alison Tyler

"Toss out the roses and box of candies. This isn't a prolonged seduction. This is slammed against the wall in an alleyway sex, and it's all that much hotter for it."
—*Erotica Readers & Writers Association*
ISBN 978-1-57344-331-9 $14.95

**Afternoon Delight**
*Erotica for Couples*
Edited by Alison Tyler

"Alison Tyler evokes a world of heady sensuality where fantasies are fearlessly explored and dreams gloriously realized."—Barbara Pizio, Executive Editor, *Penthouse Variations*
ISBN 978-1-57344-341-8 $14.95

**Can't Help the Way That I Feel**
*Sultry Stories of African American Love, Lust and Fantasy*
Edited by Lori Bryant-Woolridge

Some temptations are just too tantalizing to ignore in this collection of delicious stories edited by Emmy award-winning and *Essence* bestselling author Lori Bryant-Woolridge.
ISBN 978-1-57344-386-9 $14.95

Ordering is easy! Call us toll free or fax us to place your MC/VISA order.
You can also mail the order form below with payment to:
Cleis Press, 2246 Sixth St., Berkeley, CA 94710.

## ORDER FORM

| QTY | TITLE | PRICE |
|-----|-------|-------|
| _____ | _____ | _____ |
| _____ | _____ | _____ |
| _____ | _____ | _____ |
| _____ | _____ | _____ |
| _____ | _____ | _____ |
| _____ | _____ | _____ |
| _____ | _____ | _____ |
| _____ | _____ | _____ |

|  | SUBTOTAL | _____ |
|--|----------|---------|
|  | SHIPPING | _____ |
|  | SALES TAX | _____ |
|  | TOTAL | _____ |

Add $3.95 postage/handling for the first book ordered and $1.00 for each additional book. Outside North America, please contact us for shipping rates. California residents add 9.75% sales tax. Payment in U.S. dollars only.

**★ Free book of equal or lesser value. Shipping and applicable sales tax extra.**

**Cleis Press • Phone: (800) 780-2279 • Fax: 510-845-8001**
**orders@cleispress.com • www.cleispress.com**
**You'll find more great books on our website**

**Follow us on Twitter @cleispress • Friend/fan us on Facebook**